Office XP
in an *instant*

Visual

From
*maran*Graphics®

&

Hungry Minds™

Best-Selling Books • Digital Downloads • e-books • Answer Networks •
e-Newsletters • Branded Web Sites • e-learning

New York, NY ♦ Cleveland, OH ♦ Indianapolis, IN

Office XP In an Instant

Published by
Hungry Minds, Inc.
909 Third Avenue
New York, NY 10022
www.hungryminds.com

Copyright© 2001 by maranGraphics Inc.
5755 Coopers Avenue
Mississauga, Ontario, Canada
L4Z 1R9

Library of Congress Control Number: 2001093185
ISBN: 0-7645-3637-0
Printed in the United States of America
10 9 8 7 6 5 4 3 2 1

1B/ST/QZ/QR/MG

Distributed in the United States by Hungry Minds, Inc.
Distributed by CDG Books Canada Inc. for Canada; by Transworld Publishers Limited in the United Kingdom; by IDG Norge Books for Norway; by IDG Sweden Books for Sweden; by IDG Books Australia Publishing Corporation Pty. Ltd. for Australia and New Zealand; by TransQuest Publishers Pte Ltd. for Singapore, Malaysia, Thailand, Indonesia, and Hong Kong; by Gotop Information Inc. for Taiwan; by ICG Muse, Inc. for Japan; by Intersoft for South Africa; by Eyrolles for France; by International Thomson Publishing for Germany, Austria and Switzerland; by Distribuidora Cuspide for Argentina; by LR International for Brazil; by Galileo Libros for Chile; by Ediciones ZETA S.C.R. Ltda. for Peru; by WS Computer Publishing Corporation, Inc. for the Philippines; by Contemporanea de Ediciones for Venezuela; by Express Computer Distributors for the Caribbean and West Indies; by Micronesia Media Distributor, Inc. for Micronesia; by Chips Computadoras S.A. de C.V. for Mexico; by Editorial Norma de Panama S.A. for Panama; by American Bookshops for Finland.
For corporate orders, please call maranGraphics at 800-469-6616 or fax 905-890-9434.
For general information on Hungry Minds' products and services, please contact our Customer Care Department within the U.S. at 800-762-2974, outside the U.S. at 317-572-3993 or fax 317-572-4002.
For sales inquiries and reseller information, including discounts, premium and bulk quantity sales, and foreign-language translations, please contact our Customer Care Department at 800-434-3422, fax 317-572-4002, or write to Hungry Minds, Inc., Attn: Customer Care Department, 10475 Crosspoint Boulevard, Indianapolis, IN 46256.
For information on licensing foreign or domestic rights, please contact our Sub-Rights Customer Care Department at 212-844-5000.
For information on using Hungry Minds' products and services in the classroom or for ordering examination copies, please contact our Educational Sales Department at 800-434-2086 or fax 317-572-4005.
For press review copies, author interviews, or other publicity information, please contact our Public Relations department at 317-572-3168 or fax 317-572-4168.
For authorization to photocopy items for corporate, personal, or educational use, please contact Copyright Clearance Center, 222 Rosewood Drive, Danvers, MA 01923, or fax 978-750-4470.

Trademark Acknowledgments

Permissions

Some comments from our readers...

"I have to praise you and your company on the fine products you turn out. I have twelve of the *Teach Yourself VISUALLY* and *Simplified* books in my house. They were instrumental in helping me pass a difficult computer course. Thank you for creating books that are easy to follow."

—*Gordon Justin (Brielle, NJ)*

"I commend your efforts and your success. I teach in an outreach program for the Dr. Eugene Clark Library in Lockhart, TX. Your *Teach Yourself VISUALLY* books are incredible and I use them in my computer classes. All my students love them!"

—*Michele Schalin (Lockhart, TX)*

"Thank you so much for helping people like me learn about computers. The Maran family is just what the doctor ordered. Thank you, thank you, thank you."

—*Carol Moten (New Kensington, PA)*

"I would like to take this time to compliment maranGraphics on creating such great books. Thank you for making it clear. Keep up the good work."

—*Kirk Santoro (Burbank, CA)*

"I write to extend my thanks and appreciation for your books. They are clear, easy to follow, and straight to the point. Keep up the good work!"

—*Seward Kollie (Dakar, Senegal)*

"What fantastic teaching books you have produced! Congratulations to you and your staff. You deserve the Nobel prize in Education in the Software category. Thanks for helping me to understand computers."

—*Bruno Tonon (Melbourne, Australia)*

"Over time, I have bought a number of your 'Read Less, Learn More' books. For me, they are THE way to learn anything easily."

—*José A. Mazón (Cuba, NY)*

"I was introduced to maranGraphics about four years ago and YOU ARE THE GREATEST THING THAT EVER HAPPENED TO INTRODUCTORY COMPUTER BOOKS!"

—*Glenn Nettleton (Huntsville, AL)*

"Compliments To The Chef!! Your books are extraordinary! Or, simply put, Extra-Ordinary, meaning way above the rest! THANK YOU THANK YOU THANK YOU! for creating these."

—*Christine J. Manfrin (Castle Rock, CO)*

"I'm a grandma who was pushed by an 11-year-old grandson to join the computer age. I found myself hopelessly confused and frustrated until I discovered the Visual series. I'm no expert by any means now, but I'm a lot further along than I would have been otherwise. Thank you!"

—*Carol Louthain (Logansport, IN)*

"Thank you, thank you, thank you...for making it so easy for me to break into this high-tech world. I now own four of your books. I recommend them to anyone who is a beginner like myself. Now... if you could just do one for programming VCRs, it would make my day!"

—*Gay O'Donnell (Calgary, Alberta, Canada)*

"You're marvelous! I am greatly in your debt."

—*Patrick Baird (Lacey, WA)*

**maranGraphics is a family-run business
located near Toronto, Canada.**

At maranGraphics, we believe in producing great computer books—one book at a time.

Each maranGraphics book uses the award-winning communication process that we have been developing over the last 25 years. Using this process, we organize screen shots and text in a way that makes it easy for you to learn new concepts and tasks.

We spend hours deciding the best way to perform each task, so you don't have to!

Our clear, easy-to-follow screen shots and instructions walk you through each task from beginning to end.

We want to thank you for purchasing what we feel are the best computer books money can buy. We hope you enjoy using this book as much as we enjoyed creating it!

Sincerely,

The Maran Family

Please visit us on the Web at:

www.maran.com

CREDITS

Author:
Ruth Maran

Director of Copy Development:
Wanda Lawrie

Copy Editor:
Roderick Anatalio

Technical Consultant:
Paul Whitehead

Project Manager:
Judy Maran

Editorial Review:
Kelleigh Johnson

Editors:
Teri Lynn Pinsent
Roxanne Van Damme
Roderick Anatalio
Norm Schumacher
Megan Kirby
Stacey Morrison
Raquel Scott
Cathy Lo

Screen Captures:
Teri Lynn Pinsent

Layout Artists:
Paul Baker
Treena Lees
Hee-Jin Park

Screen Artist:
Darryl Grossi

Indexer:
Stacey Morrison

Permissions Coordinator:
Jennifer Amaral

Senior Vice President and Publisher, Hungry Minds Technology Publishing Group:
Richard Swadley

Publishing Director, Hungry Minds Technology Publishing Group:
Barry Pruett

Editorial Support, Hungry Minds Technology Publishing Group:
Jennifer Dorsey
Sandy Rodrigues
Lindsay Sandman

Post Production:
Robert Maran

ACKNOWLEDGMENTS

Thanks to the dedicated staff of maranGraphics, including
Jennifer Amaral, Roderick Anatalio, Paul Baker,
Darryl Grossi, Kelleigh Johnson, Megan Kirby, Wanda Lawrie,
Treena Lees, Cathy Lo, Jill Maran, Judy Maran, Robert Maran,
Ruth Maran, Russ Marini, Suzana G. Miokovic, Stacey Morrison,
Hee-Jin Park, Teri Lynn Pinsent, Steven Schaerer, Norm Schumacher,
Raquel Scott, Roxanne Van Damme and Paul Whitehead.

Finally, to Richard Maran who originated the easy-to-use
graphic format of this guide. Thank you for your
inspiration and guidance.

TABLE OF CONTENTS

TABLE OF CONTENTS

TABLE OF CONTENTS

INTRODUCTION TO MICROSOFT OFFICE XP

Microsoft® Office XP is a suite of programs that you can use to accomplish various tasks. All Microsoft Office XP programs share a common design and work in a similar way. Once you learn one program, you can easily learn the others.

MICROSOFT OFFICE XP PROGRAMS

WORD

Word is a word processing program that you can use to create documents such as letters, reports, essays and memos. Word offers many features that can help you efficiently enter and edit text in a document. For example, Word can help you enter common words and phrases into a document and find and correct spelling errors. There are many formatting features available in Word that you can use to enhance the appearance of the documents you create. You can change the font, size and color of text. You can also add page numbers, clip art images and tables to documents.

EXCEL

Excel is a spreadsheet program that allows you to organize, analyze and attractively present data, such as a budget or sales report. Excel allows you to quickly enter and edit data in a worksheet. You can use formulas and functions to perform calculations and analyze the data you enter. You can enhance the appearance of a worksheet by formatting numbers and changing the color of cells. When you want to graphically display worksheet data, Excel can help you create a colorful chart based on the data.

POWERPOINT

PowerPoint is a program that helps you plan, organize and design professional presentations. You can use the features in PowerPoint to edit and organize text in a presentation. PowerPoint allows you to add objects, such as pictures, charts and diagrams, to a presentation to add visual interest to the presentation. You can further enhance a presentation by changing the color scheme and adding slide transitions. PowerPoint also allows you to create notes that you can use as a guide when delivering a presentation.

ACCESS

Access is a database program that allows you to store and manage large collections of information. Access allows you to efficiently add, edit, view and organize the information stored in a database. Many people use databases to store personal information such as addresses and recipes. Companies often use databases to store information such as customer orders and expenses. You can use Access to create database objects such as tables, forms, queries and reports.

in an *instant*

OUTLOOK

Outlook is an information management program that allows you to manage several different types of information. You can use the Inbox feature to send and receive e-mail messages. The Calendar feature helps you keep track of appointments. You can use the Contacts feature to store information about your friends and colleagues. The Tasks feature allows you to create an electronic to-do list. You can use the Notes feature to create electronic notes that are similar to paper sticky notes.

SPEECH RECOGNITION

The speech recognition feature offered by Microsoft Office XP allows you to use your voice to enter text into an Office program. You can also use your voice to select commands from menus and toolbars and choose options in dialog boxes.

MICROSOFT OFFICE XP EDITIONS

There are several editions of Microsoft Office XP available. The available Microsoft Office XP editions include Standard, Professional and Developer. Each edition contains a different combination of programs. The Standard edition is useful for home users who require basic Office programs to accomplish day-to-day tasks.

The Professional edition is suited to users who require a database program in addition to the standard Office programs. The Developer edition is designed for professional software developers and includes tools for building and managing Web sites and Office-based applications.

Programs	Microsoft Office XP Editions		
	Standard	Professional	Developer
Word	✔	✔	✔
Excel	✔	✔	✔
PowerPoint	✔	✔	✔
Access		✔	✔
Outlook	✔	✔	✔
FrontPage*			✔
Developer Tools*			✔
SharePoint Team Services*			✔

* FrontPage is a program you can use to create and publish Web pages.

* Developer Tools are a collection of programs that are useful for software developers.

* SharePoint Team Services help users share information and work together on projects using a network.

START A PROGRAM

You can start an Office program to perform a task such as creating a letter, analyzing financial data or designing a presentation. When you start an Office program, a button for the program appears on the taskbar.

START A PROGRAM

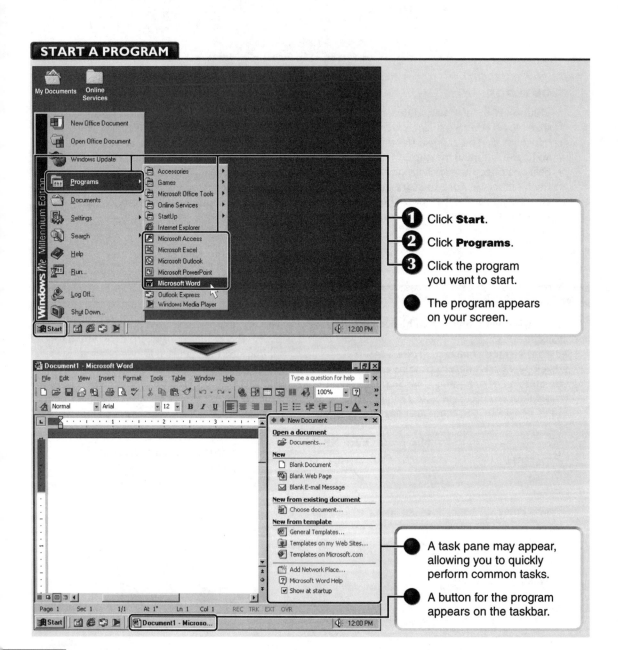

1 Click **Start**.

2 Click **Programs**.

3 Click the program you want to start.

● The program appears on your screen.

● A task pane may appear, allowing you to quickly perform common tasks.

● A button for the program appears on the taskbar.

EXIT A PROGRAM

When you finish using a program, you can exit the program. You should always exit all programs before turning off your computer. Properly exiting your programs can help prevent data loss.

EXIT A PROGRAM

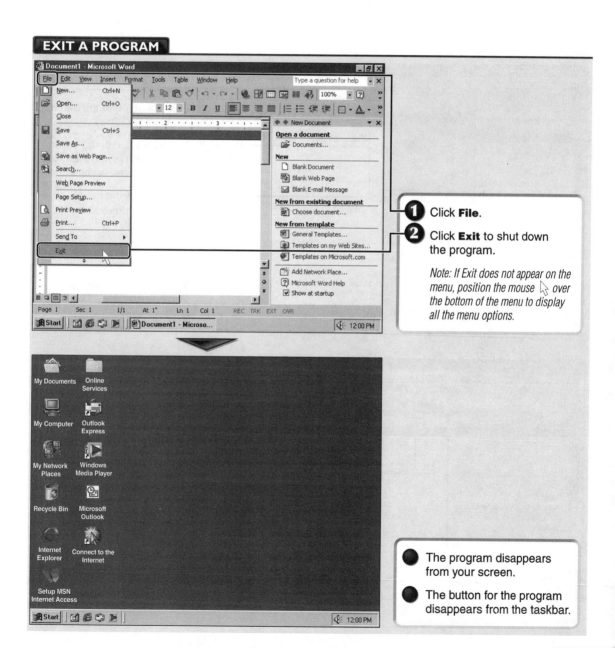

① Click **File**.

② Click **Exit** to shut down the program.

Note: If Exit does not appear on the menu, position the mouse over the bottom of the menu to display all the menu options.

● The program disappears from your screen.

● The button for the program disappears from the taskbar.

SELECT A COMMAND

You can select a command from a menu or toolbar to perform a task in an Office program. When you display a menu, a short version of the menu appears, displaying the most commonly used commands. As you work with most Office programs, the toolbars automatically change to remove buttons you rarely use and display the buttons you use most often.

SELECT A COMMAND

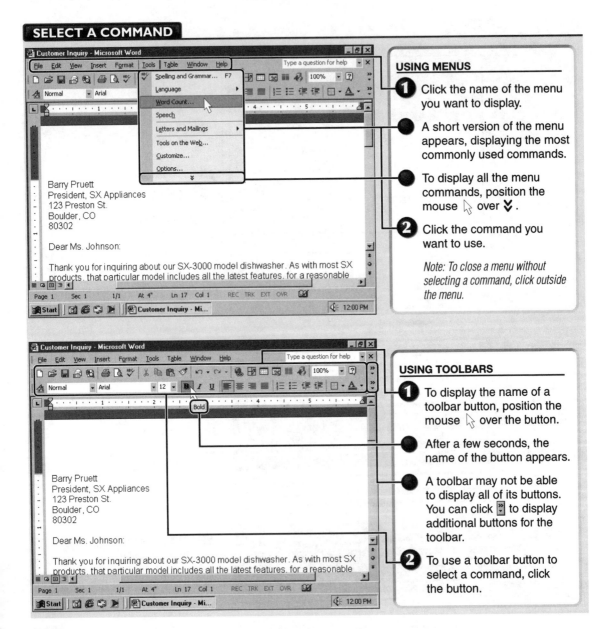

USING MENUS

① Click the name of the menu you want to display.

● A short version of the menu appears, displaying the most commonly used commands.

● To display all the menu commands, position the mouse ⃕ over ☒.

② Click the command you want to use.

Note: To close a menu without selecting a command, click outside the menu.

USING TOOLBARS

① To display the name of a toolbar button, position the mouse ⃕ over the button.

● After a few seconds, the name of the button appears.

● A toolbar may not be able to display all of its buttons. You can click ☒ to display additional buttons for the toolbar.

② To use a toolbar button to select a command, click the button.

DISPLAY OR HIDE A TOOLBAR

Each Office program offers several toolbars that you can display or hide at any time. Each toolbar contains buttons that help you quickly perform common tasks. When you first start an Office program, one or more toolbars automatically appear on your screen. You can choose which toolbars to display based on the tasks you perform most often.

DISPLAY OR HIDE A TOOLBAR

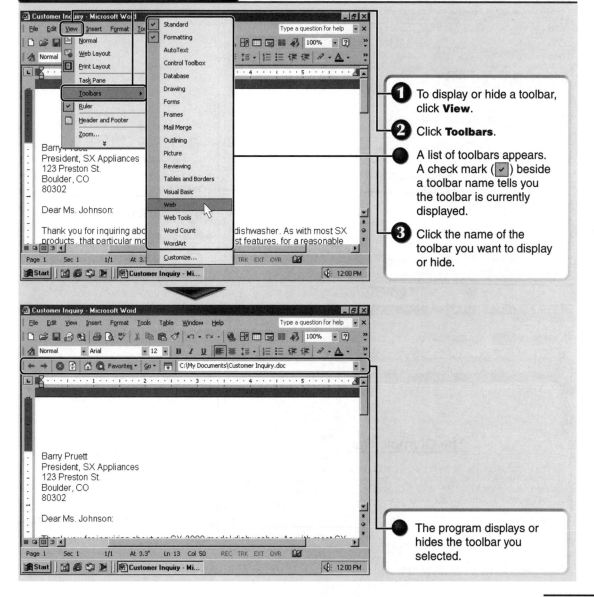

① To display or hide a toolbar, click **View**.

② Click **Toolbars**.

● A list of toolbars appears. A check mark (✓) beside a toolbar name tells you the toolbar is currently displayed.

③ Click the name of the toolbar you want to display or hide.

● The program displays or hides the toolbar you selected.

7

USING THE TASK PANE

Many Office programs offer task panes that you can use to perform common tasks, such as opening a file or searching for a file on your computer. You can display or hide a task pane at any time. When you start an Office program or perform a task, a task pane may automatically appear.

USING THE TASK PANE

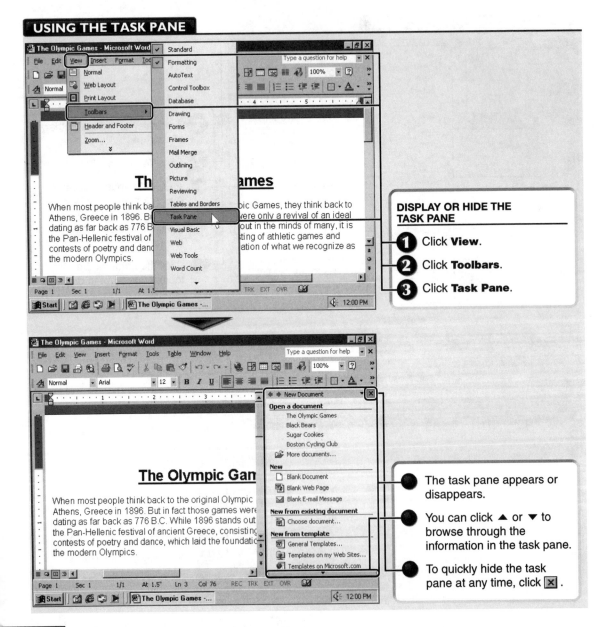

DISPLAY OR HIDE THE TASK PANE

① Click **View**.

② Click **Toolbars**.

③ Click **Task Pane**.

● The task pane appears or disappears.

● You can click ▲ or ▼ to browse through the information in the task pane.

● To quickly hide the task pane at any time, click ⊠.

in an *instant*

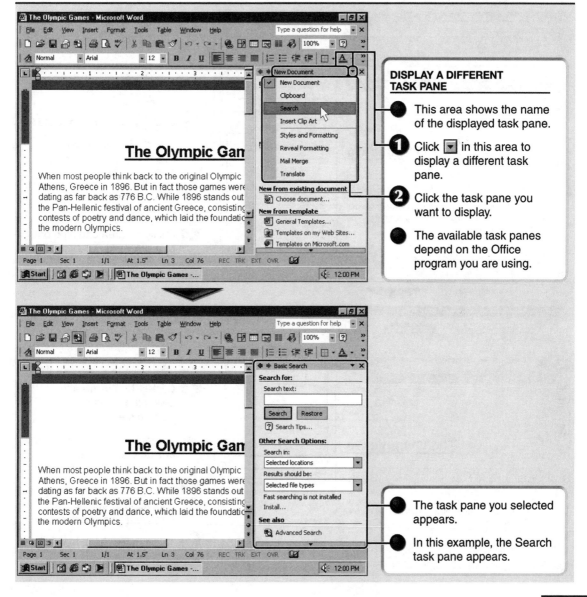

DISPLAY A DIFFERENT TASK PANE

● This area shows the name of the displayed task pane.

1 Click ▼ in this area to display a different task pane.

2 Click the task pane you want to display.

● The available task panes depend on the Office program you are using.

● The task pane you selected appears.

● In this example, the Search task pane appears.

SEARCH FOR A FILE

If you cannot remember the name or location of a file you want to work with, you can search for the file. You can specify words the file you want to find contains. The Office program will search the contents of files and the names of files for the words you specify.

SEARCH FOR A FILE

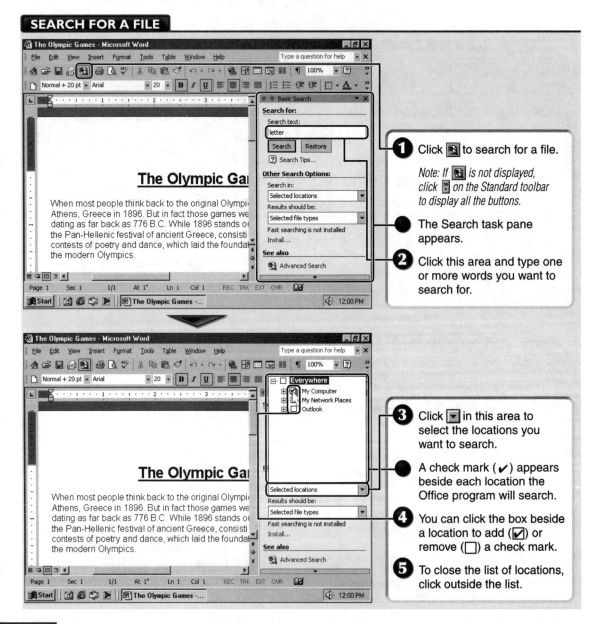

1 Click 🔍 to search for a file.

Note: If 🔍 is not displayed, click 📋 on the Standard toolbar to display all the buttons.

The Search task pane appears.

2 Click this area and type one or more words you want to search for.

3 Click ▼ in this area to select the locations you want to search.

A check mark (✔) appears beside each location the Office program will search.

4 You can click the box beside a location to add (☑) or remove (☐) a check mark.

5 To close the list of locations, click outside the list.

in an instant

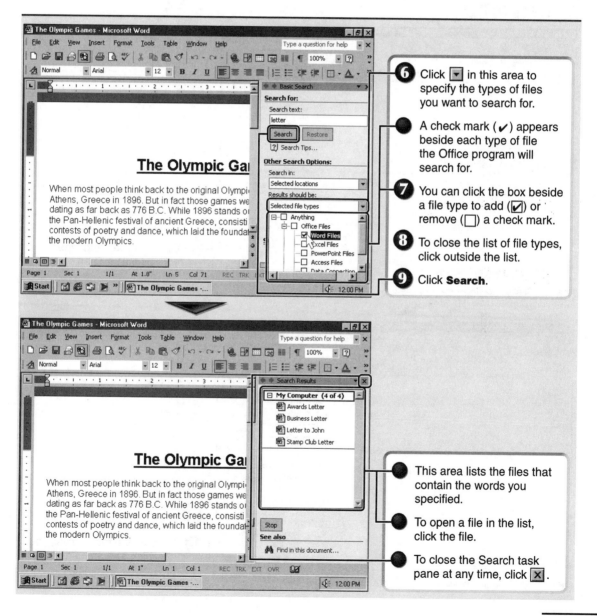

6 Click ⬇ in this area to specify the types of files you want to search for.

● A check mark (✔) appears beside each type of file the Office program will search for.

7 You can click the box beside a file type to add (☑) or remove (☐) a check mark.

8 To close the list of file types, click outside the list.

9 Click **Search**.

● This area lists the files that contain the words you specified.

● To open a file in the list, click the file.

● To close the Search task pane at any time, click ⊠.

GETTING HELP

If you do not know how to perform a task in an Office program, you can ask a question to find help information for the task. Asking a question allows you to quickly find help information of interest.

GETTING HELP

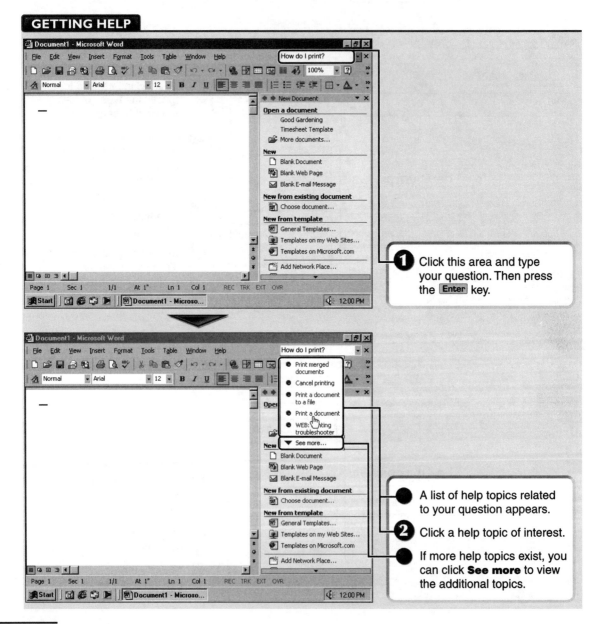

1 Click this area and type your question. Then press the `Enter` key.

● A list of help topics related to your question appears.

2 Click a help topic of interest.

● If more help topics exist, you can click **See more** to view the additional topics.

in an instant

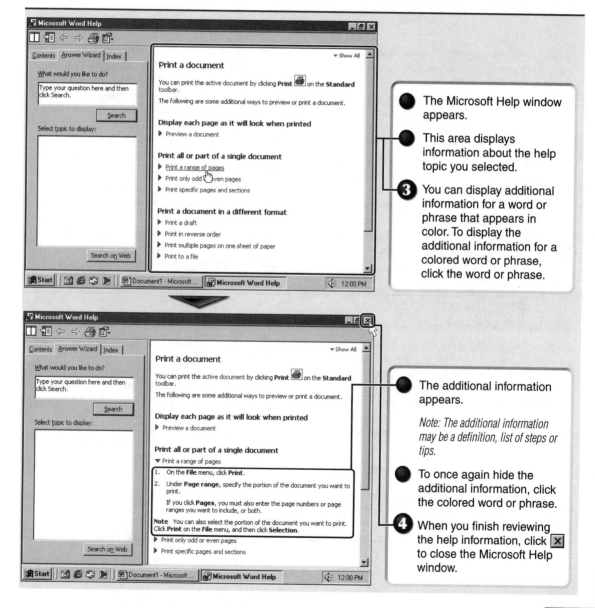

The Microsoft Help window appears.

This area displays information about the help topic you selected.

3 You can display additional information for a word or phrase that appears in color. To display the additional information for a colored word or phrase, click the word or phrase.

The additional information appears.

Note: The additional information may be a definition, list of steps or tips.

To once again hide the additional information, click the colored word or phrase.

4 When you finish reviewing the help information, click ☒ to close the Microsoft Help window.

INTRODUCTION TO WORD

Word is a word processing program you can use to efficiently produce professional-looking documents, such as letters, reports and memos.

INTRODUCTION TO WORD

EDIT TEXT

Word offers many time-saving features to help you edit text in a document. You can easily add or delete text, re-arrange paragraphs and check for spelling and grammar errors. Word remembers the last changes you made to a document, so you can undo changes you regret.

Word allows you to quickly find and replace every occurrence of a word in a document, which is ideal if you have frequently misspelled a word. You can also have Word track the editing changes that are made to a document. This is useful when two or more people are working with the same document.

FORMAT TEXT

You can format text in a document to enhance the appearance of the text. You can use various font sizes, styles and colors to help make important text stand out. You can also change the amount of space between lines of text or align text in different ways. If you want to make one area of a document look exactly like another, you can copy the formatting of text.

Formatting text can help you organize the information in a document. You can use tabs to line up columns of information or use bullets to separate items in a list. When you no longer want text to display formatting, you can quickly remove all the formatting you applied to the text.

FORMAT DOCUMENTS

Word's formatting features can help you change the appearance of a document. You can add page numbers to each page in a document or separate a document into sections. You can also add a watermark to the pages in a document to add interest to the document or identify the status of the document.

Changing the margins in a document allows you to accommodate specialty paper, such as letterhead. To create a title page for a document, you can vertically center text on a page.

CREATE TABLES

You can create tables to neatly display columns of information in a document. To improve the layout of a table you create, you can change the height of rows and the width of columns in the table. You can also add rows or columns to a table to include additional information in the table. Word offers several ready-to-use designs you can choose from to instantly enhance the appearance of a table.

THE WORD WINDOW

The Word window displays many items you can use to create and work with your documents, such as menus, toolbars and a task pane.

THE WORD WINDOW

Title Bar

Shows the name of the displayed document.

Menu Bar

Provides access to lists of commands available in Word and displays an area where you can type a question to get help information.

Standard Toolbar

Contains buttons you can use to select common commands, such as Save and Print.

Formatting Toolbar

Contains buttons you can use to select common formatting commands, such as Bold and Italic.

Task Pane

Contains links you can select to perform common tasks, such as opening or creating a document.

Document Views

Provides access to four different views of your documents.

Status Bar

Provides information about the area of the document displayed on the screen and the position of the insertion point.

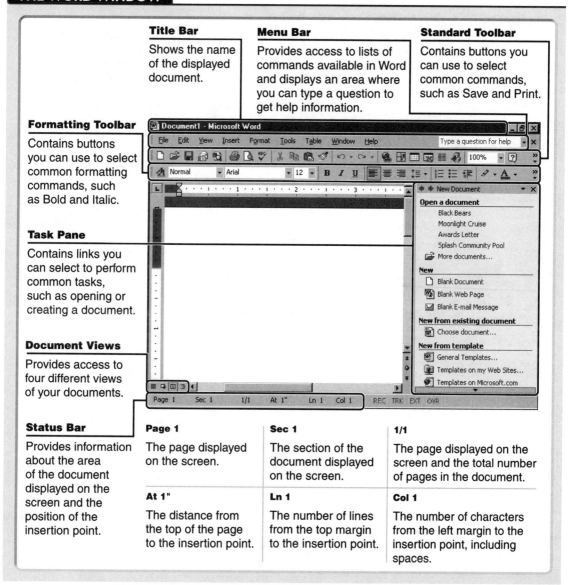

Page 1	Sec 1	1/1
The page displayed on the screen.	The section of the document displayed on the screen.	The page displayed on the screen and the total number of pages in the document.

At 1"	Ln 1	Col 1
The distance from the top of the page to the insertion point.	The number of lines from the top margin to the insertion point.	The number of characters from the left margin to the insertion point, including spaces.

ENTER TEXT

Word allows you to type text into your document quickly and easily. The text you type will appear where the insertion point flashes on your screen. As you type, Word checks your document for errors and automatically corrects any common spelling errors that are found.

ENTER TEXT

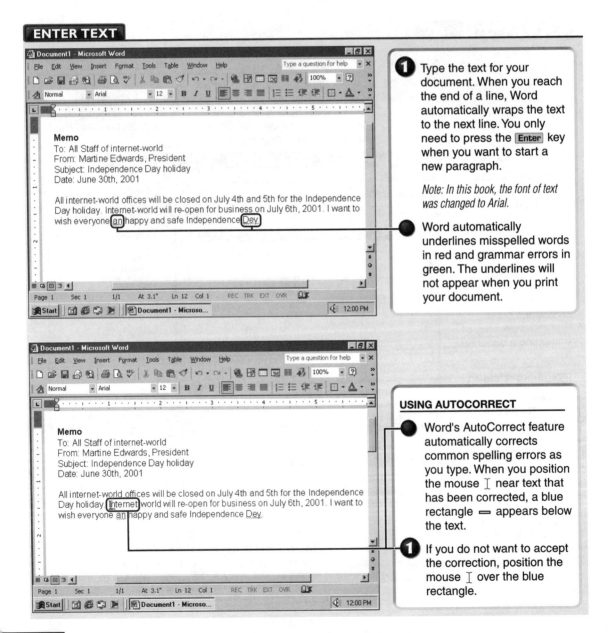

1 Type the text for your document. When you reach the end of a line, Word automatically wraps the text to the next line. You only need to press the **Enter** key when you want to start a new paragraph.

Note: In this book, the font of text was changed to Arial.

● Word automatically underlines misspelled words in red and grammar errors in green. The underlines will not appear when you print your document.

USING AUTOCORRECT

● Word's AutoCorrect feature automatically corrects common spelling errors as you type. When you position the mouse I near text that has been corrected, a blue rectangle ═ appears below the text.

1 If you do not want to accept the correction, position the mouse I over the blue rectangle.

16

in an *instant*

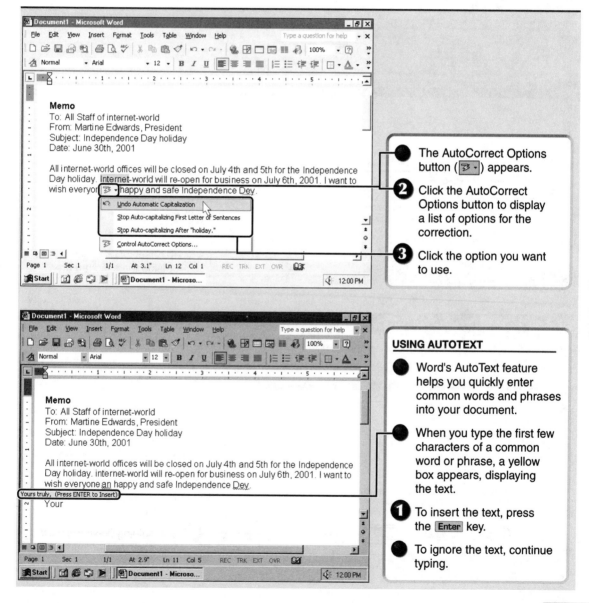

The AutoCorrect Options button ( ) appears.

2 Click the AutoCorrect Options button to display a list of options for the correction.

3 Click the option you want to use.

USING AUTOTEXT

Word's AutoText feature helps you quickly enter common words and phrases into your document.

When you type the first few characters of a common word or phrase, a yellow box appears, displaying the text.

1 To insert the text, press the Enter key.

To ignore the text, continue typing.

SELECT TEXT

Before performing many tasks in Word, you must select the text you want to work with. You can select a word, sentence, paragraph or any amount of text in a document. Selected text appears highlighted on your screen.

SELECT TEXT

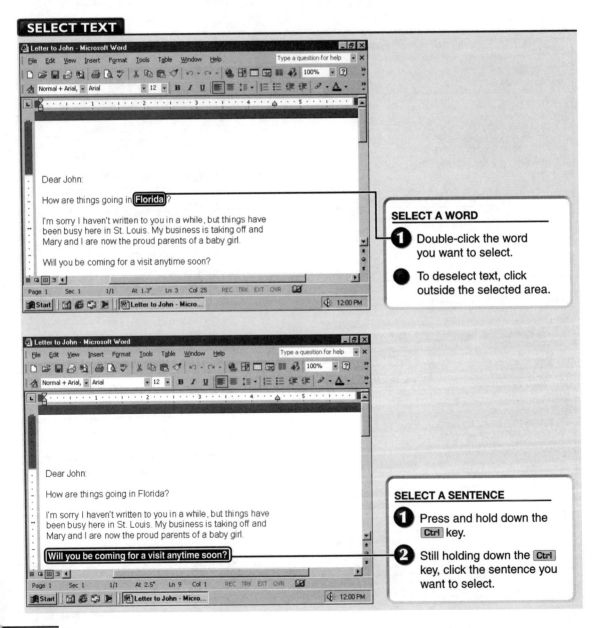

SELECT A WORD

1 Double-click the word you want to select.

● To deselect text, click outside the selected area.

SELECT A SENTENCE

1 Press and hold down the **Ctrl** key.

2 Still holding down the **Ctrl** key, click the sentence you want to select.

in an instant

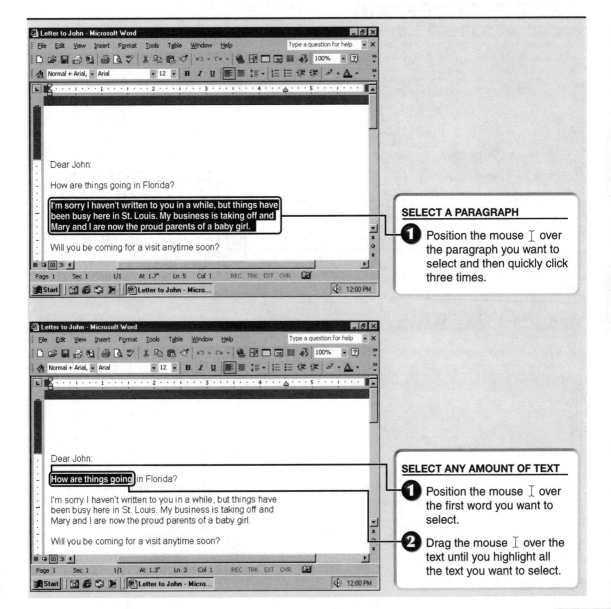

MOVE THROUGH A DOCUMENT

You can easily move to another location in your document. If your document contains a lot of text, your computer screen may not be able to display all the text at once. You must scroll through your document to view other parts of the document.

MOVE THROUGH A DOCUMENT

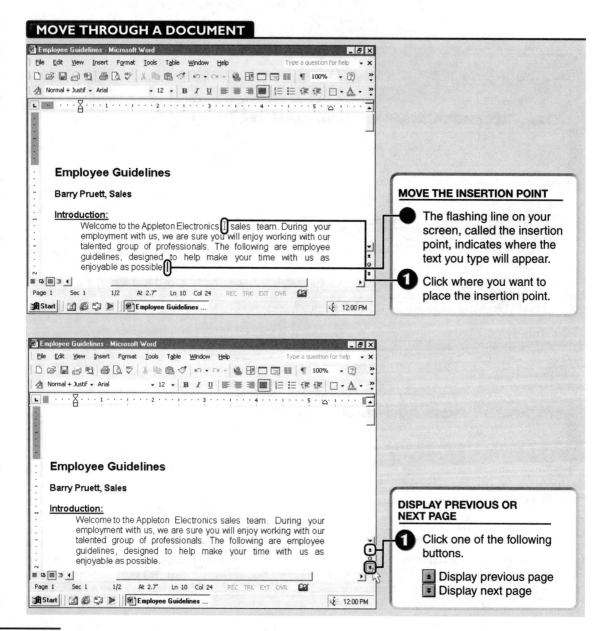

MOVE THE INSERTION POINT

The flashing line on your screen, called the insertion point, indicates where the text you type will appear.

1 Click where you want to place the insertion point.

DISPLAY PREVIOUS OR NEXT PAGE

1 Click one of the following buttons.

⬆ Display previous page
⬇ Display next page

in an *instant*

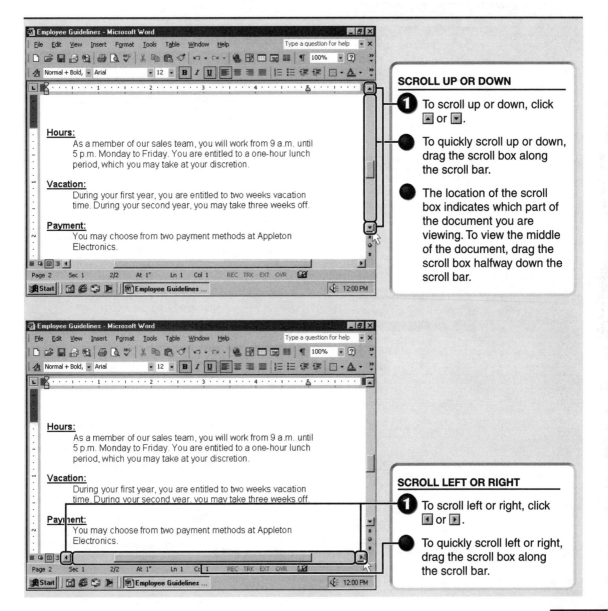

SCROLL UP OR DOWN

1. To scroll up or down, click ▲ or ▼.

● To quickly scroll up or down, drag the scroll box along the scroll bar.

● The location of the scroll box indicates which part of the document you are viewing. To view the middle of the document, drag the scroll box halfway down the scroll bar.

SCROLL LEFT OR RIGHT

1. To scroll left or right, click ◄ or ►.

● To quickly scroll left or right, drag the scroll box along the scroll bar.

CHANGE VIEW OF DOCUMENT

Word offers four different views that you can use to display your document. You can choose the view that best suits your needs. When you first start Word, documents appear in the Print Layout view.

CHANGE VIEW OF DOCUMENT

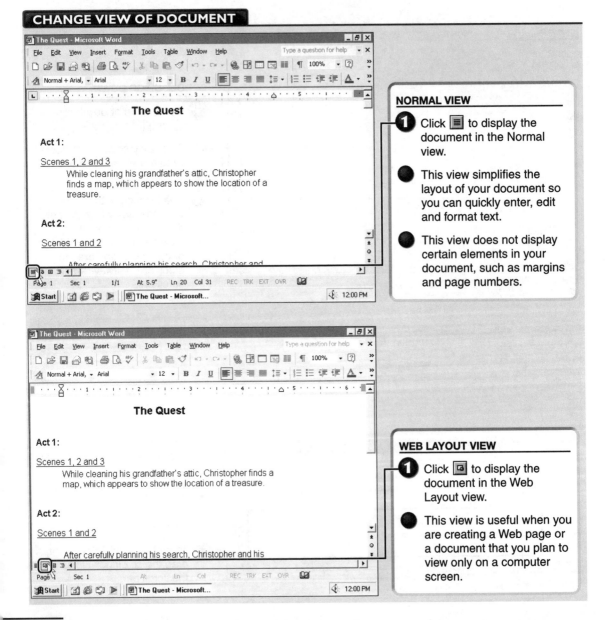

NORMAL VIEW

1 Click 🔳 to display the document in the Normal view.

● This view simplifies the layout of your document so you can quickly enter, edit and format text.

● This view does not display certain elements in your document, such as margins and page numbers.

WEB LAYOUT VIEW

1 Click 🔳 to display the document in the Web Layout view.

● This view is useful when you are creating a Web page or a document that you plan to view only on a computer screen.

in an *Instant*

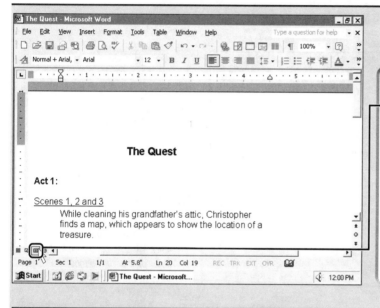

PRINT LAYOUT VIEW

1 Click 🔲 to display the document in the Print Layout view.

● This view is useful when you want to see how your document will appear on a printed page.

● This view displays all elements in your document, such as margins and page numbers.

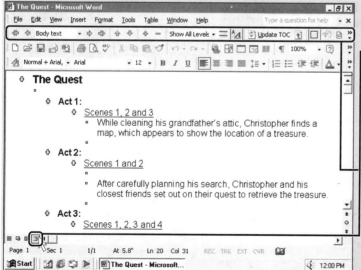

OUTLINE VIEW

1 Click 🔳 to display the document in the Outline view.

● This view is useful when you want to review and work with the structure of your document.

● This area displays the Outlining toolbar, which allows you to collapse your document to see only the headings or expand your document to see all the headings and text.

SAVE A DOCUMENT

You can save your document to store it for future use. Saving a document allows you to later review and edit the document. You should regularly save changes you make to a document to avoid losing your work.

SAVE A DOCUMENT

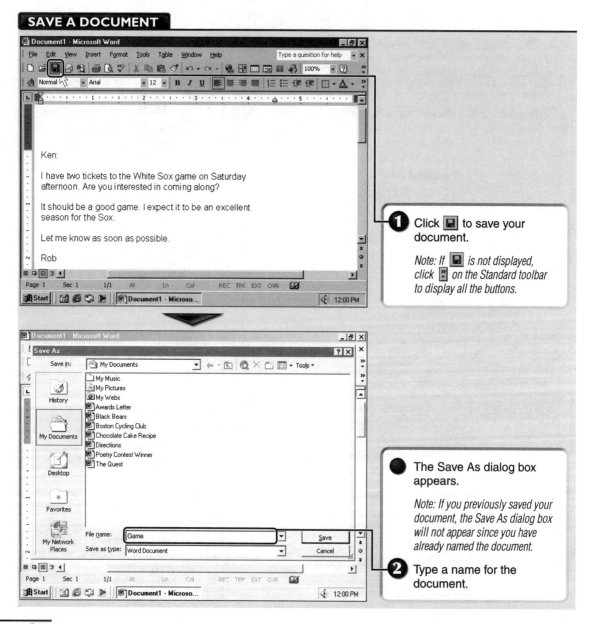

1 Click 🖫 to save your document.

Note: If 🖫 is not displayed, click 👋 on the Standard toolbar to display all the buttons.

● The Save As dialog box appears.

Note: If you previously saved your document, the Save As dialog box will not appear since you have already named the document.

2 Type a name for the document.

in an instant

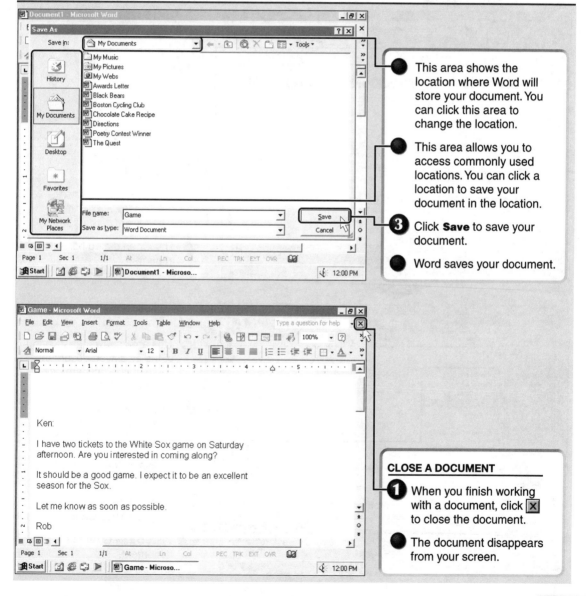

This area shows the location where Word will store your document. You can click this area to change the location.

This area allows you to access commonly used locations. You can click a location to save your document in the location.

3 Click **Save** to save your document.

Word saves your document.

CLOSE A DOCUMENT

1 When you finish working with a document, click ☒ to close the document.

The document disappears from your screen.

OPEN A DOCUMENT

You can open a saved document to view the document on your screen. This allows you to review and make changes to the document. You can have more than one document open at a time.

OPEN A DOCUMENT

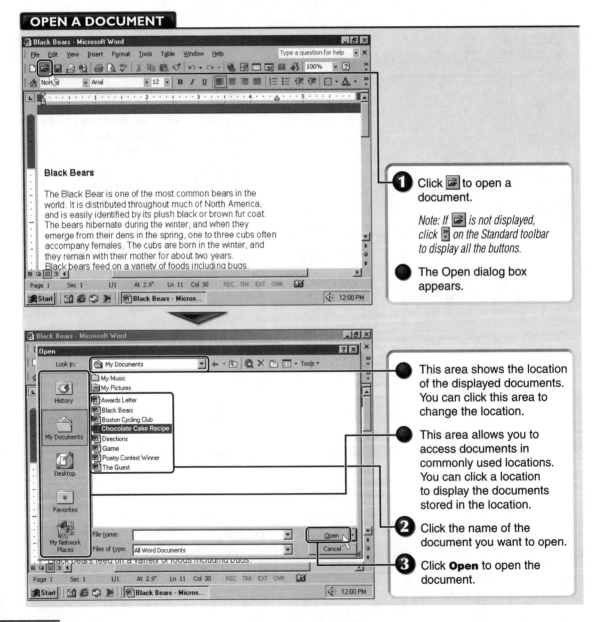

1 Click 📂 to open a document.

Note: If 📂 is not displayed, click 🔽 on the Standard toolbar to display all the buttons.

● The Open dialog box appears.

● This area shows the location of the displayed documents. You can click this area to change the location.

● This area allows you to access documents in commonly used locations. You can click a location to display the documents stored in the location.

2 Click the name of the document you want to open.

3 Click **Open** to open the document.

in an instant

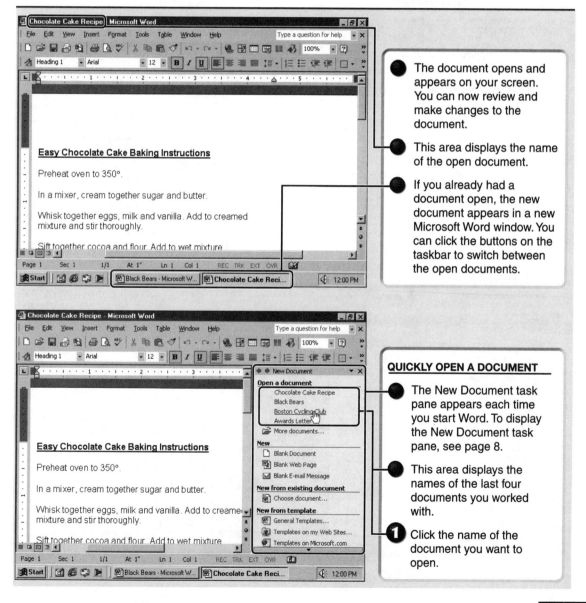

● The document opens and appears on your screen. You can now review and make changes to the document.

● This area displays the name of the open document.

● If you already had a document open, the new document appears in a new Microsoft Word window. You can click the buttons on the taskbar to switch between the open documents.

QUICKLY OPEN A DOCUMENT

● The New Document task pane appears each time you start Word. To display the New Document task pane, see page 8.

● This area displays the names of the last four documents you worked with.

1 Click the name of the document you want to open.

PREVIEW A DOCUMENT

You can use the Print Preview feature to see how your document will look when printed, which allows you to confirm that the document will print the way you want. When using the Print Preview feature, you can magnify an area of a page in your document. This allows you to view the area in more detail.

PREVIEW A DOCUMENT

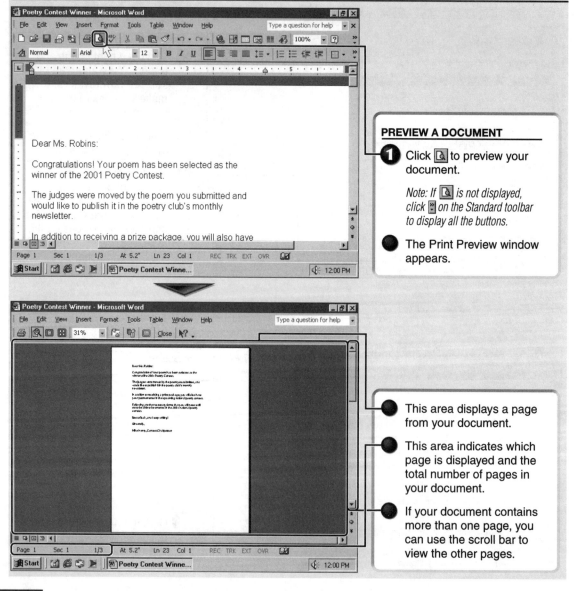

PREVIEW A DOCUMENT

1️⃣ Click 🔍 to preview your document.

Note: If 🔍 is not displayed, click 🔽 on the Standard toolbar to display all the buttons.

● The Print Preview window appears.

● This area displays a page from your document.

● This area indicates which page is displayed and the total number of pages in your document.

● If your document contains more than one page, you can use the scroll bar to view the other pages.

in an *instant*

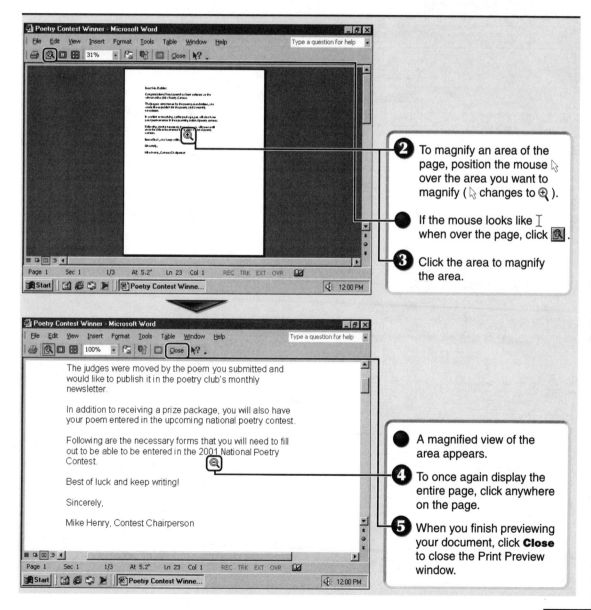

2 To magnify an area of the page, position the mouse ⬉ over the area you want to magnify (⬉ changes to ⊕).

● If the mouse looks like Ⅰ when over the page, click 🔍 .

3 Click the area to magnify the area.

● A magnified view of the area appears.

4 To once again display the entire page, click anywhere on the page.

5 When you finish previewing your document, click **Close** to close the Print Preview window.

PRINT A DOCUMENT

You can produce a paper copy of the document displayed on your screen. Word allows you to print the entire document, specific pages or selected text in the document. Before printing your document, make sure the printer is turned on and contains an adequate supply of paper.

PRINT A DOCUMENT

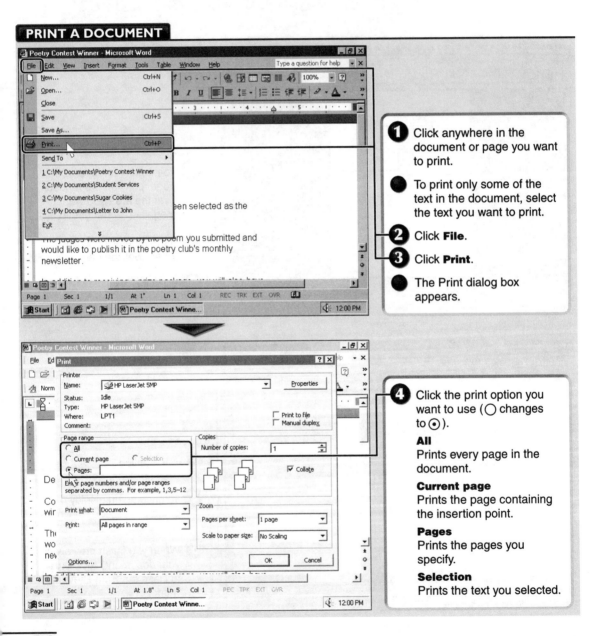

1 Click anywhere in the document or page you want to print.

■ To print only some of the text in the document, select the text you want to print.

2 Click **File**.

3 Click **Print**.

■ The Print dialog box appears.

4 Click the print option you want to use (○ changes to ⊙).

All
Prints every page in the document.

Current page
Prints the page containing the insertion point.

Pages
Prints the pages you specify.

Selection
Prints the text you selected.

in an *instant*

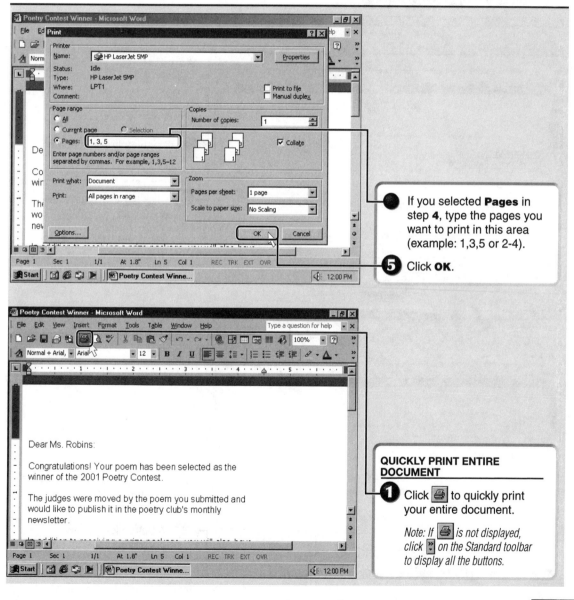

If you selected **Pages** in step **4**, type the pages you want to print in this area (example: 1,3,5 or 2-4).

5 Click **OK**.

QUICKLY PRINT ENTIRE DOCUMENT

1 Click 🖨 to quickly print your entire document.

Note: If 🖨 is not displayed, click ›› on the Standard toolbar to display all the buttons.

CREATE A NEW DOCUMENT

You can create a new document to start writing a new letter, memo or report. Each document is like a separate piece of paper. Creating a new document is like placing a new piece of paper on your screen.

CREATE A NEW DOCUMENT

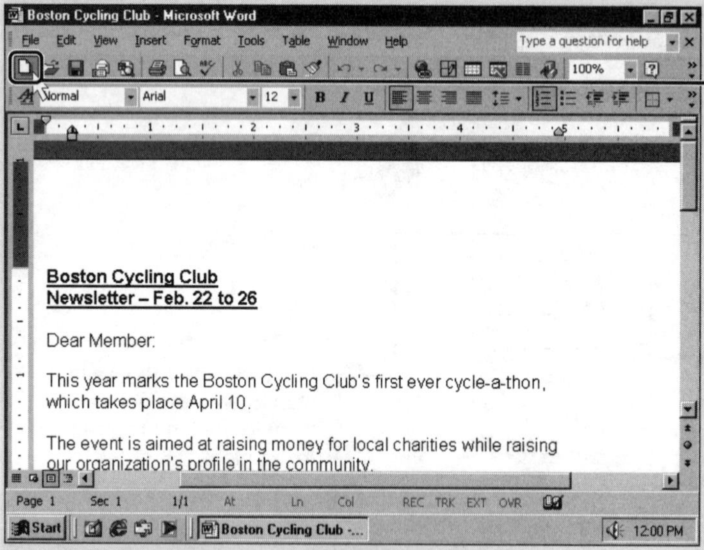

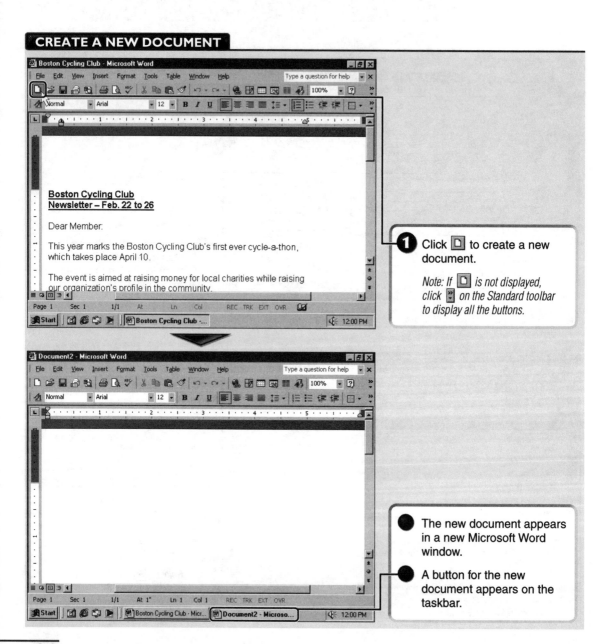

1. Click ▢ to create a new document.

Note: If ▢ is not displayed, click » on the Standard toolbar to display all the buttons.

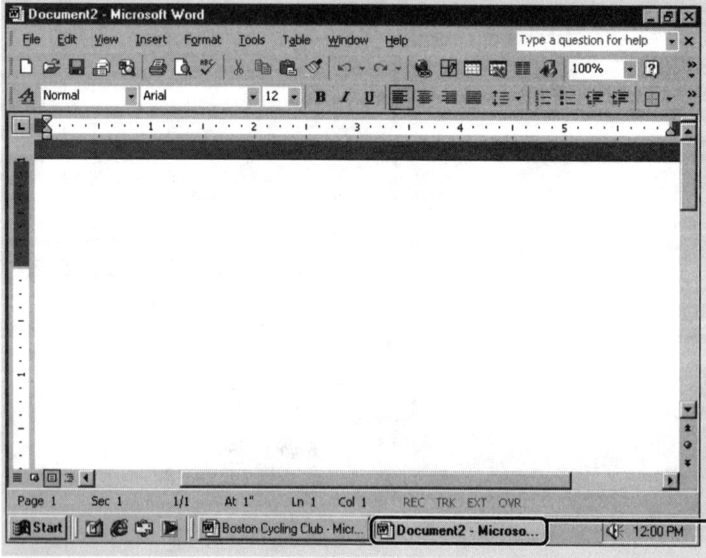

- The new document appears in a new Microsoft Word window.
- A button for the new document appears on the taskbar.

SWITCH BETWEEN DOCUMENTS

You can have several documents open at once. Word allows you to easily switch from one open document to another. Switching between documents is useful when you are working on several related documents.

SWITCH BETWEEN DOCUMENTS

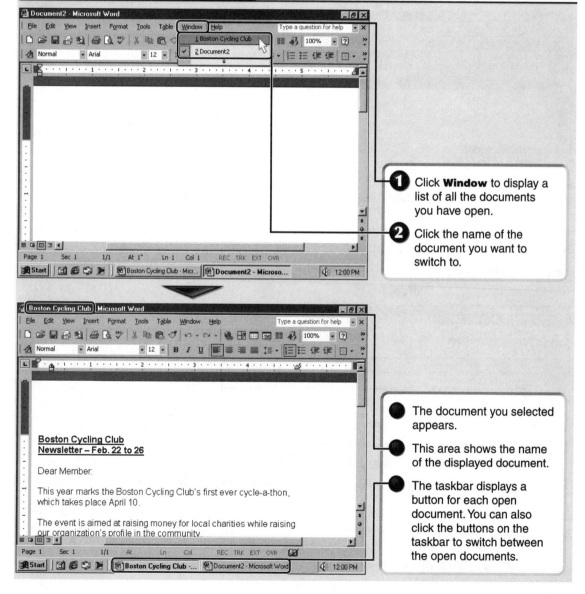

1 Click **Window** to display a list of all the documents you have open.

2 Click the name of the document you want to switch to.

● The document you selected appears.

● This area shows the name of the displayed document.

● The taskbar displays a button for each open document. You can also click the buttons on the taskbar to switch between the open documents.

E-MAIL A DOCUMENT

You can e-mail the document displayed on your screen to a friend, family member or colleague. When sending an e-mail message, you must specify the e-mail address of each person you want to receive the message. You can also send a copy of the message to people who are not directly involved but would be interested in the message.

E-MAIL A DOCUMENT

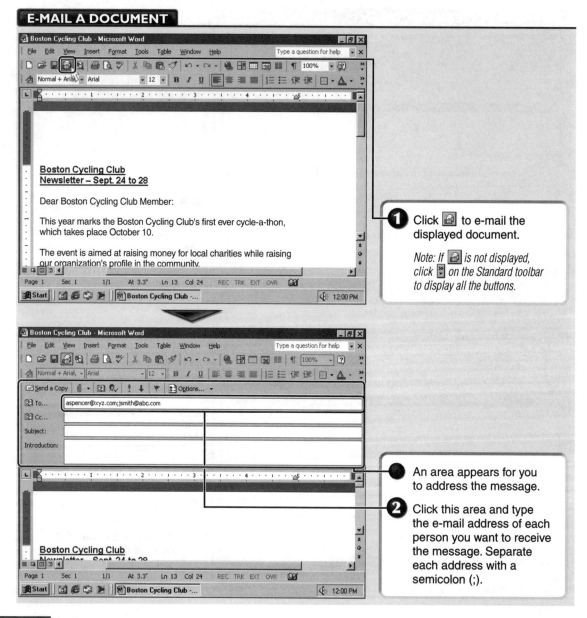

1 Click 🖃 to e-mail the displayed document.

Note: If 🖃 is not displayed, click ➤ on the Standard toolbar to display all the buttons.

■ An area appears for you to address the message.

2 Click this area and type the e-mail address of each person you want to receive the message. Separate each address with a semicolon (;).

in an *instant*

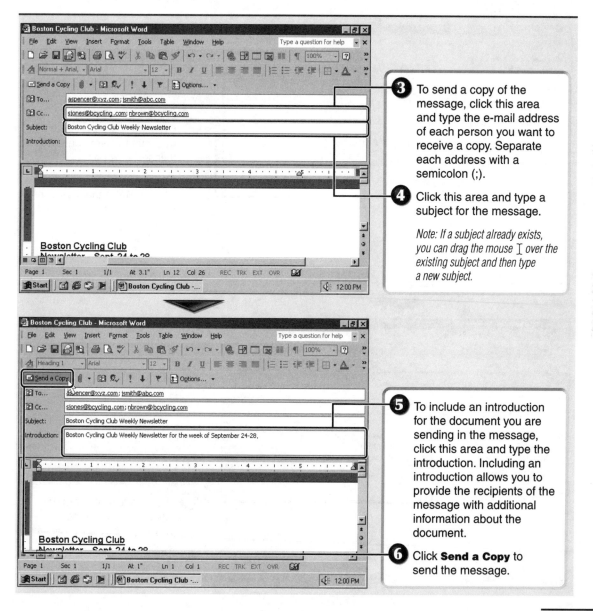

3 To send a copy of the message, click this area and type the e-mail address of each person you want to receive a copy. Separate each address with a semicolon (;).

4 Click this area and type a subject for the message.

Note: If a subject already exists, you can drag the mouse I over the existing subject and then type a new subject.

5 To include an introduction for the document you are sending in the message, click this area and type the introduction. Including an introduction allows you to provide the recipients of the message with additional information about the document.

6 Click **Send a Copy** to send the message.

INSERT TEXT

You can easily insert new text and blank spaces into your document. When you insert new text or blank spaces into a document, the existing text moves to make room for the text or spaces you add.

INSERT TEXT

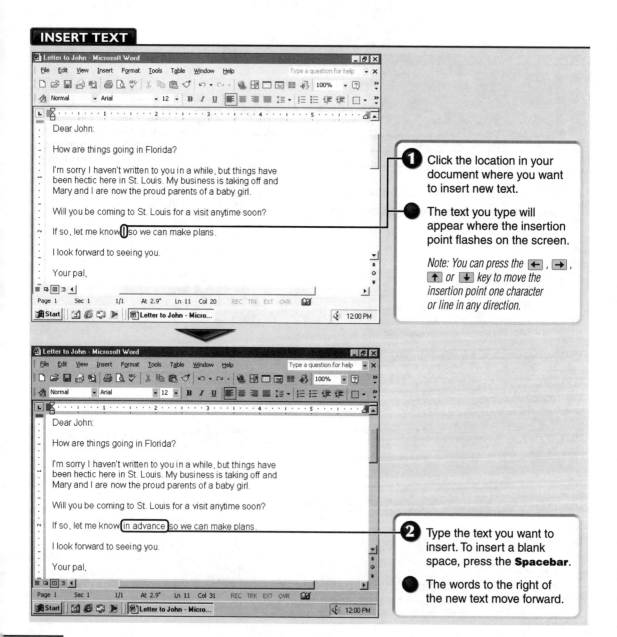

1 Click the location in your document where you want to insert new text.

■ The text you type will appear where the insertion point flashes on the screen.

Note: You can press the ←, →, ↑ or ↓ key to move the insertion point one character or line in any direction.

2 Type the text you want to insert. To insert a blank space, press the **Spacebar**.

■ The words to the right of the new text move forward.

DELETE TEXT

You can remove text you no longer need from your document. You can remove any amount of text, such as a word, sentence or paragraph. When you remove text from a document, the remaining text in the line or paragraph will move to fill the empty space.

DELETE TEXT

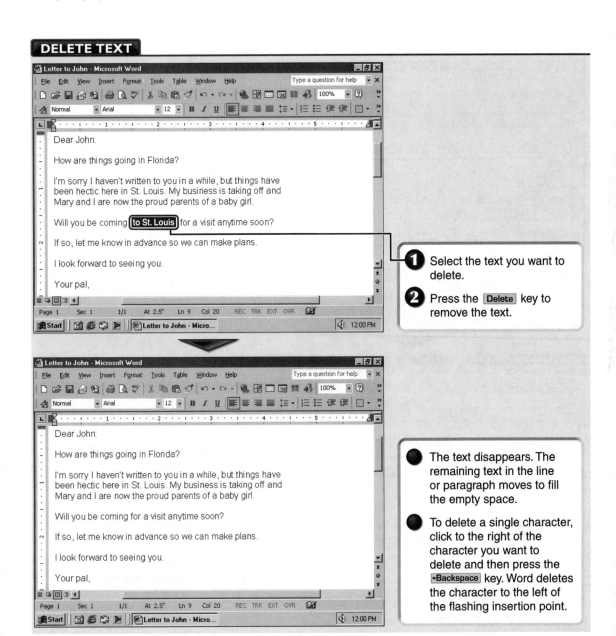

1 Select the text you want to delete.

2 Press the `Delete` key to remove the text.

■ The text disappears. The remaining text in the line or paragraph moves to fill the empty space.

■ To delete a single character, click to the right of the character you want to delete and then press the `◆Backspace` key. Word deletes the character to the left of the flashing insertion point.

MOVE OR COPY TEXT

You can move or copy text to a new location in your document. Moving text allows you to rearrange text in your document. Copying text allows you to repeat information in your document without having to retype the text.

MOVE OR COPY TEXT

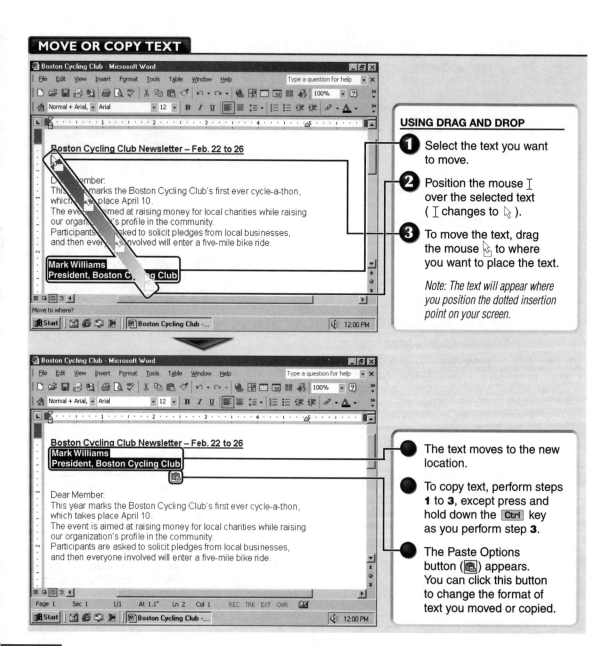

USING DRAG AND DROP

1 Select the text you want to move.

2 Position the mouse I over the selected text (I changes to ⇗).

3 To move the text, drag the mouse ⇗ to where you want to place the text.

Note: The text will appear where you position the dotted insertion point on your screen.

● The text moves to the new location.

● To copy text, perform steps **1** to **3**, except press and hold down the **Ctrl** key as you perform step **3**.

● The Paste Options button (🖺) appears. You can click this button to change the format of text you moved or copied.

in an instant

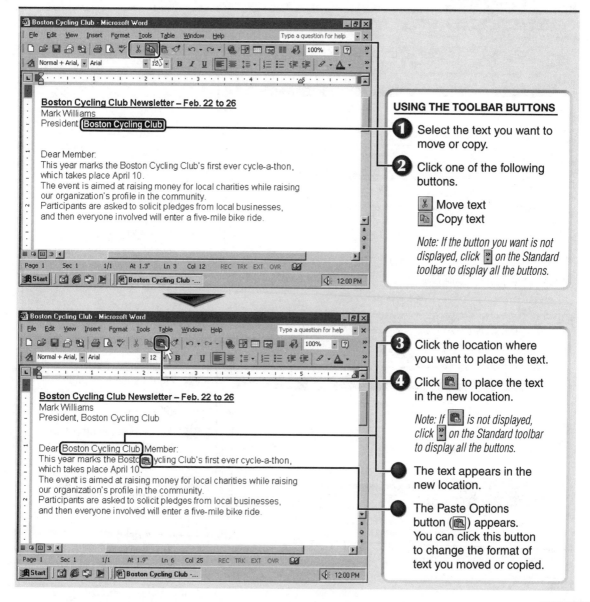

USING THE TOOLBAR BUTTONS

1. Select the text you want to move or copy.

2. Click one of the following buttons.

   ✄ Move text
   📋 Copy text

   Note: If the button you want is not displayed, click ʺ on the Standard toolbar to display all the buttons.

3. Click the location where you want to place the text.

4. Click 📋 to place the text in the new location.

   Note: If 📋 is not displayed, click ʺ on the Standard toolbar to display all the buttons.

● The text appears in the new location.

● The Paste Options button (📋) appears. You can click this button to change the format of text you moved or copied.

UNDO CHANGES

Word remembers the last changes you made to your document. If you regret these changes, you can cancel them by using the Undo feature. The Undo feature can cancel your last editing and formatting changes.

UNDO CHANGES

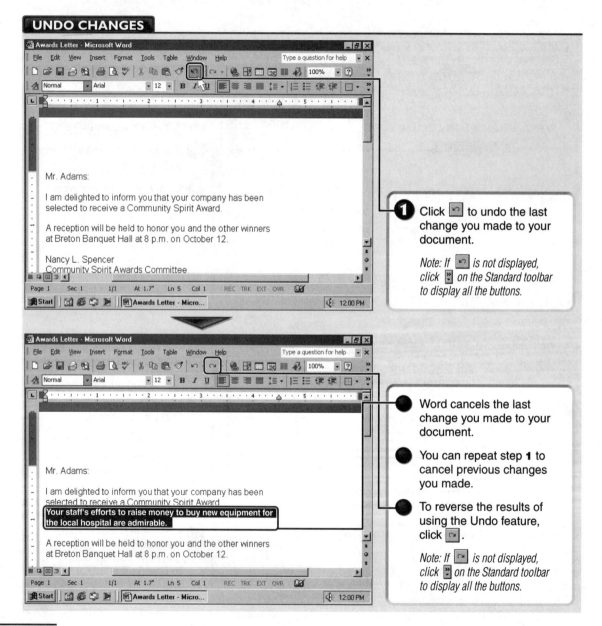

1 Click 🔄 to undo the last change you made to your document.

Note: If 🔄 is not displayed, click ⏵ on the Standard toolbar to display all the buttons.

■ Word cancels the last change you made to your document.

■ You can repeat step **1** to cancel previous changes you made.

■ To reverse the results of using the Undo feature, click 🔄.

Note: If 🔄 is not displayed, click ⏵ on the Standard toolbar to display all the buttons.

COUNT WORDS IN A DOCUMENT

You can have Word count the number of words in your document. When counting the number of words in a document, Word also counts the number of pages, characters, paragraphs and lines in the document.

COUNT WORDS IN A DOCUMENT

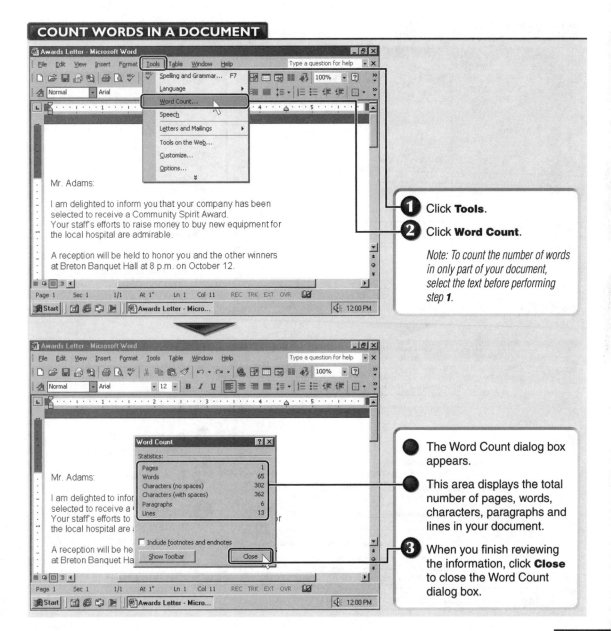

① Click **Tools**.

② Click **Word Count**.

Note: To count the number of words in only part of your document, select the text before performing step 1.

● The Word Count dialog box appears.

● This area displays the total number of pages, words, characters, paragraphs and lines in your document.

③ When you finish reviewing the information, click **Close** to close the Word Count dialog box.

FIND AND REPLACE TEXT

You can find and replace every occurrence of a word
or phrase in your document. This is useful if you have
frequently misspelled a name. For example, you can
quickly change all occurrences of McDonald to Macdonald.

FIND AND REPLACE TEXT

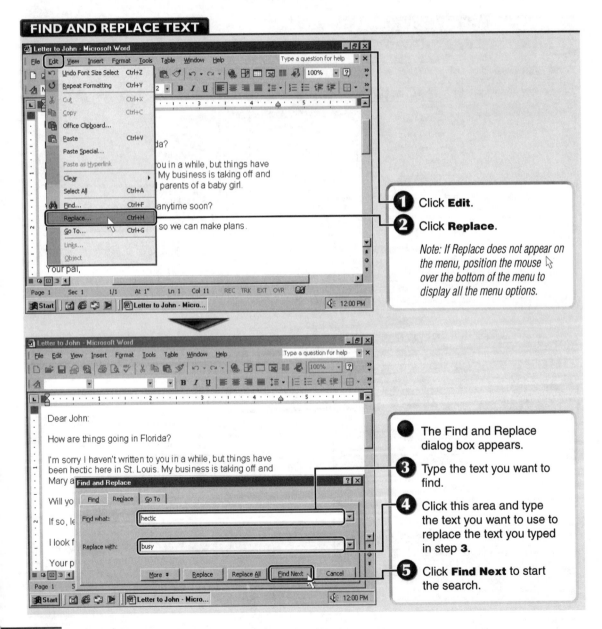

1 Click **Edit**.

2 Click **Replace**.

Note: If Replace does not appear on the menu, position the mouse over the bottom of the menu to display all the menu options.

● The Find and Replace dialog box appears.

3 Type the text you want to find.

4 Click this area and type the text you want to use to replace the text you typed in step **3**.

5 Click **Find Next** to start the search.

in an *instant*

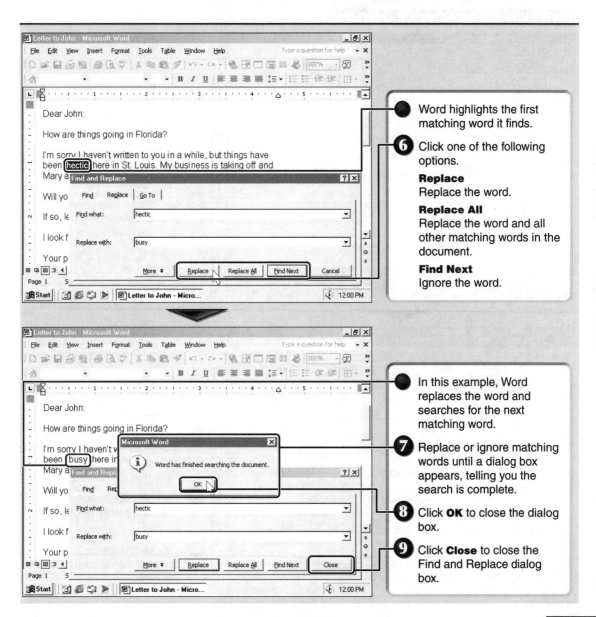

Word highlights the first matching word it finds.

⬤6 Click one of the following options.

Replace
Replace the word.

Replace All
Replace the word and all other matching words in the document.

Find Next
Ignore the word.

In this example, Word replaces the word and searches for the next matching word.

⬤7 Replace or ignore matching words until a dialog box appears, telling you the search is complete.

⬤8 Click **OK** to close the dialog box.

⬤9 Click **Close** to close the Find and Replace dialog box.

CHECK SPELLING AND GRAMMAR

You can find and correct all the spelling and grammar errors in your document. Word compares every word in your document to words in its dictionary. If a word does not exist in the dictionary, the word is considered misspelled.

CHECK SPELLING AND GRAMMAR

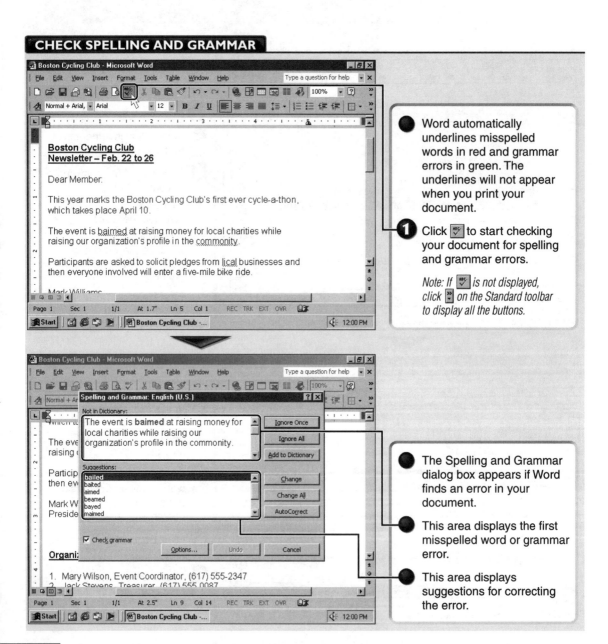

● Word automatically underlines misspelled words in red and grammar errors in green. The underlines will not appear when you print your document.

1 Click 🔤 to start checking your document for spelling and grammar errors.

Note: If 🔤 is not displayed, click ☒ on the Standard toolbar to display all the buttons.

● The Spelling and Grammar dialog box appears if Word finds an error in your document.

● This area displays the first misspelled word or grammar error.

● This area displays suggestions for correcting the error.

in an *instant*

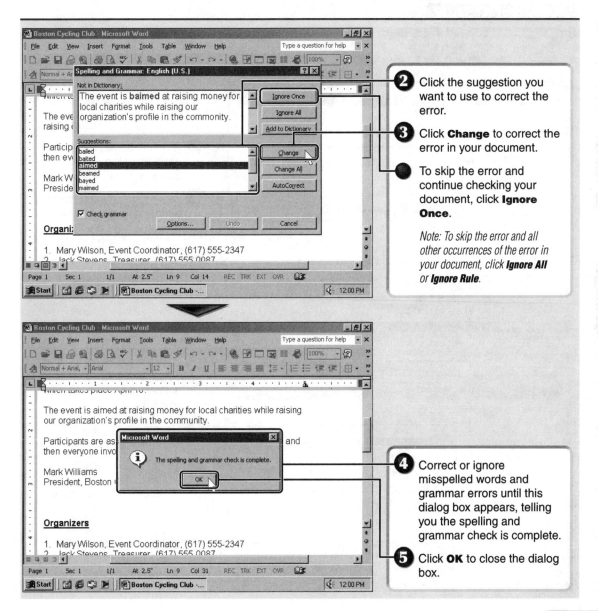

2 Click the suggestion you want to use to correct the error.

3 Click **Change** to correct the error in your document.

To skip the error and continue checking your document, click **Ignore Once**.

*Note: To skip the error and all other occurrences of the error in your document, click **Ignore All** or **Ignore Rule**.*

4 Correct or ignore misspelled words and grammar errors until this dialog box appears, telling you the spelling and grammar check is complete.

5 Click **OK** to close the dialog box.

45

USING SMART TAGS

Word labels certain types of information, such as dates and addresses, with smart tags. You can use a smart tag to perform an action, such as scheduling a meeting for a date or displaying a map for an address.

USING SMART TAGS

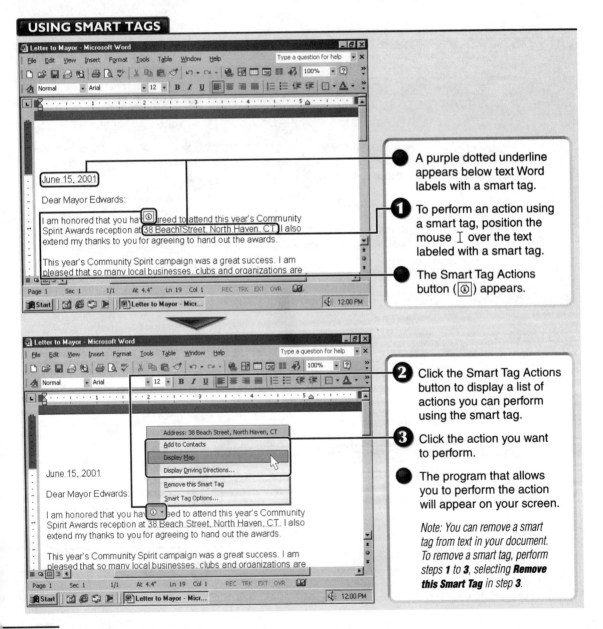

● A purple dotted underline appears below text Word labels with a smart tag.

1 To perform an action using a smart tag, position the mouse I over the text labeled with a smart tag.

● The Smart Tag Actions button (⑤) appears.

2 Click the Smart Tag Actions button to display a list of actions you can perform using the smart tag.

3 Click the action you want to perform.

● The program that allows you to perform the action will appear on your screen.

*Note: You can remove a smart tag from text in your document. To remove a smart tag, perform steps 1 to 3, selecting **Remove this Smart Tag** in step 3.*

in an *instant*

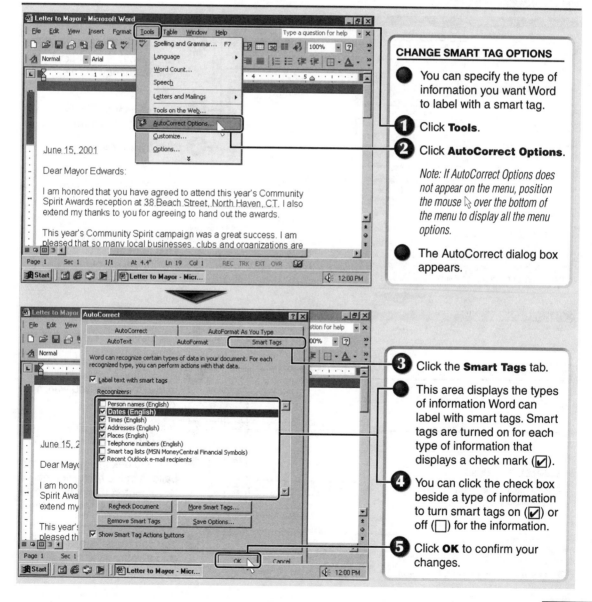

CHANGE SMART TAG OPTIONS

● You can specify the type of information you want Word to label with a smart tag.

1 Click **Tools**.

2 Click **AutoCorrect Options**.

Note: If AutoCorrect Options does not appear on the menu, position the mouse ⩗ over the bottom of the menu to display all the menu options.

● The AutoCorrect dialog box appears.

3 Click the **Smart Tags** tab.

● This area displays the types of information Word can label with smart tags. Smart tags are turned on for each type of information that displays a check mark (☑).

4 You can click the check box beside a type of information to turn smart tags on (☑) or off (☐) for the information.

5 Click **OK** to confirm your changes.

TRACK CHANGES

Word can keep track of the changes that are made to a document. This is useful when multiple people are working with the same document. You can review the changes that have been made to a document and choose whether to accept or reject each change.

TRACK CHANGES

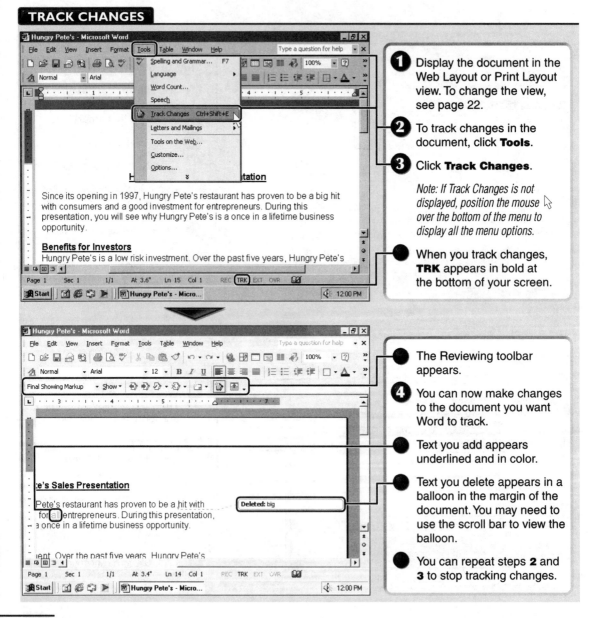

1 Display the document in the Web Layout or Print Layout view. To change the view, see page 22.

2 To track changes in the document, click **Tools**.

3 Click **Track Changes**.

Note: If Track Changes is not displayed, position the mouse over the bottom of the menu to display all the menu options.

■ When you track changes, **TRK** appears in bold at the bottom of your screen.

■ The Reviewing toolbar appears.

4 You can now make changes to the document you want Word to track.

■ Text you add appears underlined and in color.

■ Text you delete appears in a balloon in the margin of the document. You may need to use the scroll bar to view the balloon.

■ You can repeat steps **2** and **3** to stop tracking changes.

in an instant

REVIEW TRACKED CHANGES

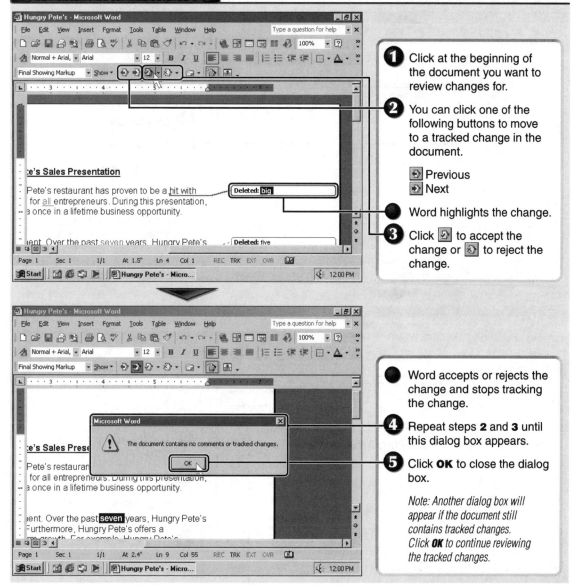

1 Click at the beginning of the document you want to review changes for.

2 You can click one of the following buttons to move to a tracked change in the document.

⬅ Previous
➡ Next

● Word highlights the change.

3 Click 🕗 to accept the change or 🕗 to reject the change.

● Word accepts or rejects the change and stops tracking the change.

4 Repeat steps **2** and **3** until this dialog box appears.

5 Click **OK** to close the dialog box.

*Note: Another dialog box will appear if the document still contains tracked changes. Click **OK** to continue reviewing the tracked changes.*

ADD A CLIP ART IMAGE

You can add a clip art image to your document. Adding a clip art image can make your document more interesting and entertaining. After you add a clip art image, you can resize the image to suit your document. You can also delete a clip art image you no longer need.

ADD A CLIP ART IMAGE

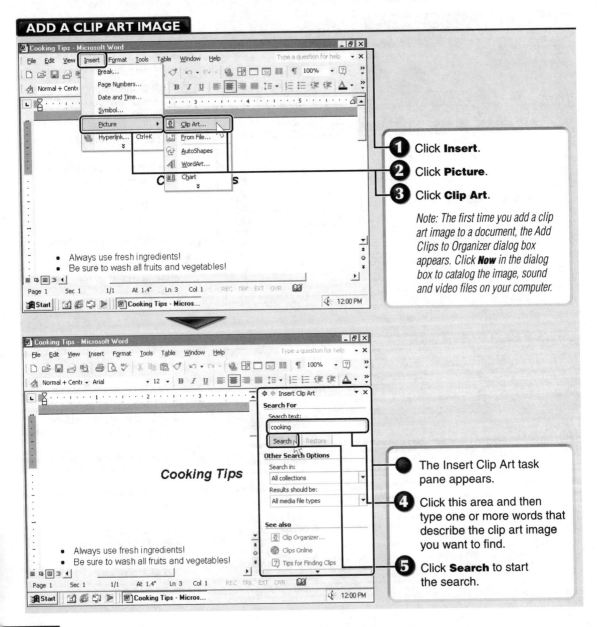

1 Click **Insert**.

2 Click **Picture**.

3 Click **Clip Art**.

*Note: The first time you add a clip art image to a document, the Add Clips to Organizer dialog box appears. Click **Now** in the dialog box to catalog the image, sound and video files on your computer.*

■ The Insert Clip Art task pane appears.

4 Click this area and then type one or more words that describe the clip art image you want to find.

5 Click **Search** to start the search.

in an instant

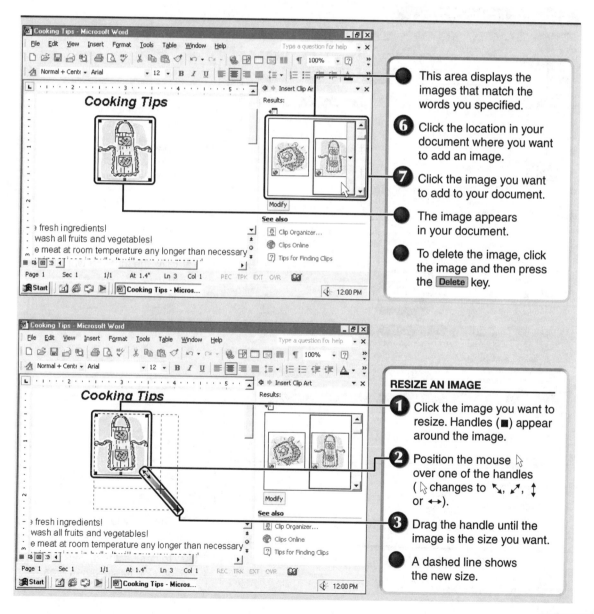

This area displays the images that match the words you specified.

6 Click the location in your document where you want to add an image.

7 Click the image you want to add to your document.

The image appears in your document.

To delete the image, click the image and then press the Delete key.

RESIZE AN IMAGE

1 Click the image you want to resize. Handles (■) appear around the image.

2 Position the mouse ⌖ over one of the handles (⌖ changes to ⬉, ⬈, ↕ or ↔).

3 Drag the handle until the image is the size you want.

A dashed line shows the new size.

CHANGE FONT OF TEXT

You can change the font of text to enhance the appearance of your document. Word provides a list of fonts for you to choose from. The fonts you have used most recently appear at the top of the list.

CHANGE FONT OF TEXT

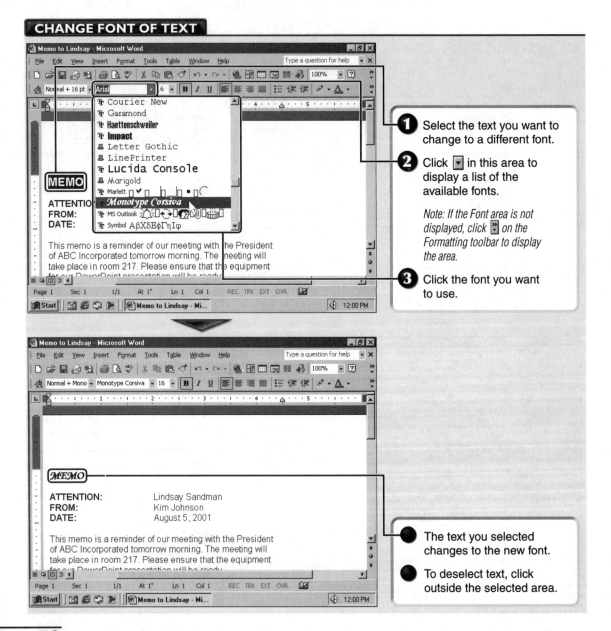

1 Select the text you want to change to a different font.

2 Click ▼ in this area to display a list of the available fonts.

Note: If the Font area is not displayed, click ⯮ on the Formatting toolbar to display the area.

3 Click the font you want to use.

● The text you selected changes to the new font.

● To deselect text, click outside the selected area.

CHANGE SIZE OF TEXT

You can increase or decrease the size of text in your document. Larger text is easier to read, but smaller text allows you to fit more information on a page. Word measures the size of text in points. There are approximately 72 points in an inch.

CHANGE SIZE OF TEXT

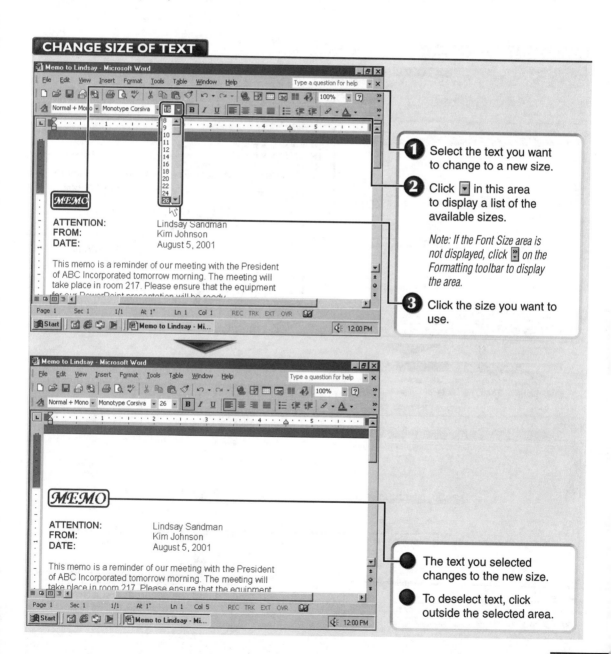

1 Select the text you want to change to a new size.

2 Click ▾ in this area to display a list of the available sizes.

Note: If the Font Size area is not displayed, click ⚏ on the Formatting toolbar to display the area.

3 Click the size you want to use.

● The text you selected changes to the new size.

● To deselect text, click outside the selected area.

CHANGE TEXT COLOR

You can change the color of text to draw attention to headings or important information in your document. Changing the color of text also allows you to enhance the appearance of your document. Word provides several colors for you to choose from.

CHANGE TEXT COLOR

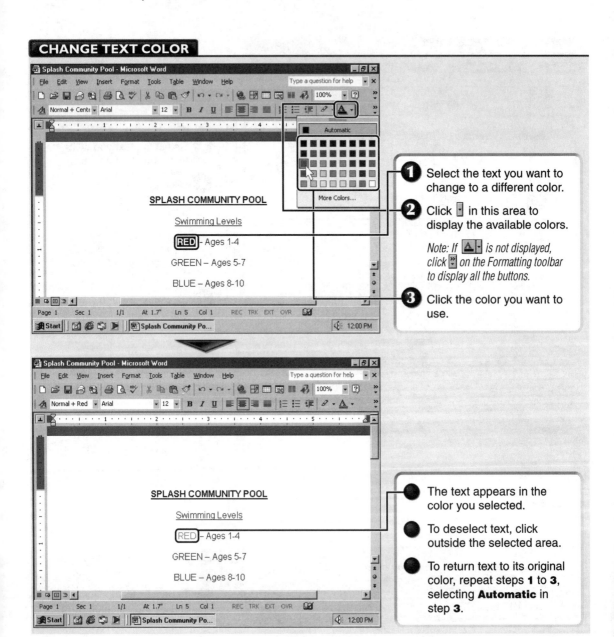

1 Select the text you want to change to a different color.

2 Click ∙ in this area to display the available colors.

Note: If ▲∙ is not displayed, click ▸▸ on the Formatting toolbar to display all the buttons.

3 Click the color you want to use.

● The text appears in the color you selected.

● To deselect text, click outside the selected area.

● To return text to its original color, repeat steps **1** to **3**, selecting **Automatic** in step **3**.

You can highlight text that you want to stand out in your document. Highlighting text is useful for marking information you want to review or verify later. If you plan to print your document on a black-and-white printer, use a light highlight color so you will be able to easily read the printed text.

HIGHLIGHT TEXT

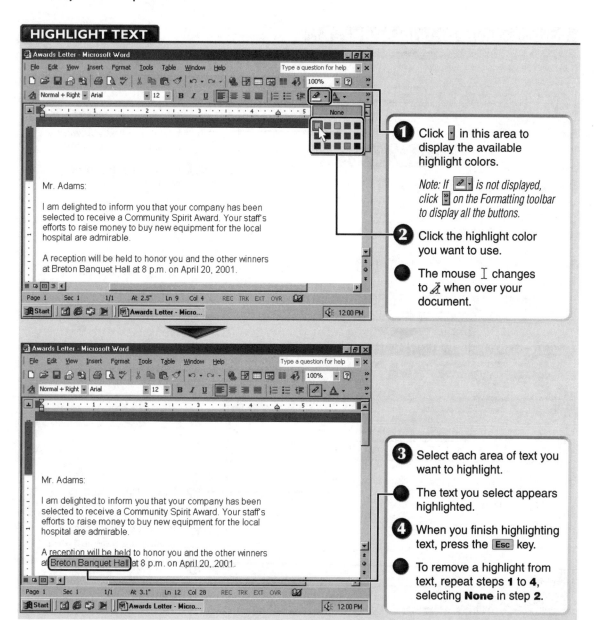

1 Click ▾ in this area to display the available highlight colors.

Note: If ✏▾ is not displayed, click » on the Formatting toolbar to display all the buttons.

2 Click the highlight color you want to use.

● The mouse I changes to ✏ when over your document.

3 Select each area of text you want to highlight.

● The text you select appears highlighted.

4 When you finish highlighting text, press the Esc key.

● To remove a highlight from text, repeat steps 1 to 4, selecting **None** in step 2.

BOLD, ITALICIZE OR UNDERLINE TEXT

You can bold, italicize or underline text to emphasize information in your document. For example, you can bold titles or important words to make them stand out from the rest of the text in your document.

BOLD, ITALICIZE OR UNDERLINE TEXT

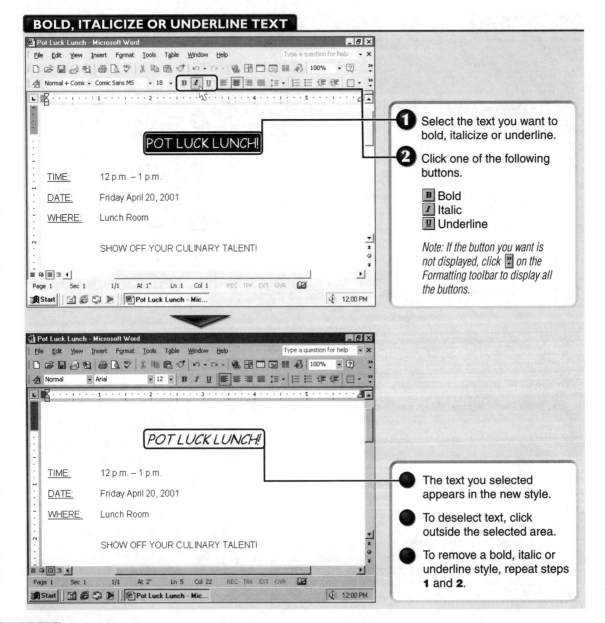

1. Select the text you want to bold, italicize or underline.

2. Click one of the following buttons.

   B Bold
   I Italic
   <u>U</u> Underline

   Note: If the button you want is not displayed, click ⊡ on the Formatting toolbar to display all the buttons.

- The text you selected appears in the new style.

- To deselect text, click outside the selected area.

- To remove a bold, italic or underline style, repeat steps **1** and **2**.

COPY FORMATTING

You can copy the formatting of text to make one area of text in your document look exactly like another. You may want to copy the formatting of text to make all the headings in your document look the same. This will give the text in your document a consistent appearance.

COPY FORMATTING

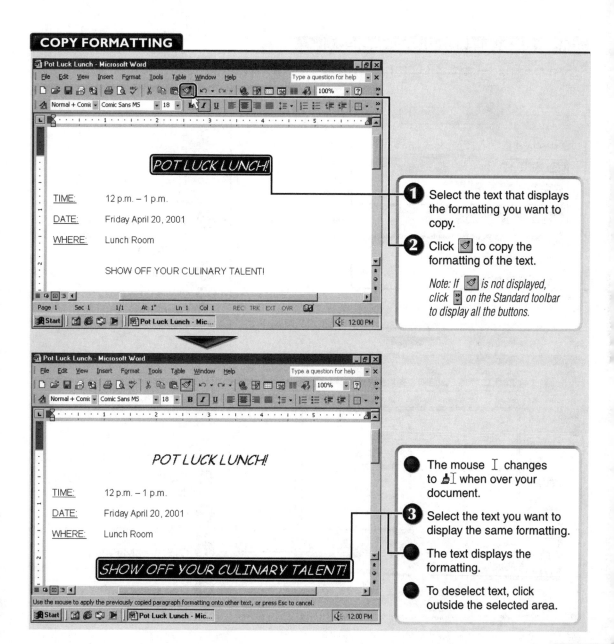

1 Select the text that displays the formatting you want to copy.

2 Click ✍ to copy the formatting of the text.

Note: If ✍ is not displayed, click ☷ on the Standard toolbar to display all the buttons.

● The mouse I changes to 🖌I when over your document.

3 Select the text you want to display the same formatting.

● The text displays the formatting.

● To deselect text, click outside the selected area.

CREATE A BULLETED OR NUMBERED LIST

You can separate items in a list by beginning each item
with a bullet or number. Bulleted lists are useful for items
in no particular order, such as items in a shopping list.
Numbered lists are useful for items in a specific order,
such as instructions in a recipe.

CREATE A BULLETED OR NUMBERED LIST

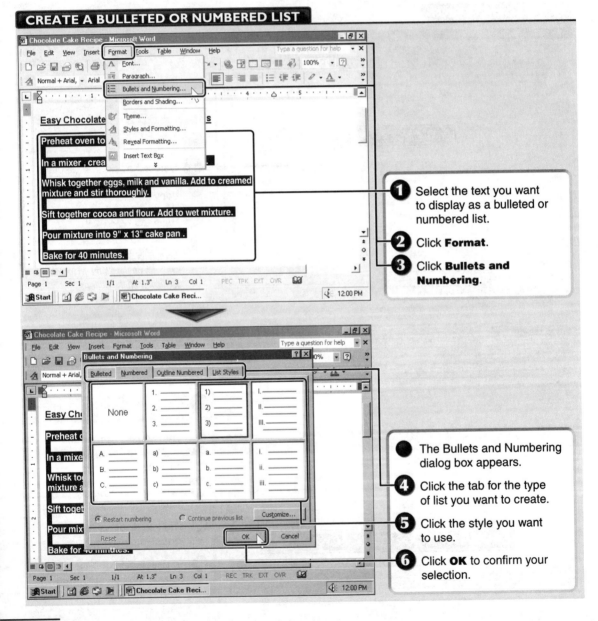

1. Select the text you want to display as a bulleted or numbered list.

2. Click **Format**.

3. Click **Bullets and Numbering**.

■ The Bullets and Numbering dialog box appears.

4. Click the tab for the type of list you want to create.

5. Click the style you want to use.

6. Click **OK** to confirm your selection.

in an *Instant*

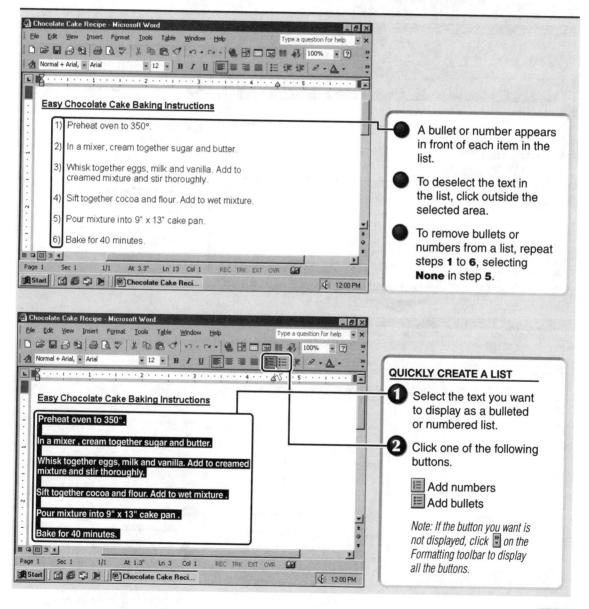

- A bullet or number appears in front of each item in the list.

- To deselect the text in the list, click outside the selected area.

- To remove bullets or numbers from a list, repeat steps **1** to **6**, selecting **None** in step **5**.

QUICKLY CREATE A LIST

1 Select the text you want to display as a bulleted or numbered list.

2 Click one of the following buttons.

≣ Add numbers
≣ Add bullets

Note: If the button you want is not displayed, click ☒ on the Formatting toolbar to display all the buttons.

CHANGE ALIGNMENT OF TEXT

You can change the alignment of text in your document. Word automatically left aligns text that you type. Changing the alignment of text is useful when you want to center a heading or right align an address.

CHANGE ALIGNMENT OF TEXT

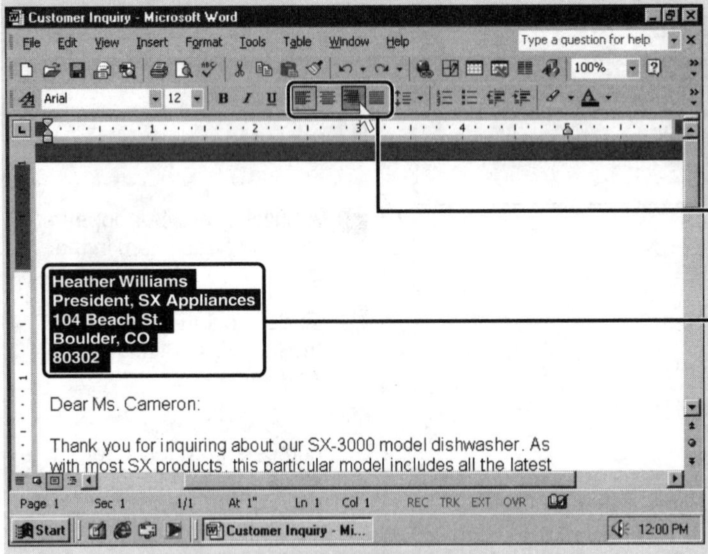

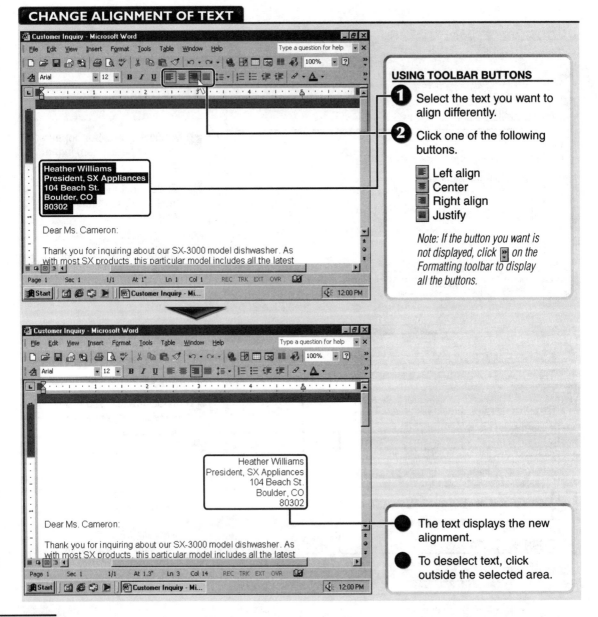

USING TOOLBAR BUTTONS

1. Select the text you want to align differently.
2. Click one of the following buttons.
   - Left align
   - Center
   - Right align
   - Justify

Note: If the button you want is not displayed, click » on the Formatting toolbar to display all the buttons.

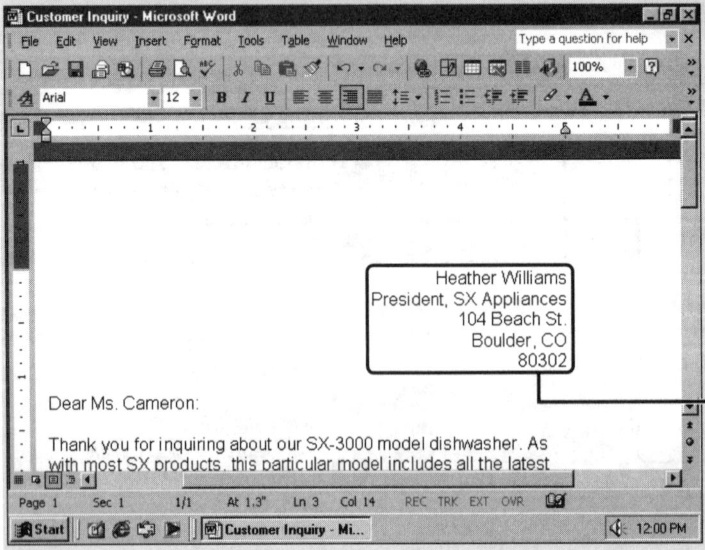

- The text displays the new alignment.
- To deselect text, click outside the selected area.

in an instant

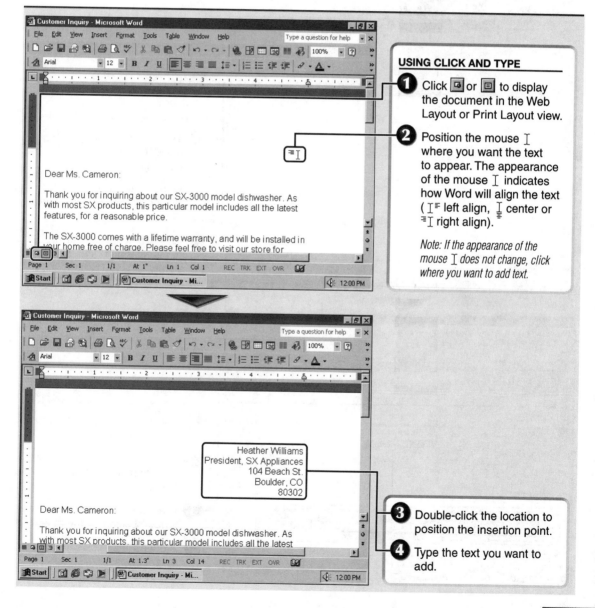

USING CLICK AND TYPE

1 Click 📄 or 📄 to display the document in the Web Layout or Print Layout view.

2 Position the mouse I where you want the text to appear. The appearance of the mouse I indicates how Word will align the text (I⁼ left align, ⫢ center or ⁼I right align).

Note: If the appearance of the mouse I does not change, click where you want to add text.

3 Double-click the location to position the insertion point.

4 Type the text you want to add.

INDENT PARAGRAPHS

You can indent text to make paragraphs in your document stand out. For example, you can indent only the first line of a paragraph to mark the beginning of the paragraph. You can also indent all but the first line of a paragraph to create a hanging indent. Hanging indents are useful when you are creating a glossary.

INDENT PARAGRAPHS

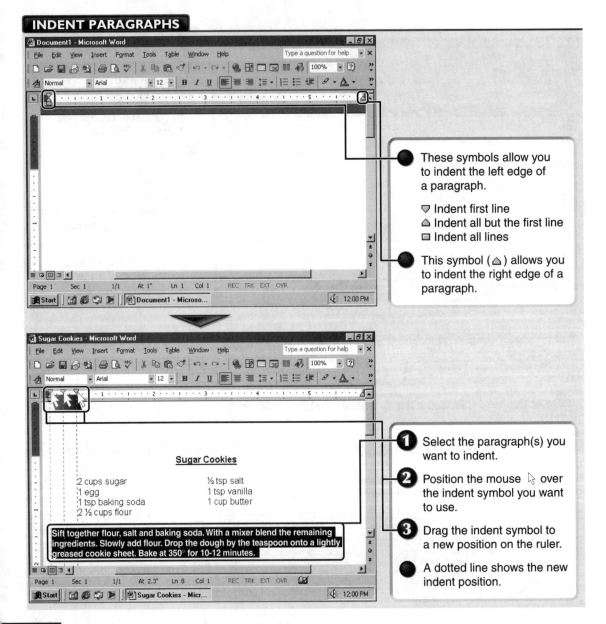

These symbols allow you to indent the left edge of a paragraph.

▽ Indent first line
△ Indent all but the first line
▭ Indent all lines

This symbol (△) allows you to indent the right edge of a paragraph.

1 Select the paragraph(s) you want to indent.

2 Position the mouse ↕ over the indent symbol you want to use.

3 Drag the indent symbol to a new position on the ruler.

■ A dotted line shows the new indent position.

Sugar Cookies

2 cups sugar ½ tsp salt
1 egg 1 tsp vanilla
1 tsp baking soda 1 cup butter
2 ½ cups flour

Sift together flour, salt and baking soda. With a mixer blend the remaining ingredients. Slowly add flour. Drop the dough by the teaspoon onto a lightly greased cookie sheet. Bake at 350° for 10-12 minutes.

in an *instant*

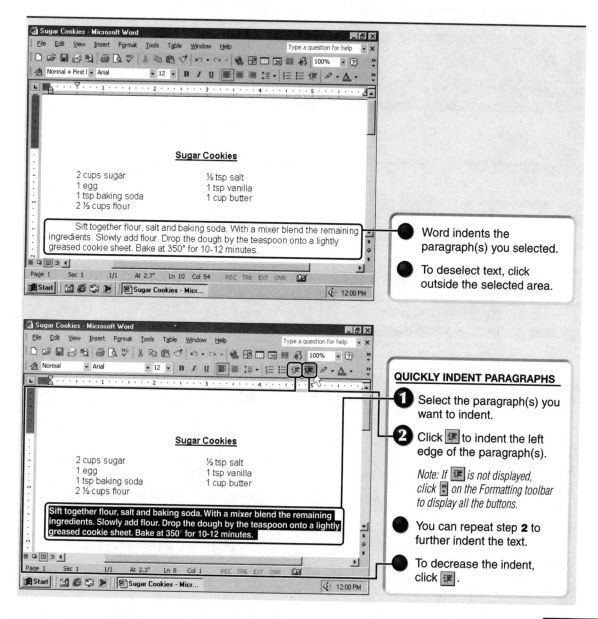

Word indents the paragraph(s) you selected.

To deselect text, click outside the selected area.

QUICKLY INDENT PARAGRAPHS

1 Select the paragraph(s) you want to indent.

2 Click 🔲 to indent the left edge of the paragraph(s).

Note: If 🔲 is not displayed, click »̣ on the Formatting toolbar to display all the buttons.

You can repeat step **2** to further indent the text.

To decrease the indent, click 🔲.

CHANGE TAB SETTINGS

You can use tabs to line up information in your document. Word automatically places a tab every 0.5 inches across a page, but you can add tabs wherever you require them. Word offers several types of tabs that you can choose from. When you no longer need a tab you have added, you can remove it from your document.

CHANGE TAB SETTINGS

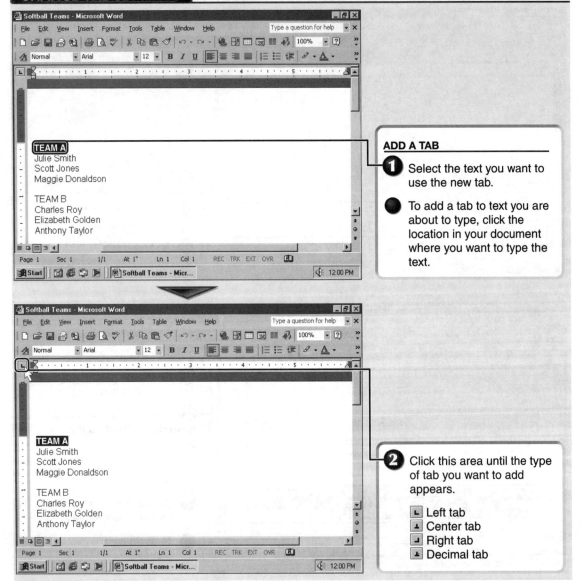

ADD A TAB

① Select the text you want to use the new tab.

● To add a tab to text you are about to type, click the location in your document where you want to type the text.

② Click this area until the type of tab you want to add appears.

- ∟ Left tab
- ⊥ Center tab
- ⅃ Right tab
- ⅃ Decimal tab

in an *instant*

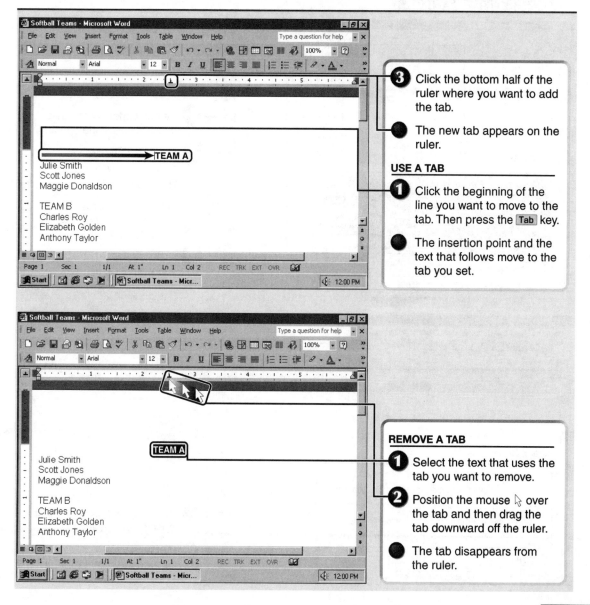

3 Click the bottom half of the ruler where you want to add the tab.

● The new tab appears on the ruler.

USE A TAB

1 Click the beginning of the line you want to move to the tab. Then press the Tab key.

● The insertion point and the text that follows move to the tab you set.

REMOVE A TAB

1 Select the text that uses the tab you want to remove.

2 Position the mouse ⬚ over the tab and then drag the tab downward off the ruler.

● The tab disappears from the ruler.

CHANGE LINE SPACING

You can change the amount of space between the lines of text in your document. Changing the line spacing can make a document easier to review and edit. Word automatically uses single line spacing for text you type into a document.

CHANGE LINE SPACING

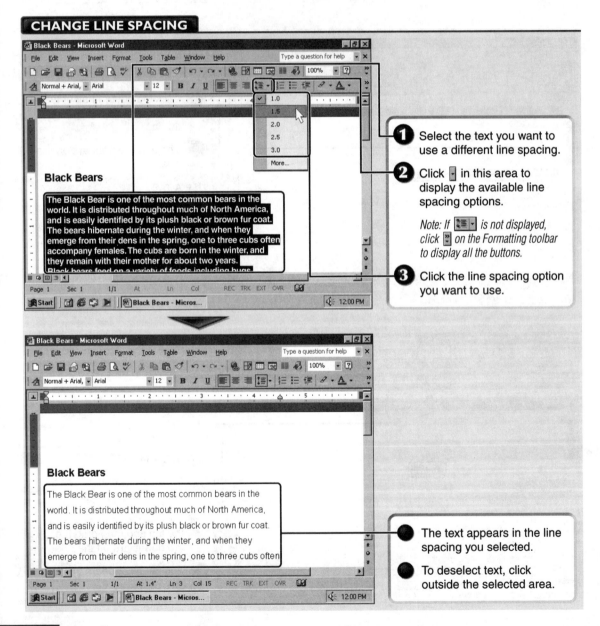

1 Select the text you want to use a different line spacing.

2 Click ⊡ in this area to display the available line spacing options.

Note: If ⊞⊡ is not displayed, click ⊡ on the Formatting toolbar to display all the buttons.

3 Click the line spacing option you want to use.

● The text appears in the line spacing you selected.

● To deselect text, click outside the selected area.

REMOVE FORMATTING FROM TEXT

You can remove the formatting you applied to text in your document. For example, you can remove the font style and color you applied to text. Word allows you to remove the formatting you applied to a word, sentence, paragraph or your entire document.

REMOVE FORMATTING FROM TEXT

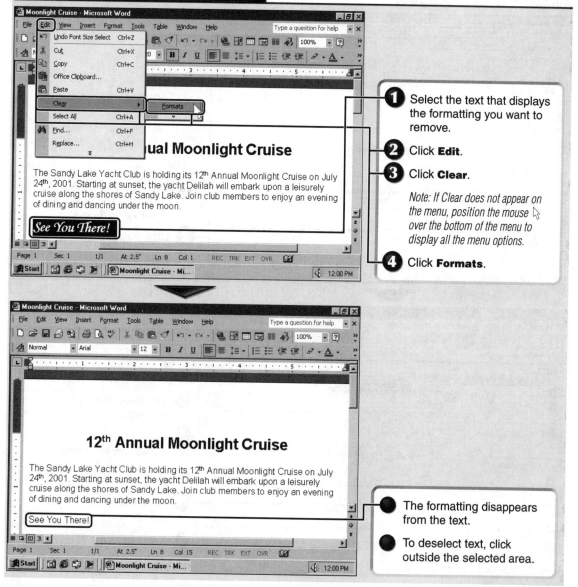

1 Select the text that displays the formatting you want to remove.

2 Click **Edit**.

3 Click **Clear**.

Note: If Clear does not appear on the menu, position the mouse over the bottom of the menu to display all the menu options.

4 Click **Formats**.

● The formatting disappears from the text.

● To deselect text, click outside the selected area.

INSERT A PAGE BREAK

If you want to start a new page at a specific location in your document, you can insert a page break. A page break indicates where one page ends and another begins. Inserting a page break is useful when you want a heading to appear at the top of a new page.

INSERT A PAGE BREAK

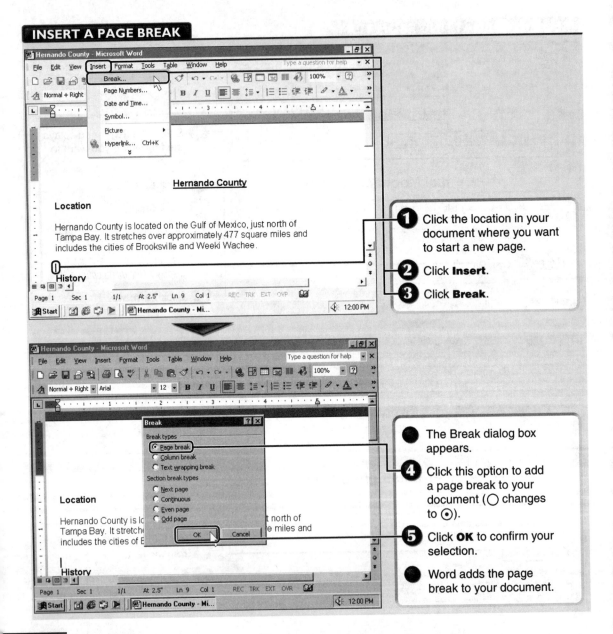

1 Click the location in your document where you want to start a new page.

2 Click **Insert**.

3 Click **Break**.

■ The Break dialog box appears.

4 Click this option to add a page break to your document (○ changes to ⊙).

5 Click **OK** to confirm your selection.

■ Word adds the page break to your document.

in an *instant*

DELETE A PAGE BREAK

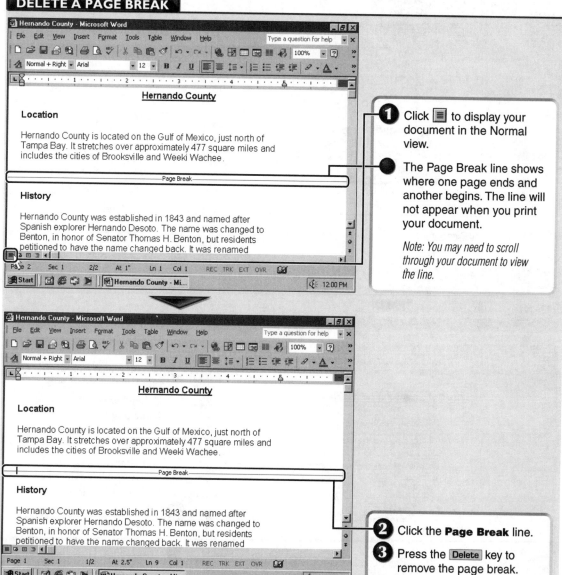

1 Click 🔳 to display your document in the Normal view.

● The Page Break line shows where one page ends and another begins. The line will not appear when you print your document.

Note: You may need to scroll through your document to view the line.

2 Click the **Page Break** line.

3 Press the Delete key to remove the page break.

INSERT A SECTION BREAK

You can insert section breaks to divide your document into sections. Dividing your document into sections allows you to apply formatting to only part of your document. For example, you may want to vertically center text or change the margins for only part of your document.

INSERT A SECTION BREAK

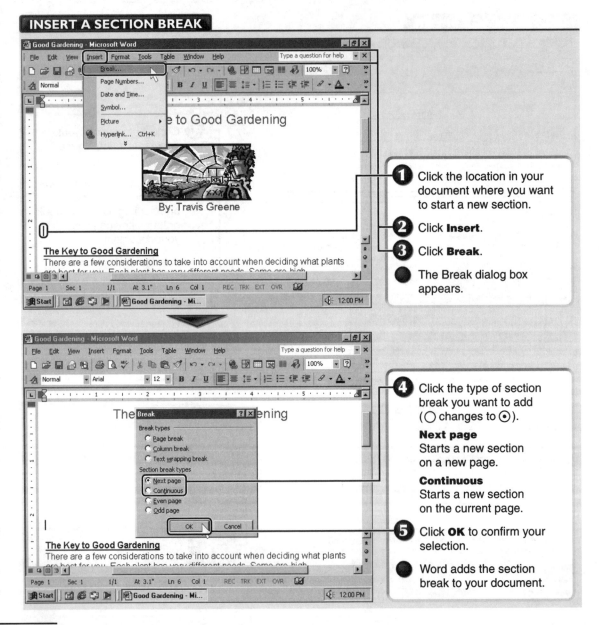

1 Click the location in your document where you want to start a new section.

2 Click **Insert**.

3 Click **Break**.

● The Break dialog box appears.

4 Click the type of section break you want to add (○ changes to ⊙).

Next page
Starts a new section on a new page.

Continuous
Starts a new section on the current page.

5 Click **OK** to confirm your selection.

● Word adds the section break to your document.

in an *instant*

DELETE A SECTION BREAK

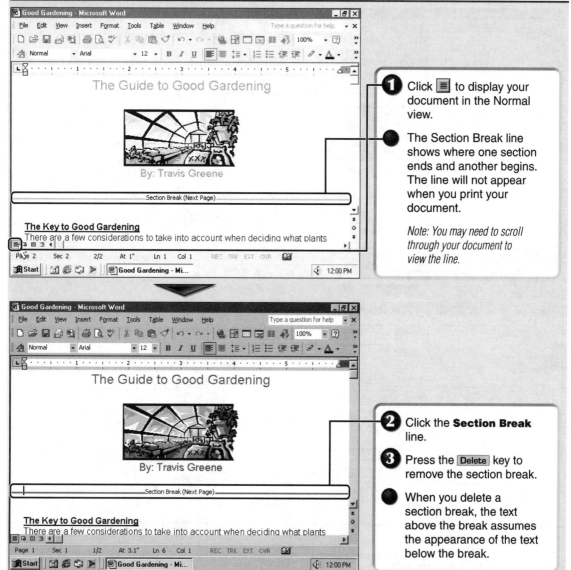

1 Click ▤ to display your document in the Normal view.

● The Section Break line shows where one section ends and another begins. The line will not appear when you print your document.

Note: You may need to scroll through your document to view the line.

2 Click the **Section Break** line.

3 Press the Delete key to remove the section break.

● When you delete a section break, the text above the break assumes the appearance of the text below the break.

CENTER TEXT ON A PAGE

You can vertically center the text in your document. This is useful when creating title pages and short memos. After vertically centering text, you can use the Print Preview feature to see how the centered text will appear on a printed page.

CENTER TEXT ON A PAGE

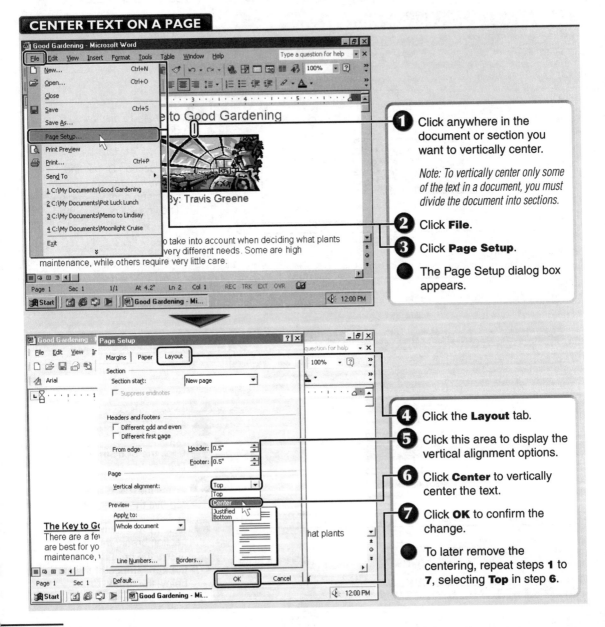

1 Click anywhere in the document or section you want to vertically center.

Note: To vertically center only some of the text in a document, you must divide the document into sections.

2 Click **File**.

3 Click **Page Setup**.

● The Page Setup dialog box appears.

4 Click the **Layout** tab.

5 Click this area to display the vertical alignment options.

6 Click **Center** to vertically center the text.

7 Click **OK** to confirm the change.

● To later remove the centering, repeat steps **1** to **7**, selecting **Top** in step **6**.

CHANGE MARGINS

A margin is the amount of space between the text in your document and the edge of your paper. You can change the margins to suit your needs. Changing margins lets you accommodate letterhead and other specialty paper. Word automatically sets the top and bottom margins to 1 inch and the left and right margins to 1.25 inches.

CHANGE MARGINS

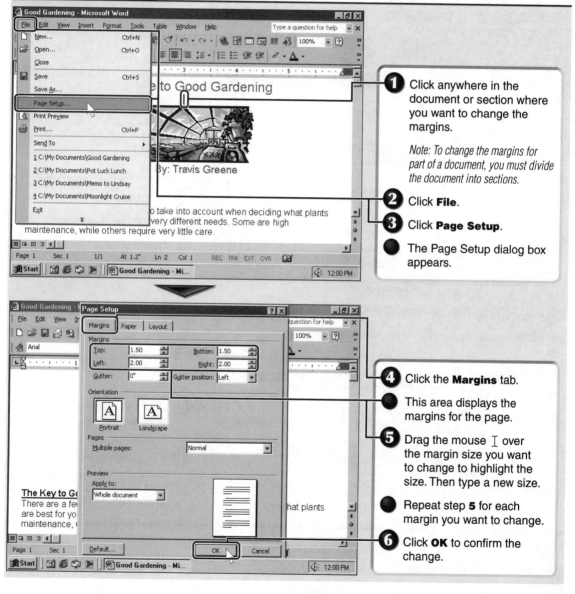

1 Click anywhere in the document or section where you want to change the margins.

Note: To change the margins for part of a document, you must divide the document into sections.

2 Click **File**.

3 Click **Page Setup**.

■ The Page Setup dialog box appears.

4 Click the **Margins** tab.

■ This area displays the margins for the page.

5 Drag the mouse I over the margin size you want to change to highlight the size. Then type a new size.

■ Repeat step **5** for each margin you want to change.

6 Click **OK** to confirm the change.

ADD PAGE NUMBERS

You can have Word number the pages in your document. To view the page numbers on your screen, your document must be displayed in the Print Layout view. If you later make changes that affect the pages in your document, such as adding or removing text, Word will automatically adjust the page numbers for you.

ADD PAGE NUMBERS

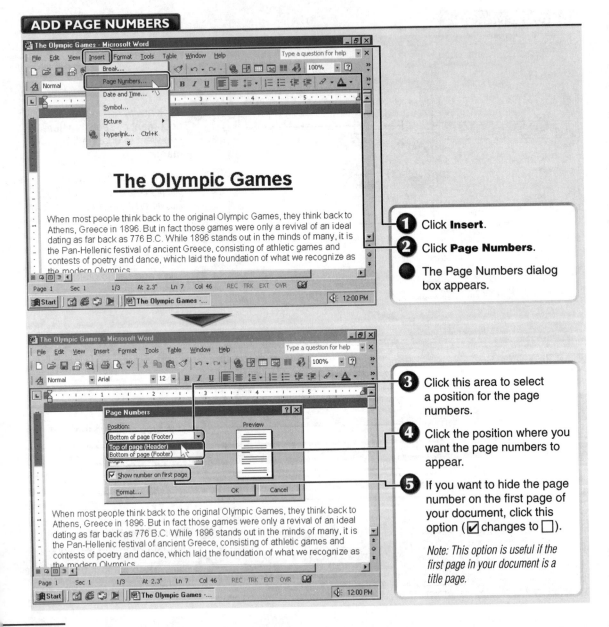

1 Click **Insert**.

2 Click **Page Numbers**.

● The Page Numbers dialog box appears.

3 Click this area to select a position for the page numbers.

4 Click the position where you want the page numbers to appear.

5 If you want to hide the page number on the first page of your document, click this option (☑ changes to ☐).

Note: This option is useful if the first page in your document is a title page.

in an *instant*

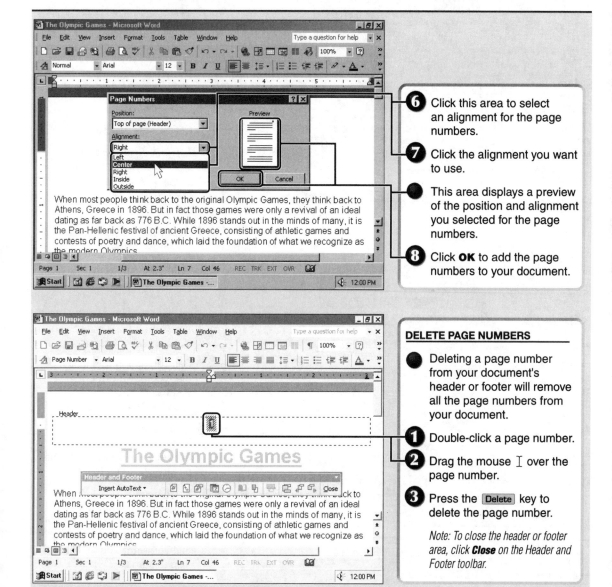

6 Click this area to select an alignment for the page numbers.

7 Click the alignment you want to use.

This area displays a preview of the position and alignment you selected for the page numbers.

8 Click **OK** to add the page numbers to your document.

DELETE PAGE NUMBERS

Deleting a page number from your document's header or footer will remove all the page numbers from your document.

1 Double-click a page number.

2 Drag the mouse I over the page number.

3 Press the Delete key to delete the page number.

*Note: To close the header or footer area, click **Close** on the Header and Footer toolbar.*

ADD A WATERMARK

You can display a faint picture or text behind the information in your document. This can add interest or identify the status of the document. Common text watermarks include ASAP, Confidential, Copy, Personal, Sample and Urgent. Word can only display watermarks in the Print Layout view.

ADD A WATERMARK

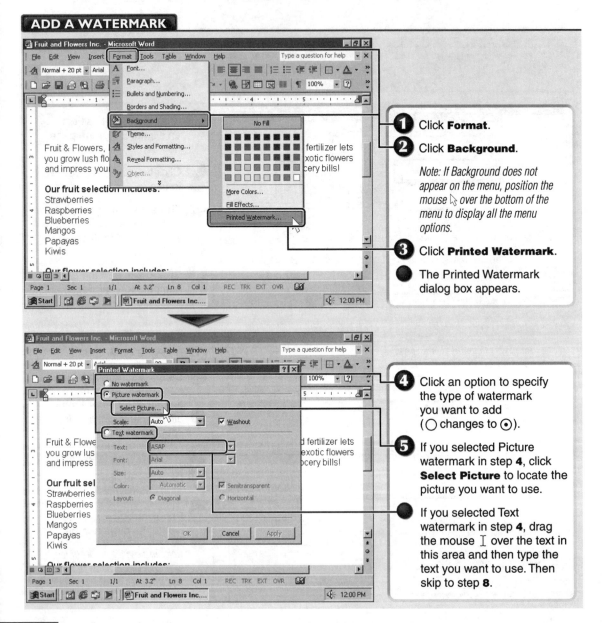

1 Click **Format**.

2 Click **Background**.

Note: If Background does not appear on the menu, position the mouse over the bottom of the menu to display all the menu options.

3 Click **Printed Watermark**.

● The Printed Watermark dialog box appears.

4 Click an option to specify the type of watermark you want to add (○ changes to ●).

5 If you selected Picture watermark in step **4**, click **Select Picture** to locate the picture you want to use.

● If you selected Text watermark in step **4**, drag the mouse I over the text in this area and then type the text you want to use. Then skip to step **8**.

in an *Instant*

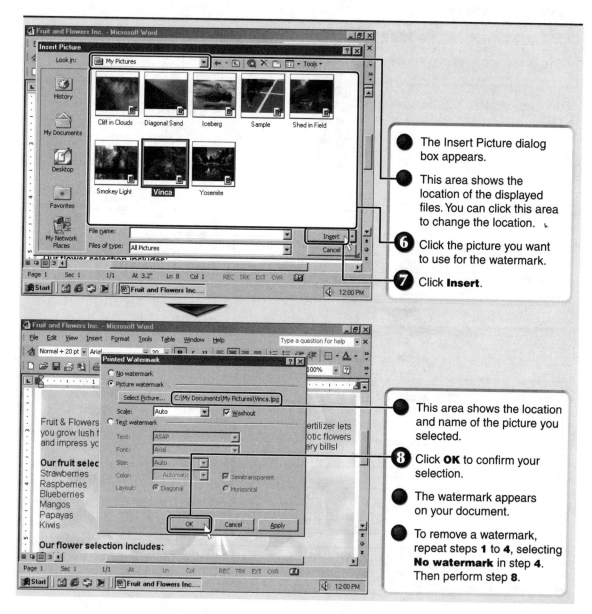

The Insert Picture dialog box appears.

This area shows the location of the displayed files. You can click this area to change the location.

6 Click the picture you want to use for the watermark.

7 Click **Insert**.

This area shows the location and name of the picture you selected.

8 Click **OK** to confirm your selection.

The watermark appears on your document.

To remove a watermark, repeat steps **1** to **4**, selecting **No watermark** in step **4**. Then perform step **8**.

CREATE A TABLE

You can create a table to neatly display information in your document. A table is made up of rows, columns and cells. You can edit and format the text you enter into a table as you would edit and format any text in your document.

CREATE A TABLE

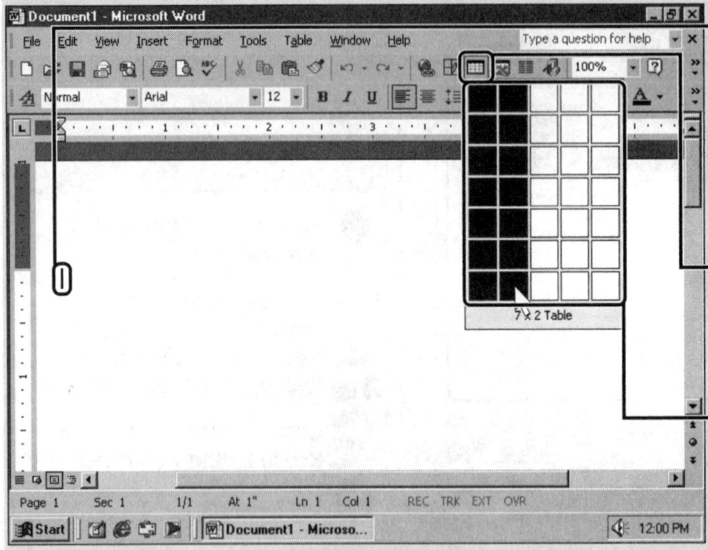

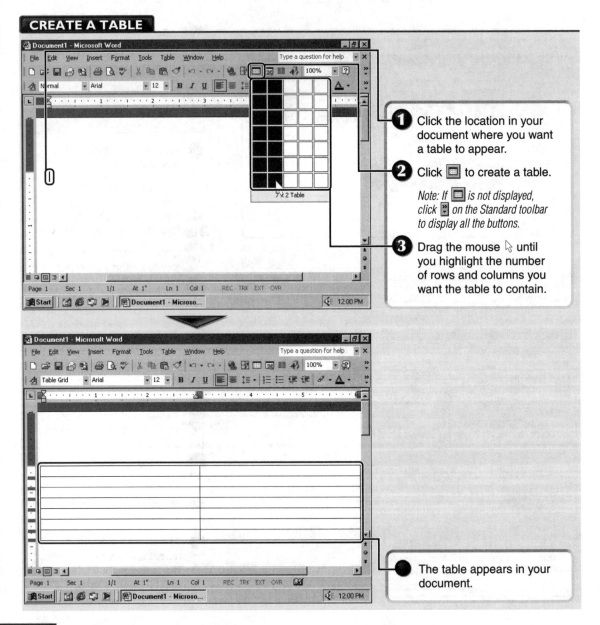

1 Click the location in your document where you want a table to appear.

2 Click ▦ to create a table.

Note: If ▦ is not displayed, click » on the Standard toolbar to display all the buttons.

3 Drag the mouse ↖ until you highlight the number of rows and columns you want the table to contain.

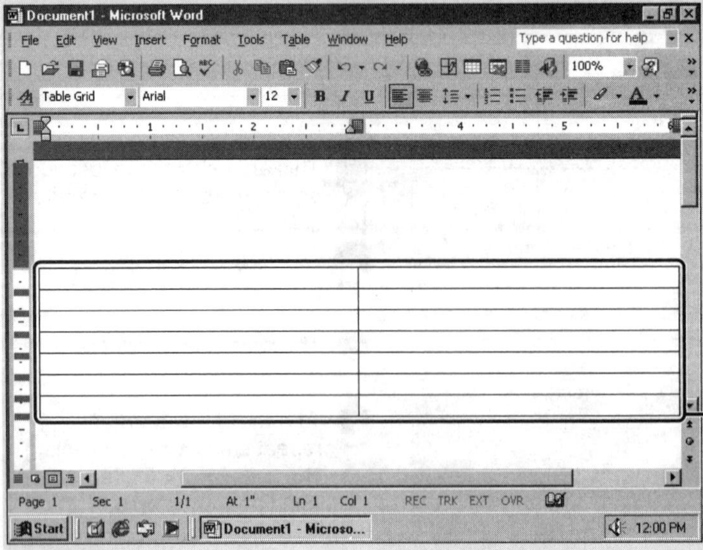

● The table appears in your document.

in an instant

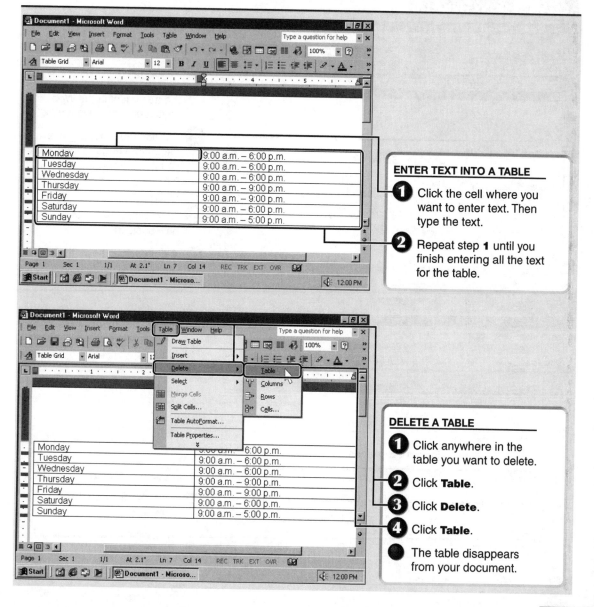

ENTER TEXT INTO A TABLE

1 Click the cell where you want to enter text. Then type the text.

2 Repeat step **1** until you finish entering all the text for the table.

DELETE A TABLE

1 Click anywhere in the table you want to delete.

2 Click **Table**.

3 Click **Delete**.

4 Click **Table**.

● The table disappears from your document.

CHANGE ROW HEIGHT OR COLUMN WIDTH

You can change the height of rows and the width of columns to improve the layout of your table. When you change a row height or column width, all the cells in the row or column are affected. You cannot change the height or width of a single cell.

CHANGE ROW HEIGHT

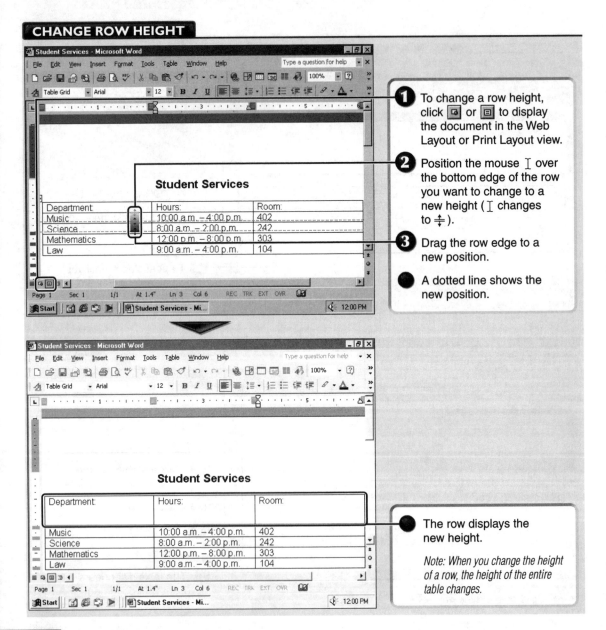

1 To change a row height, click 🔲 or 🔲 to display the document in the Web Layout or Print Layout view.

2 Position the mouse I over the bottom edge of the row you want to change to a new height (I changes to ⇕).

3 Drag the row edge to a new position.

● A dotted line shows the new position.

● The row displays the new height.

Note: When you change the height of a row, the height of the entire table changes.

in an *instant*

CHANGE COLUMN WIDTH

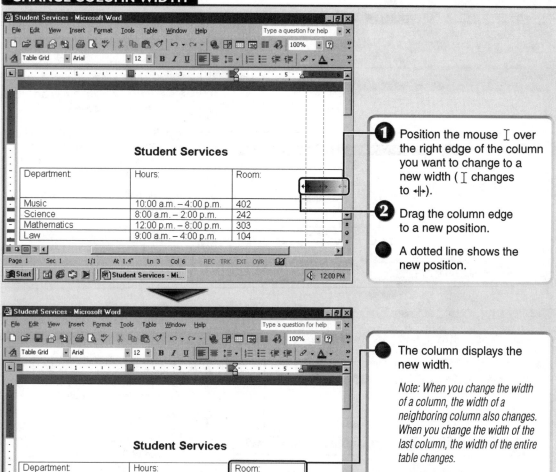

1 Position the mouse I over the right edge of the column you want to change to a new width (I changes to +‖+).

2 Drag the column edge to a new position.

● A dotted line shows the new position.

● The column displays the new width.

Note: When you change the width of a column, the width of a neighboring column also changes. When you change the width of the last column, the width of the entire table changes.

FIT LONGEST ITEM

1 To quickly change a column width to fit the longest item in the column, double-click the right edge of the column.

ADD A ROW OR COLUMN

You can add a row or column to your table to insert additional information. You can also delete a row or column you no longer need. When you delete a row or column from your table, all the information in the row or column is also deleted.

ADD A ROW

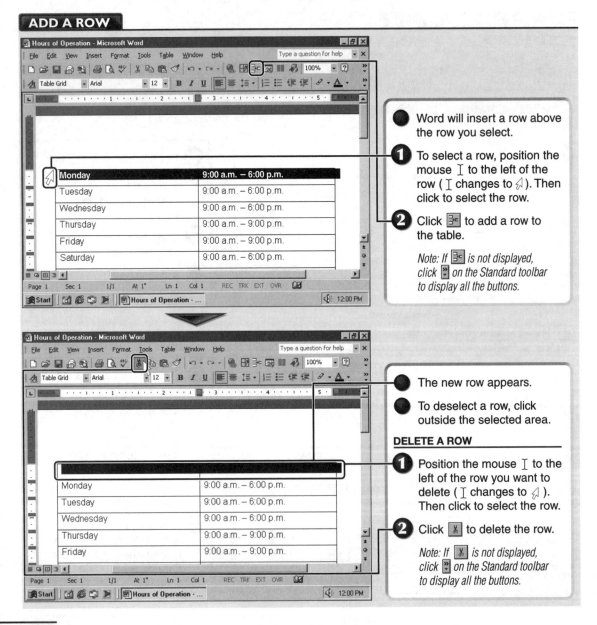

● Word will insert a row above the row you select.

1 To select a row, position the mouse I to the left of the row (I changes to ⟨⟩). Then click to select the row.

2 Click ⬚ to add a row to the table.

Note: If ⬚ is not displayed, click ⟫ on the Standard toolbar to display all the buttons.

● The new row appears.

● To deselect a row, click outside the selected area.

DELETE A ROW

1 Position the mouse I to the left of the row you want to delete (I changes to ⟨⟩). Then click to select the row.

2 Click ✂ to delete the row.

Note: If ✂ is not displayed, click ⟫ on the Standard toolbar to display all the buttons.

in an instant

ADD A COLUMN

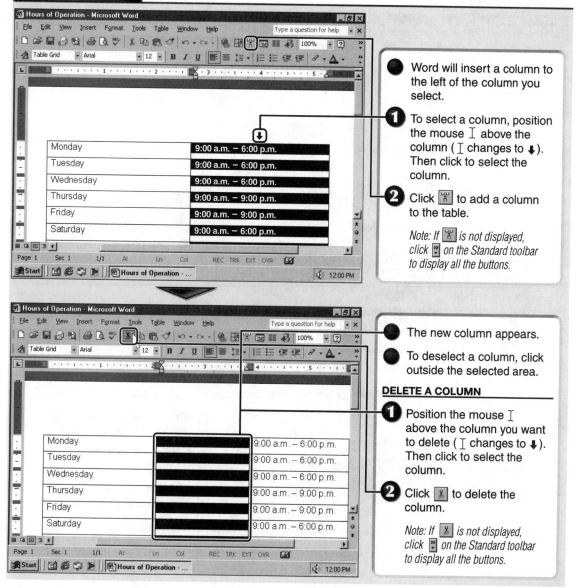

Word will insert a column to the left of the column you select.

1 To select a column, position the mouse I above the column (I changes to ↓). Then click to select the column.

2 Click 🖽 to add a column to the table.

Note: If 🖽 is not displayed, click » on the Standard toolbar to display all the buttons.

The new column appears.

To deselect a column, click outside the selected area.

DELETE A COLUMN

1 Position the mouse I above the column you want to delete (I changes to ↓). Then click to select the column.

2 Click ✂ to delete the column.

Note: If ✂ is not displayed, click » on the Standard toolbar to display all the buttons.

FORMAT A TABLE

Word offers many ready-to-use designs that you can choose from to give your table a professional appearance. Each design offers options you can use to apply special formats to the heading row, first column, last row and last column in your table.

FORMAT A TABLE

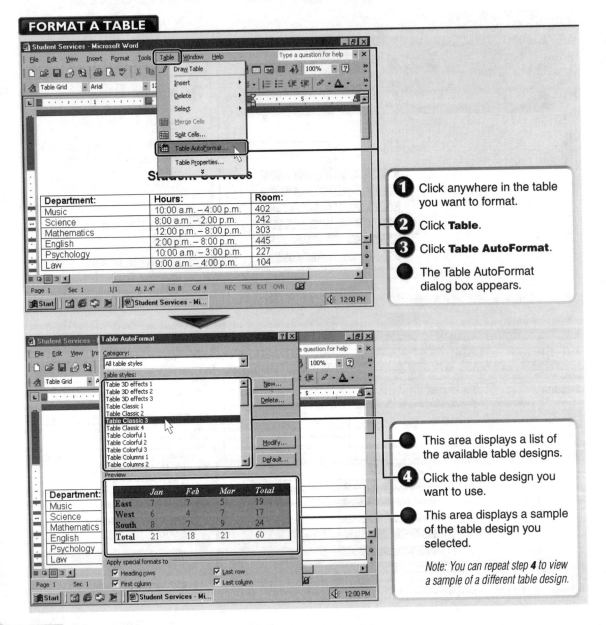

1 Click anywhere in the table you want to format.

2 Click **Table**.

3 Click **Table AutoFormat**.

■ The Table AutoFormat dialog box appears.

■ This area displays a list of the available table designs.

4 Click the table design you want to use.

■ This area displays a sample of the table design you selected.

Note: You can repeat step 4 to view a sample of a different table design.

in an instant

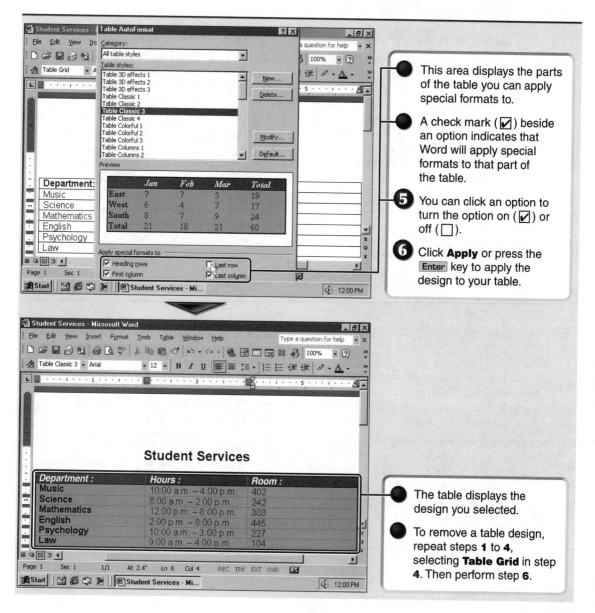

This area displays the parts of the table you can apply special formats to.

A check mark (☑) beside an option indicates that Word will apply special formats to that part of the table.

5 You can click an option to turn the option on (☑) or off (☐).

6 Click **Apply** or press the Enter key to apply the design to your table.

The table displays the design you selected.

To remove a table design, repeat steps **1** to **4**, selecting **Table Grid** in step **4**. Then perform step **6**.

INTRODUCTION TO EXCEL

Excel is a spreadsheet program you can use to organize, analyze and attractively present data, such as a budget or sales report.

INTRODUCTION TO EXCEL

ENTER AND EDIT DATA

Excel allows you to efficiently enter and edit data in a worksheet. Excel can help you quickly enter data by completing a series of numbers or text for you. When you want to re-arrange the data in a worksheet, you can move or copy data to a new location in the worksheet. You can also insert new rows and columns into a worksheet to accommodate new data. Excel remembers the last changes you made to a worksheet, so you can undo changes you regret.

You can store data on more than one worksheet and easily switch between worksheets to work with the data. Excel also makes it easy to add a worksheet to store new data or delete a worksheet you no longer need.

USE FORMULAS AND FUNCTIONS

Formulas and functions allow you to perform calculations and analyze data in a worksheet. Common calculations include finding the sum, average or total number of values in a list.

If you change a value used in a formula or function, Excel will automatically redo the calculation for you and display the new result. When Excel cannot properly calculate or display the result of a formula, the program displays an error message to help you correct the problem.

FORMAT WORKSHEETS

Excel includes many formatting features that can help you change the appearance of a worksheet. Excel allows you to change the width of columns and the height of rows to better fit the data in a worksheet.

You can bold, italicize or underline data to emphasize important data in a worksheet. You can also make data in a worksheet easier to read by changing the font and size of data or by changing the appearance of numbers to display formats such as currency and percent.

CREATE CHARTS

Excel helps you create colorful charts from worksheet data to visually display the data. If you change the worksheet data, Excel will automatically update the chart to display the changes. You can move and resize a chart to suit your needs. You can also change the chart type to present the data more effectively. Some types of charts are ideal for showing changes to values over time, while other chart types are ideal for showing percentages. When you print a chart, you can choose to print the chart with the worksheet data or on its own page.

THE EXCEL WINDOW

The Excel window displays many items you can use to work with your data, such as menus, toolbars and a task pane.

THE EXCEL WINDOW

Menu Bar

Provides access to lists of commands available in Excel and displays an area where you can type a question to get help information.

Title Bar

Shows the name of the displayed workbook.

Standard Toolbar

Contains buttons you can use to select common commands, such as Save and Print.

Formatting Toolbar

Contains buttons you can use to select common formatting commands, such as Bold and Underline.

Formula Bar

Displays the cell reference and the contents of the active cell. A cell reference identifies the location of each cell in a worksheet and consists of a column letter followed by a row number, such as A1.

Active Cell

Displays a thick border. You enter data into the active cell.

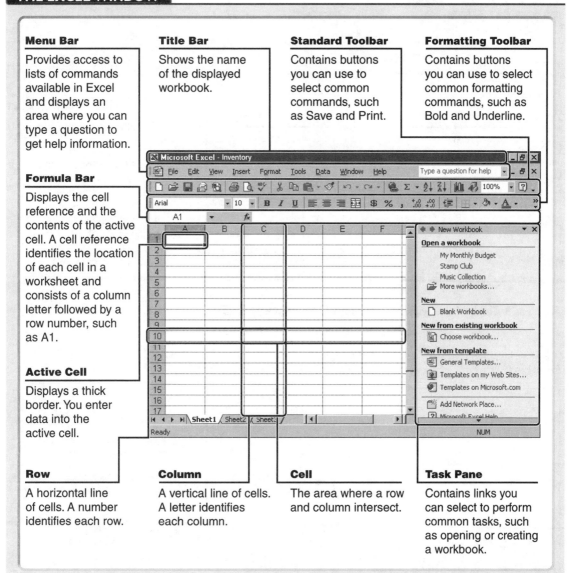

Row

A horizontal line of cells. A number identifies each row.

Column

A vertical line of cells. A letter identifies each column.

Cell

The area where a row and column intersect.

Task Pane

Contains links you can select to perform common tasks, such as opening or creating a workbook.

CHANGE THE ACTIVE CELL

You can make any cell in your worksheet the active cell. You enter data into the active cell, which displays a thick border. You can make only one cell in your worksheet active at a time.

CHANGE THE ACTIVE CELL

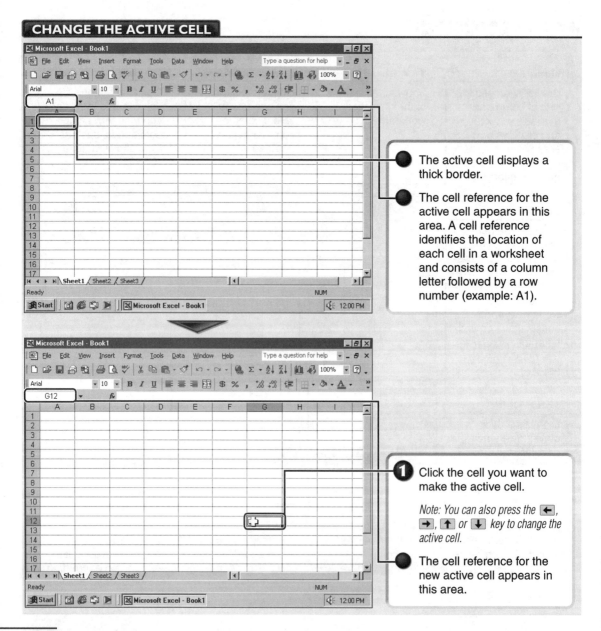

The active cell displays a thick border.

The cell reference for the active cell appears in this area. A cell reference identifies the location of each cell in a worksheet and consists of a column letter followed by a row number (example: A1).

1 Click the cell you want to make the active cell.

Note: You can also press the ←, →, ↑ or ↓ key to change the active cell.

The cell reference for the new active cell appears in this area.

SCROLL THROUGH A WORKSHEET

You can scroll through your worksheet to view other areas of the worksheet. This is useful when your worksheet contains a lot of data and your computer screen cannot display all the data at once.

SCROLL THROUGH A WORKSHEET

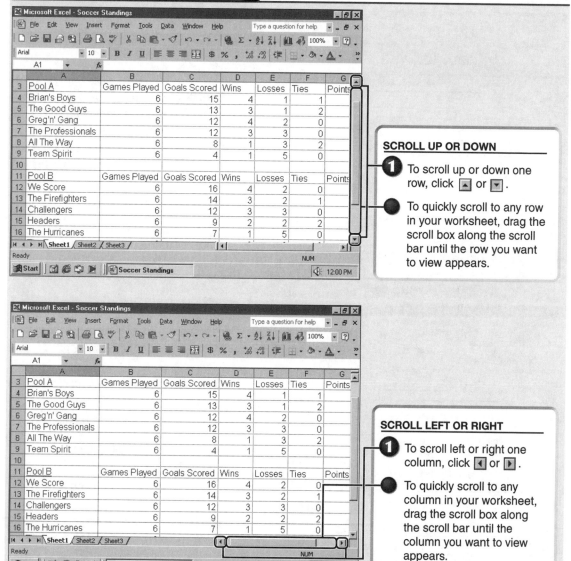

SCROLL UP OR DOWN

1 To scroll up or down one row, click ▲ or ▼.

● To quickly scroll to any row in your worksheet, drag the scroll box along the scroll bar until the row you want to view appears.

SCROLL LEFT OR RIGHT

1 To scroll left or right one column, click ◄ or ►.

● To quickly scroll to any column in your worksheet, drag the scroll box along the scroll bar until the column you want to view appears.

ENTER DATA

You can enter data into your worksheet quickly and easily. If you enter long words or large numbers, Excel may not be able to display all the data. The amount of data Excel can display in a cell depends on whether the neighboring cell contains data and the width of the column.

ENTER DATA

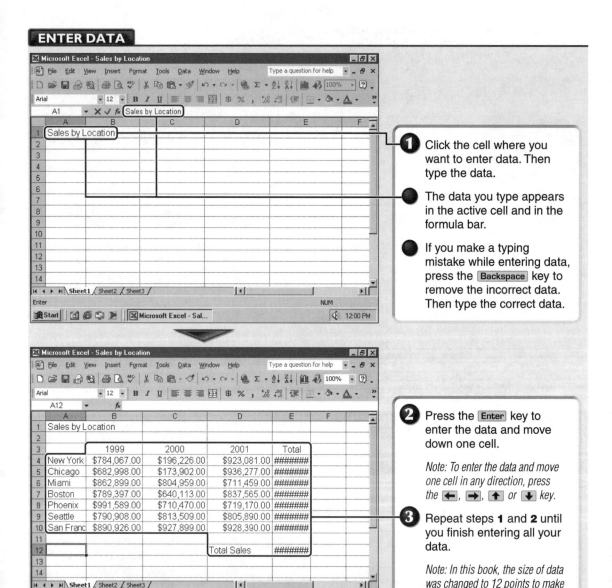

1 Click the cell where you want to enter data. Then type the data.

● The data you type appears in the active cell and in the formula bar.

● If you make a typing mistake while entering data, press the Backspace key to remove the incorrect data. Then type the correct data.

2 Press the Enter key to enter the data and move down one cell.

Note: To enter the data and move one cell in any direction, press the ←, →, ↑ or ↓ key.

3 Repeat steps **1** and **2** until you finish entering all your data.

Note: In this book, the size of data was changed to 12 points to make the data easier to read.

in an instant

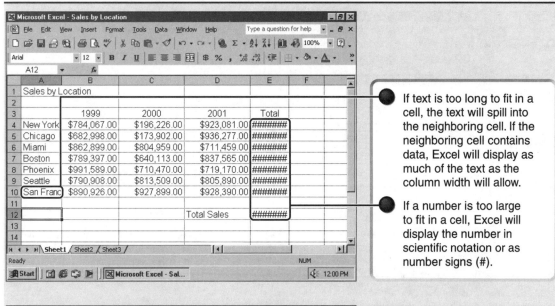

If text is too long to fit in a cell, the text will spill into the neighboring cell. If the neighboring cell contains data, Excel will display as much of the text as the column width will allow.

If a number is too large to fit in a cell, Excel will display the number in scientific notation or as number signs (#).

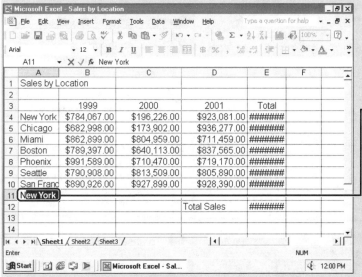

AUTOCOMPLETE

If the first few letters you type match the text in another cell in the same column, Excel will complete the text for you.

1 To enter the text Excel provides, press the Enter key.

To enter different text, continue typing.

SELECT CELLS

Before performing many tasks in Excel, you must select the cells you want to work with. You can select a cell, row, column or group of cells in a worksheet. Selected cells appear highlighted on your screen.

SELECT CELLS

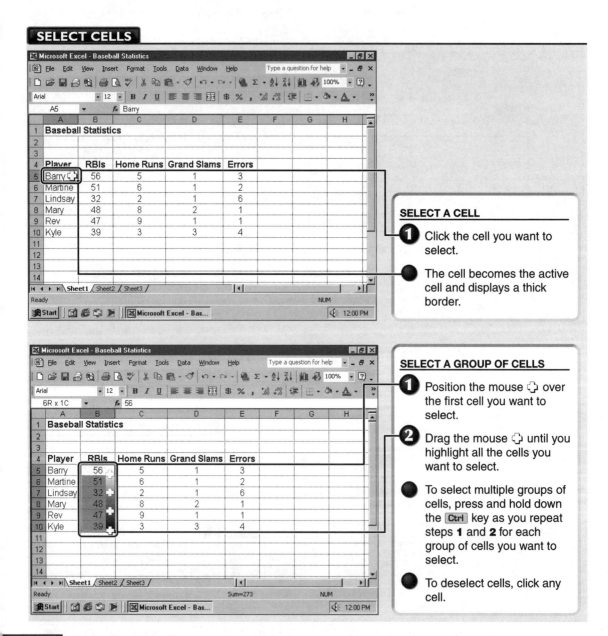

SELECT A CELL

1 Click the cell you want to select.

● The cell becomes the active cell and displays a thick border.

SELECT A GROUP OF CELLS

1 Position the mouse ⊕ over the first cell you want to select.

2 Drag the mouse ⊕ until you highlight all the cells you want to select.

● To select multiple groups of cells, press and hold down the **Ctrl** key as you repeat steps **1** and **2** for each group of cells you want to select.

● To deselect cells, click any cell.

in an *instant*

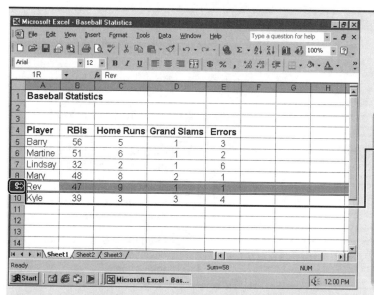

SELECT A ROW

1 Click the number of the row you want to select.

● To select multiple rows, position the mouse → over the number of the first row you want to select. Then drag the mouse → until you highlight all the rows you want to select.

SELECT A COLUMN

1 Click the letter of the column you want to select.

● To select multiple columns, position the mouse ↓ over the letter of the first column you want to select. Then drag the mouse ↓ until you highlight all the columns you want to select.

COMPLETE A SERIES

Excel can save you time by completing a text or number series for you. You can complete a series across a row or down a column in a worksheet. Excel completes a text series based on the text you enter in one cell. Excel completes a number series based on the numbers you enter in two cells.

COMPLETE A TEXT SERIES

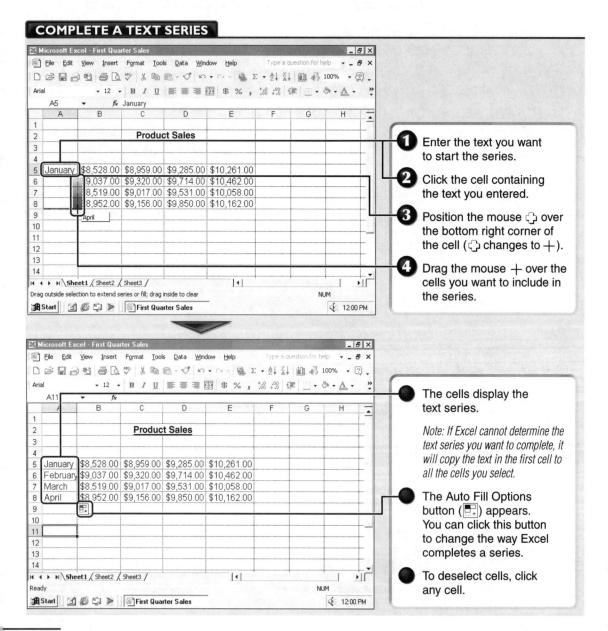

1 Enter the text you want to start the series.

2 Click the cell containing the text you entered.

3 Position the mouse ⊕ over the bottom right corner of the cell (⊕ changes to +).

4 Drag the mouse + over the cells you want to include in the series.

■ The cells display the text series.

Note: If Excel cannot determine the text series you want to complete, it will copy the text in the first cell to all the cells you select.

■ The Auto Fill Options button (■) appears. You can click this button to change the way Excel completes a series.

■ To deselect cells, click any cell.

in an **instant**

COMPLETE A NUMBER SERIES

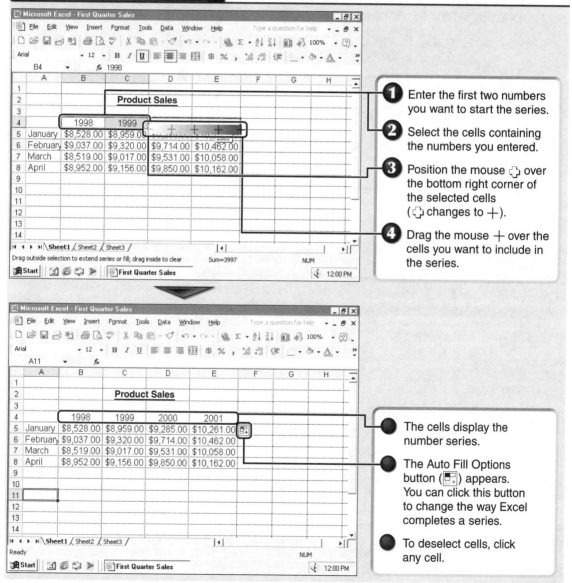

1 Enter the first two numbers you want to start the series.

2 Select the cells containing the numbers you entered.

3 Position the mouse ⟨⊹⟩ over the bottom right corner of the selected cells (⟨⊹⟩ changes to +).

4 Drag the mouse + over the cells you want to include in the series.

● The cells display the number series.

● The Auto Fill Options button (⊞) appears. You can click this button to change the way Excel completes a series.

● To deselect cells, click any cell.

95

SWITCH BETWEEN WORKSHEETS

A workbook contains several worksheets. You can easily switch from one worksheet to another. Worksheets can help you organize information in your workbook. For example, you can store information for each division of a company on a separate worksheet.

SWITCH BETWEEN WORKSHEETS

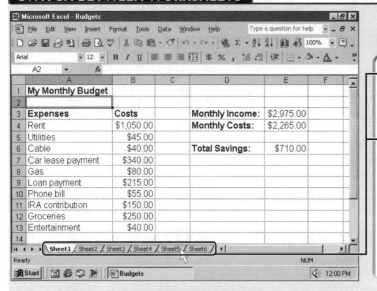

This area displays a tab for each worksheet in your workbook. The displayed worksheet has a white tab.

1 Click the tab for the worksheet you want to display.

■ The worksheet you selected appears. The contents of the other worksheets in your workbook are hidden behind the displayed worksheet.

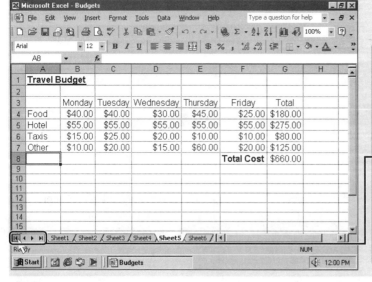

BROWSE THROUGH WORKSHEET TABS

● If you have many worksheets in your workbook, you may not be able to see all the worksheet tabs.

1 Click one of the following buttons to browse through the worksheet tabs.

◄◄	Display first tab
◄	Display previous tab
►	Display next tab
►►	Display last tab

RENAME A WORKSHEET

You can rename each worksheet in your workbook. When renaming a worksheet, you should choose a name that describes the contents of the worksheet. Descriptive names can help you identify worksheets of interest more easily.

RENAME A WORKSHEET

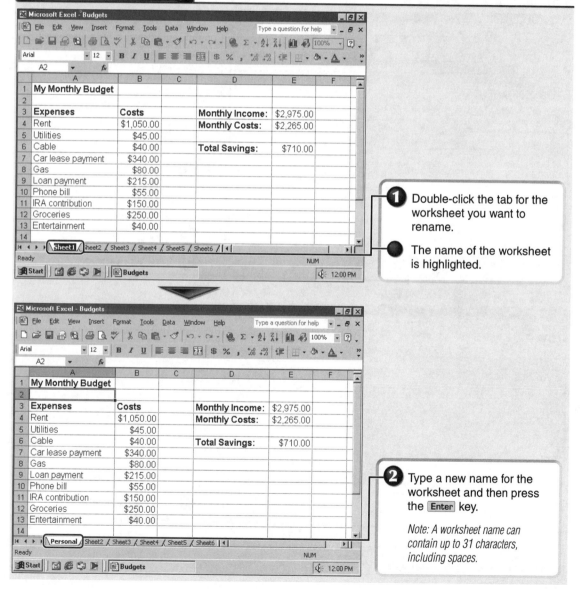

1 Double-click the tab for the worksheet you want to rename.

The name of the worksheet is highlighted.

2 Type a new name for the worksheet and then press the Enter key.

Note: A worksheet name can contain up to 31 characters, including spaces.

INSERT A WORKSHEET

You can insert a new worksheet into your workbook to include additional information in the workbook. Each workbook you create automatically contains three worksheets. You can insert as many new worksheets as you need.

INSERT A WORKSHEET

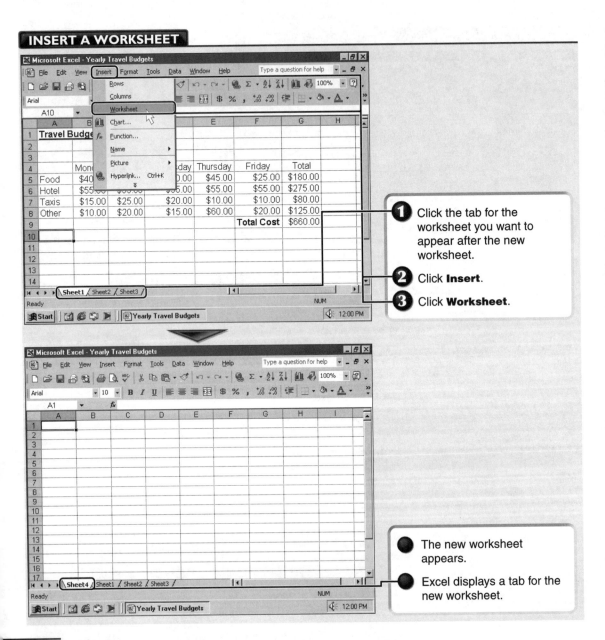

1 Click the tab for the worksheet you want to appear after the new worksheet.

2 Click **Insert**.

3 Click **Worksheet**.

● The new worksheet appears.

● Excel displays a tab for the new worksheet.

DELETE A WORKSHEET

You can remove a worksheet you no longer need from your workbook. Removing unneeded worksheets can help you organize your workbook. Once you remove a worksheet, all the data in the worksheet is permanently deleted from your workbook.

DELETE A WORKSHEET

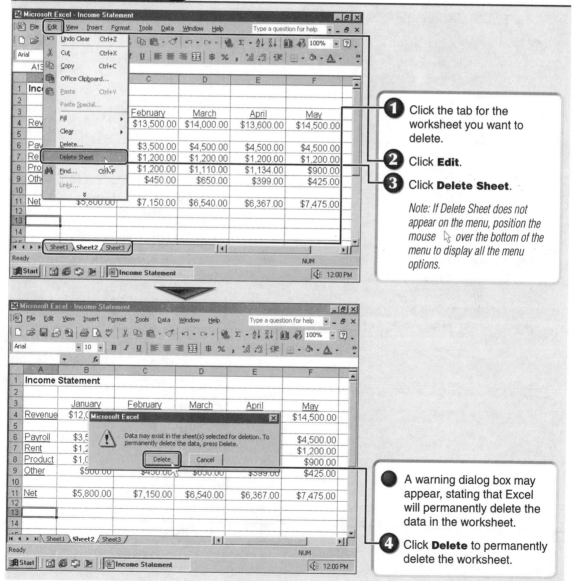

1 Click the tab for the worksheet you want to delete.

2 Click **Edit**.

3 Click **Delete Sheet**.

Note: If Delete Sheet does not appear on the menu, position the mouse ⃗ over the bottom of the menu to display all the menu options.

● A warning dialog box may appear, stating that Excel will permanently delete the data in the worksheet.

4 Click **Delete** to permanently delete the worksheet.

SAVE A WORKBOOK

You can save your workbook to store the workbook for future use. Saving a workbook allows you to later review and make changes to the workbook. You should regularly save changes you make to a workbook to avoid losing your work.

SAVE A WORKBOOK

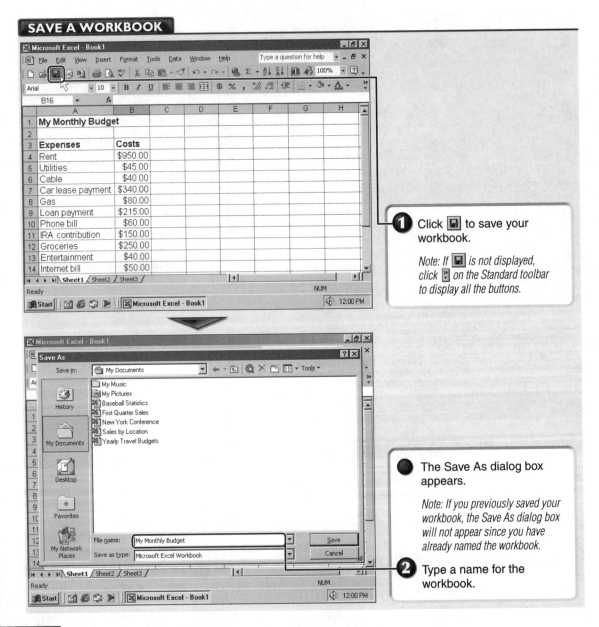

1 Click 🖫 to save your workbook.

Note: If 🖫 is not displayed, click ⚒ on the Standard toolbar to display all the buttons.

● The Save As dialog box appears.

Note: If you previously saved your workbook, the Save As dialog box will not appear since you have already named the workbook.

2 Type a name for the workbook.

in an *instant*

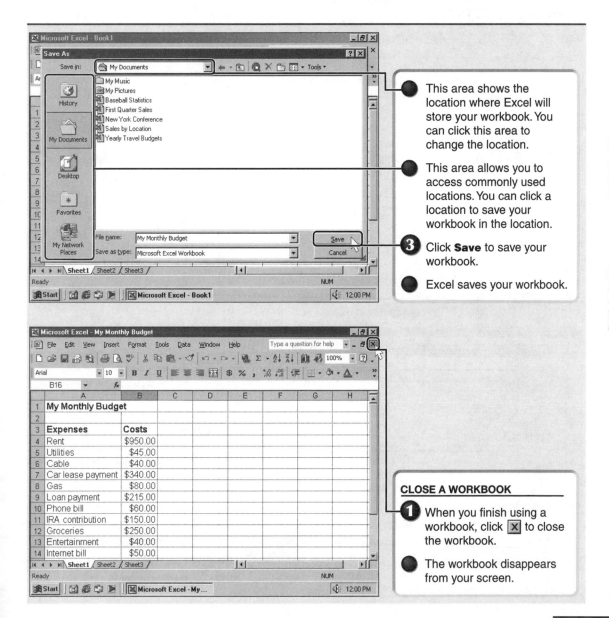

This area shows the location where Excel will store your workbook. You can click this area to change the location.

This area allows you to access commonly used locations. You can click a location to save your workbook in the location.

3 Click **Save** to save your workbook.

Excel saves your workbook.

CLOSE A WORKBOOK

1 When you finish using a workbook, click ☒ to close the workbook.

The workbook disappears from your screen.

101

OPEN A WORKBOOK

You can open a saved workbook to view the workbook on your screen. This allows you to review and make changes to the workbook. After you open a workbook, Excel displays the name of the workbook at the top of your screen. You can have several workbooks open at once.

OPEN A WORKBOOK

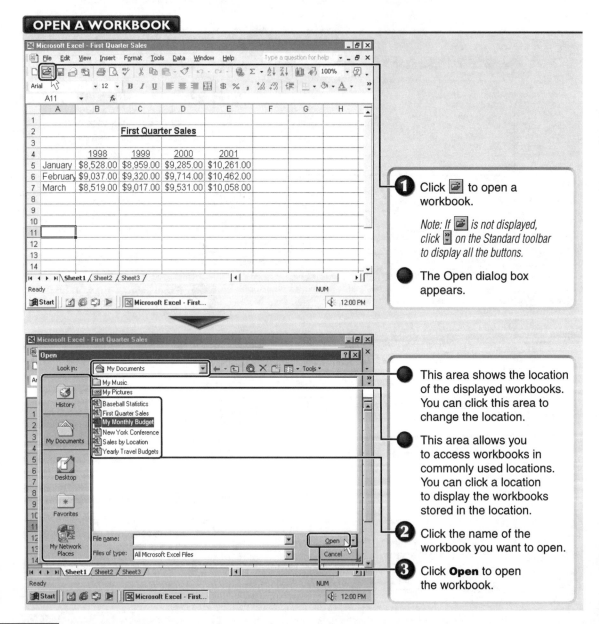

1 Click to open a workbook.

Note: If is not displayed, click on the Standard toolbar to display all the buttons.

■ The Open dialog box appears.

■ This area shows the location of the displayed workbooks. You can click this area to change the location.

■ This area allows you to access workbooks in commonly used locations. You can click a location to display the workbooks stored in the location.

2 Click the name of the workbook you want to open.

3 Click **Open** to open the workbook.

in an instant

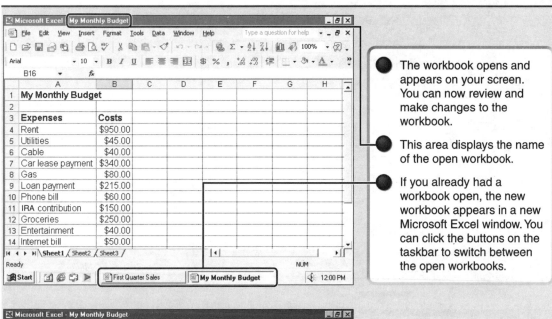

The workbook opens and appears on your screen. You can now review and make changes to the workbook.

This area displays the name of the open workbook.

If you already had a workbook open, the new workbook appears in a new Microsoft Excel window. You can click the buttons on the taskbar to switch between the open workbooks.

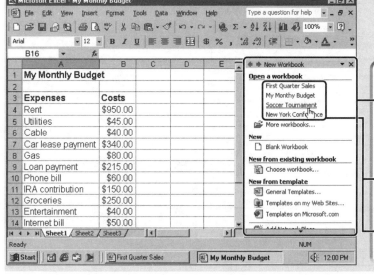

QUICKLY OPEN A WORKBOOK

The New Workbook task pane appears each time you start Excel. To display the New Workbook task pane, see page 8.

This area displays the names of the last four workbooks you worked with.

1 Click the name of the workbook you want to open.

CREATE A NEW WORKBOOK

You can create a new workbook to store new information, such as a budget or sales report. When you create a new workbook, the taskbar at the bottom of your screen displays a button for the workbook.

CREATE A NEW WORKBOOK

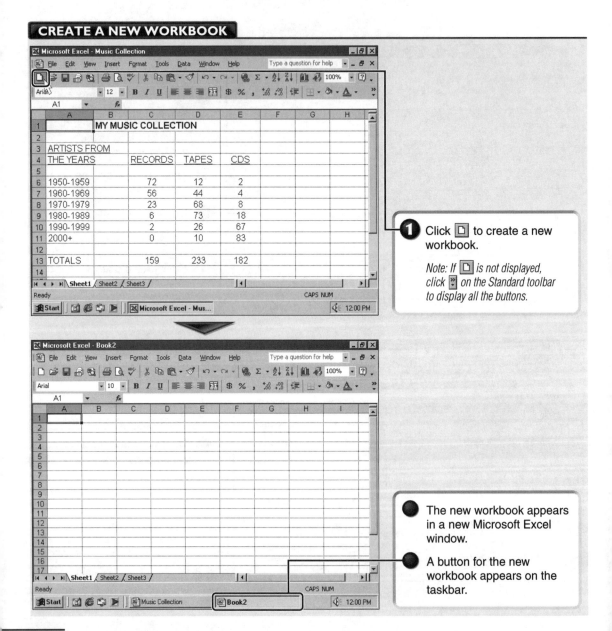

1 Click to create a new workbook.

Note: If the icon is not displayed, click the button on the Standard toolbar to display all the buttons.

● The new workbook appears in a new Microsoft Excel window.

● A button for the new workbook appears on the taskbar.

SWITCH BETWEEN WORKBOOKS

You can have several workbooks open at once. Excel allows you to easily switch from one open workbook to another. Excel displays the name of the workbook you are currently working with at the top of your screen.

SWITCH BETWEEN WORKBOOKS

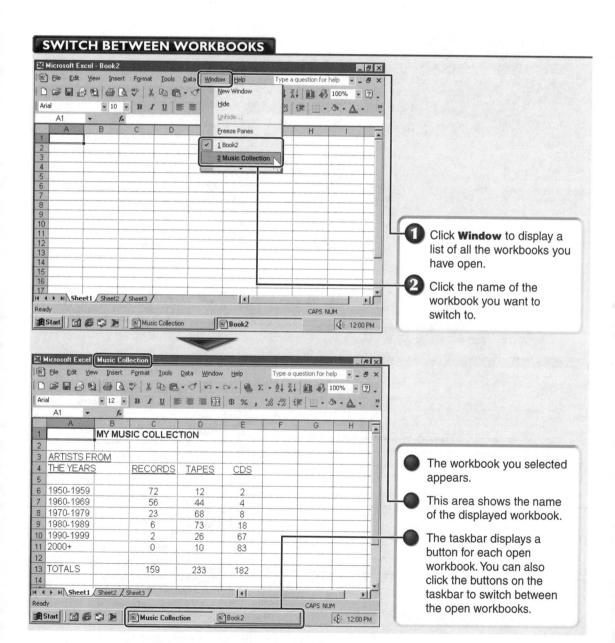

1 Click **Window** to display a list of all the workbooks you have open.

2 Click the name of the workbook you want to switch to.

● The workbook you selected appears.

● This area shows the name of the displayed workbook.

● The taskbar displays a button for each open workbook. You can also click the buttons on the taskbar to switch between the open workbooks.

105

E-MAIL A WORKSHEET

You can e-mail the worksheet displayed on your screen to a friend, family member or colleague. When sending an e-mail message, you must specify the e-mail address of each person you want to receive the message. You can also send a copy of the message to people who are not directly involved but would be interested in the message.

E-MAIL A WORKSHEET

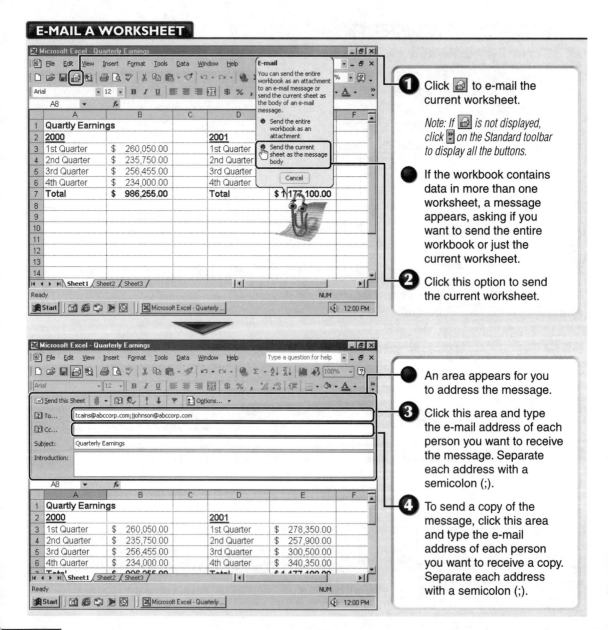

1 Click 🖃 to e-mail the current worksheet.

Note: If 🖃 is not displayed, click ⁛ on the Standard toolbar to display all the buttons.

● If the workbook contains data in more than one worksheet, a message appears, asking if you want to send the entire workbook or just the current worksheet.

2 Click this option to send the current worksheet.

● An area appears for you to address the message.

3 Click this area and type the e-mail address of each person you want to receive the message. Separate each address with a semicolon (;).

4 To send a copy of the message, click this area and type the e-mail address of each person you want to receive a copy. Separate each address with a semicolon (;).

in an *instant*

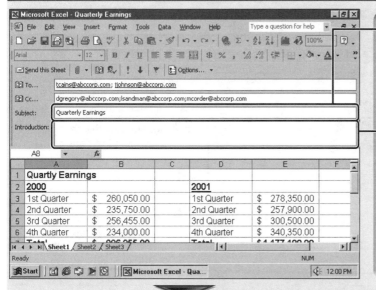

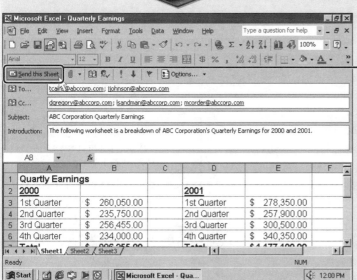

5 Click this area and type a subject for the message.

Note: If a subject already exists, you can drag the mouse I over the existing subject and then type a new subject.

6 To include an introduction for the worksheet you are sending in the message, click this area and type the introduction. Including an introduction allows you to provide the recipients of the message with additional information about the worksheet.

7 Click **Send this Sheet** to send the message.

● To e-mail an entire workbook, perform steps **1** and **2**, selecting **Send the entire workbook as an attachment** in step **2**. The Choose Profile dialog box may appear. Click **OK** to close the dialog box. Perform steps **3** to **5** and then click **Send**.

107

EDIT DATA

You can edit data in your worksheet to correct a mistake or update data. You can also delete data you no longer need. When you delete the data in a cell, Excel will not remove the formatting you applied to the cell, such as a new font or color. Any new data you enter into the cell will display the same formatting as the data you deleted.

EDIT DATA

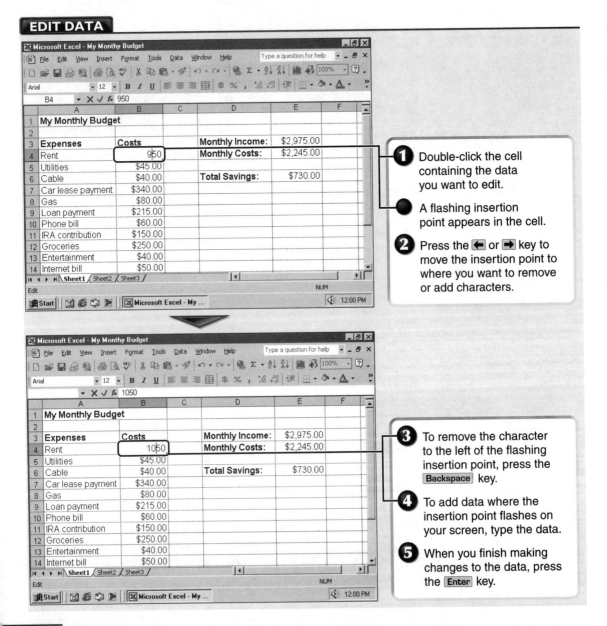

1 Double-click the cell containing the data you want to edit.

● A flashing insertion point appears in the cell.

2 Press the ← or → key to move the insertion point to where you want to remove or add characters.

3 To remove the character to the left of the flashing insertion point, press the Backspace key.

4 To add data where the insertion point flashes on your screen, type the data.

5 When you finish making changes to the data, press the Enter key.

in an *instant*

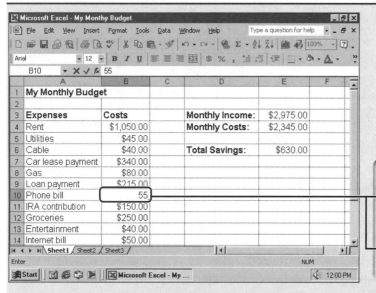

REPLACE ALL DATA IN A CELL

1 Click the cell containing the data you want to replace with new data.

2 Type the new data and then press the Enter key.

DELETE DATA

1 Select the cells containing the data you want to delete.

2 Press the Delete key.

● The data in the cells you selected disappears.

● To deselect cells, click any cell.

MOVE OR COPY DATA

You can move or copy data to a new location in your worksheet. Moving data allows you to reorganize data in your worksheet. When you move data, the data disappears from its original location. Copying data allows you to repeat data in your worksheet without having to retype the data. When you copy data, the data appears in both the original and new locations.

MOVE OR COPY DATA

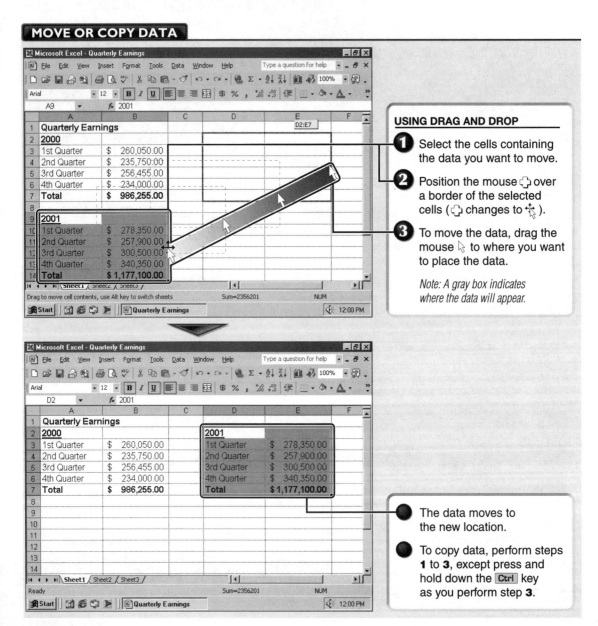

USING DRAG AND DROP

1 Select the cells containing the data you want to move.

2 Position the mouse ⊕ over a border of the selected cells (⊕ changes to ⊹).

3 To move the data, drag the mouse ⊹ to where you want to place the data.

Note: A gray box indicates where the data will appear.

■ The data moves to the new location.

■ To copy data, perform steps **1** to **3**, except press and hold down the **Ctrl** key as you perform step **3**.

in an *Instant*

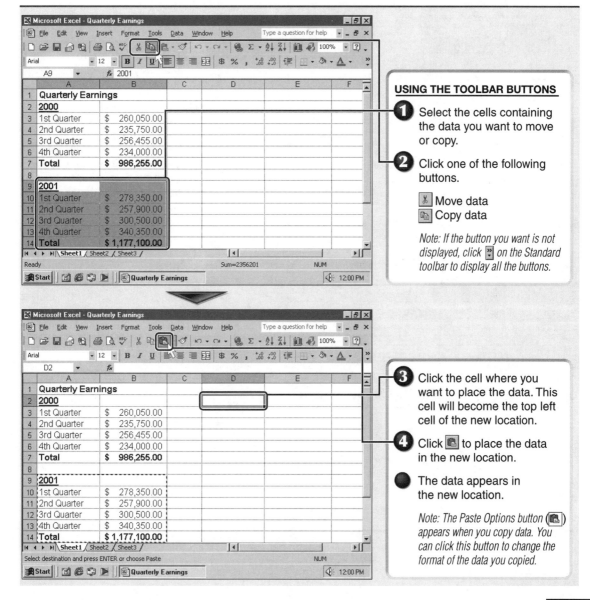

USING THE TOOLBAR BUTTONS

1 Select the cells containing the data you want to move or copy.

2 Click one of the following buttons.

✂ Move data
📋 Copy data

Note: If the button you want is not displayed, click ≫ on the Standard toolbar to display all the buttons.

3 Click the cell where you want to place the data. This cell will become the top left cell of the new location.

4 Click 📋 to place the data in the new location.

⬤ The data appears in the new location.

Note: The Paste Options button (📋) appears when you copy data. You can click this button to change the format of the data you copied.

111

INSERT A ROW OR COLUMN

You can add a row or column to your worksheet to insert additional data. Before you can add a row or column, you must select an existing row or column in your worksheet. Excel automatically updates any formulas affected by the row or column you add to your worksheet.

INSERT A ROW

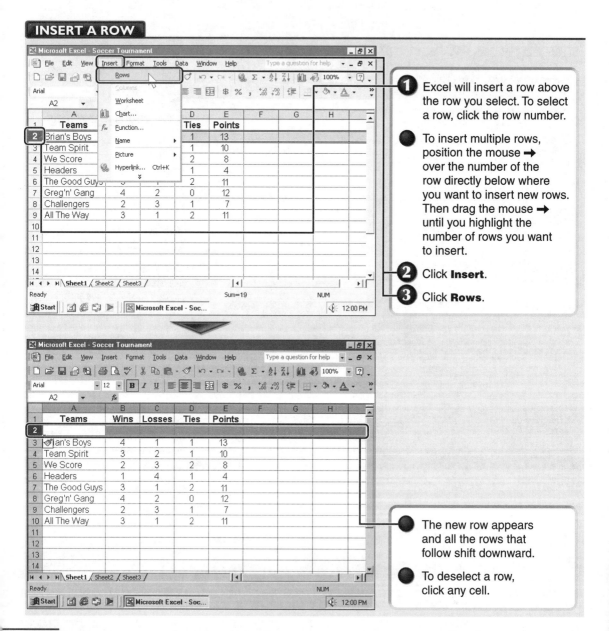

1. Excel will insert a row above the row you select. To select a row, click the row number.

● To insert multiple rows, position the mouse → over the number of the row directly below where you want to insert new rows. Then drag the mouse → until you highlight the number of rows you want to insert.

2. Click **Insert**.

3. Click **Rows**.

● The new row appears and all the rows that follow shift downward.

● To deselect a row, click any cell.

in an instant

INSERT A COLUMN

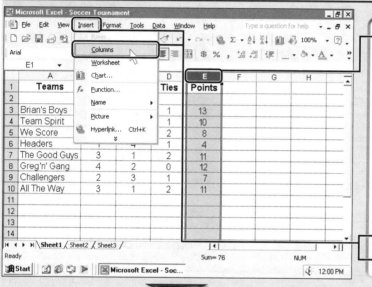

1 Excel will insert a column to the left of the column you select. To select a column, click the column letter.

● To insert multiple columns, position the mouse ↓ over the letter of the column directly to the right of where you want to insert new columns. Then drag the mouse ↓ until you highlight the number of columns you want to insert.

2 Click **Insert**.

3 Click **Columns**.

● The new column appears and all the columns that follow shift to the right.

● To deselect a column, click any cell.

DELETE A ROW OR COLUMN

You can delete a row or column to remove data you no longer want to display in your worksheet. Before deleting a row or column, you should make sure the row or column does not contain data that is used in a formula. If #REF! appears in a cell in your worksheet, you may have deleted data needed to calculate a formula.

DELETE A ROW

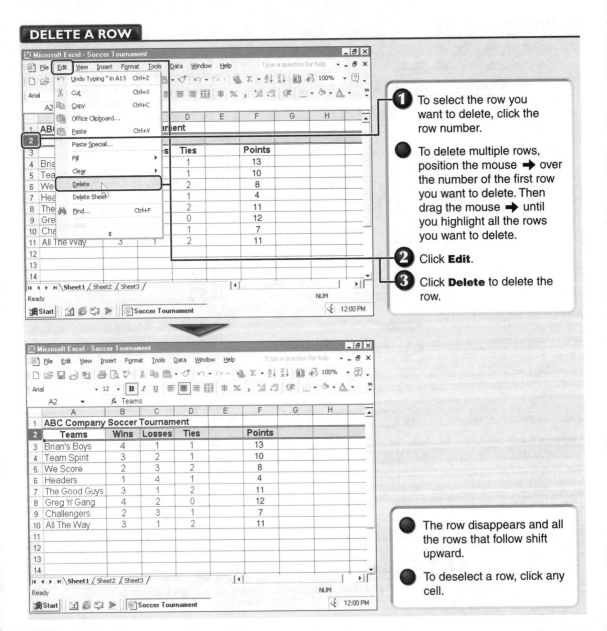

1 To select the row you want to delete, click the row number.

● To delete multiple rows, position the mouse ➡ over the number of the first row you want to delete. Then drag the mouse ➡ until you highlight all the rows you want to delete.

2 Click **Edit**.

3 Click **Delete** to delete the row.

● The row disappears and all the rows that follow shift upward.

● To deselect a row, click any cell.

in an *instant*

DELETE A COLUMN

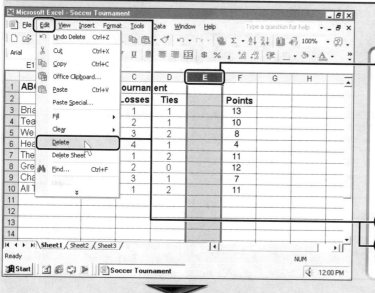

1 To select the column you want to delete, click the column letter.

● To delete multiple columns, position the mouse ↓ over the letter of the first column you want to delete. Then drag the mouse ↓ until you highlight all the columns you want to delete.

2 Click **Edit**.

3 Click **Delete** to delete the column.

● The column disappears and all the columns that follow shift to the left.

● To deselect a column, click any cell.

ZOOM IN OR OUT

You can enlarge or reduce the display of data on your screen. Excel automatically displays your worksheets in the 100% zoom setting, but you can choose the zoom setting that suits your needs. Changing the zoom setting will not affect the way data appears on a printed page.

ZOOM IN OR OUT

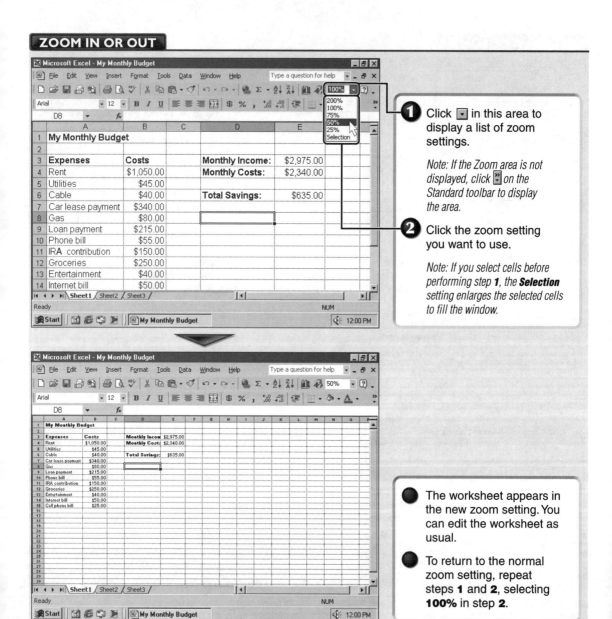

1 Click ▼ in this area to display a list of zoom settings.

Note: If the Zoom area is not displayed, click » on the Standard toolbar to display the area.

2 Click the zoom setting you want to use.

*Note: If you select cells before performing step 1, the **Selection** setting enlarges the selected cells to fill the window.*

● The worksheet appears in the new zoom setting. You can edit the worksheet as usual.

● To return to the normal zoom setting, repeat steps **1** and **2**, selecting **100%** in step **2**.

UNDO CHANGES

Excel remembers the last changes you made to your worksheet. If you regret these changes, you can cancel them by using the Undo feature. The Undo feature can cancel your last editing and formatting changes.

UNDO CHANGES

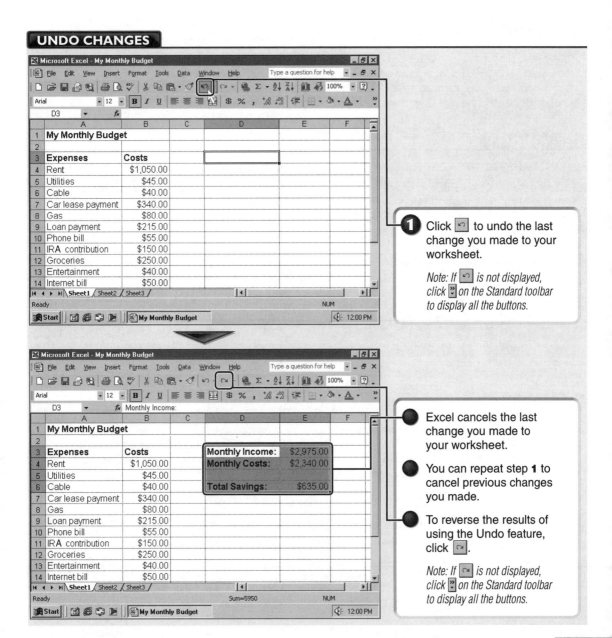

1 Click ⟲ to undo the last change you made to your worksheet.

Note: If ⟲ is not displayed, click » on the Standard toolbar to display all the buttons.

● Excel cancels the last change you made to your worksheet.

● You can repeat step **1** to cancel previous changes you made.

● To reverse the results of using the Undo feature, click ⟳.

Note: If ⟳ is not displayed, click » on the Standard toolbar to display all the buttons.

INTRODUCTION TO FORMULAS AND FUNCTIONS

A formula allows you to calculate and analyze data in your worksheet. A formula always begins with an equal sign (=).

CELL REFERENCES

When entering formulas, use cell references instead of actual data whenever possible. For example, enter the formula =A1+A2 instead of =10+20.

When you use cell references and you change a number used in a formula, Excel will automatically redo the calculation for you.

OPERATORS

ARITHMETIC OPERATORS

You can use arithmetic operators to perform mathematical calculations.

OPERATOR	DESCRIPTION
+	Addition (A1+B1)
-	Subtraction (A1-B1)
*	Multiplication (A1*B1)
/	Division (A1/B1)
%	Percent (A1%)
^	Exponentiation (A1^B1)

ORDER OF CALCULATIONS

When a formula contains more than one operator, Excel performs the calculations in a specific order.

1	Percent (%)
2	Exponentiation (^)
3	Multiplication (*) and Division (/)
4	Addition (+) and Subtraction (-)

You can use parentheses ( ) to change the order in which Excel performs calculations. Excel will perform the calculations inside the parentheses first.

FUNCTIONS

A function is a ready-to-use formula that you can use to perform a calculation on the data in your worksheet. Examples of commonly used functions include AVERAGE, COUNT, MAX and SUM.

A function always begins with an equal sign (=). The data Excel will use to calculate a function is enclosed in parentheses ( ).

SPECIFY INDIVIDUAL CELLS

When a comma (,) separates cell references in a function, Excel uses each cell to perform the calculation. For example, =SUM(A1,A2,A3) is the same as the formula =A1+A2+A3.

SPECIFY A GROUP OF CELLS

When a colon (:) separates cell references in a function, Excel uses the specified cells and all cells between them to perform the calculation. For example, =SUM(A1:A3) is the same as the formula =A1+A2+A3.

An error message appears when Excel cannot properly calculate or display the result of a formula. Errors in formulas are often the result of typing mistakes. You can edit a formula to correct an error or change the formula.

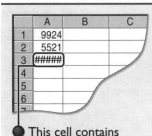

#####

The column is too narrow to display the result of the calculation. You can change the column width to display the result.

● This cell contains the formula:
=A1*A2

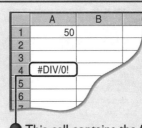

#DIV/0!

The formula divides a number by zero (0). Excel considers a blank cell to have a value of zero.

● This cell contains the formula:
=A1/A2
=50/0

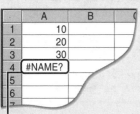

#NAME?

The formula contains a function name or cell reference Excel does not recognize.

● This cell contains the formula:
=AQ+A2+A3

In this example, the cell reference A1 was typed incorrectly.

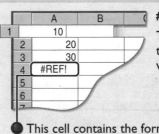

#REF!

The formula refers to a cell that is not valid.

● This cell contains the formula:
=A1+A2+A3

In this example, a row containing a cell used in the formula was deleted.

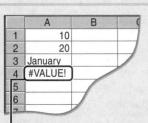

#VALUE!

The formula refers to a cell that Excel cannot use in a calculation.

● This cell contains the formula:
=A1+A2+A3

In this example, a cell used in the formula contains text.

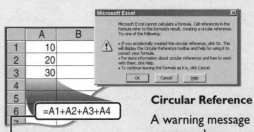

● This cell contains the formula:
=A1+A2+A3+A4

Circular Reference

A warning message appears when a formula refers to the cell containing the formula. This is called a circular reference.

ENTER A FORMULA

You can enter a formula into any cell in your worksheet. A formula helps you calculate and analyze data. When entering formulas, you should use cell references instead of actual data whenever possible. When you use cell references and you change a number used in a formula, Excel will automatically redo the calculation for you.

ENTER A FORMULA

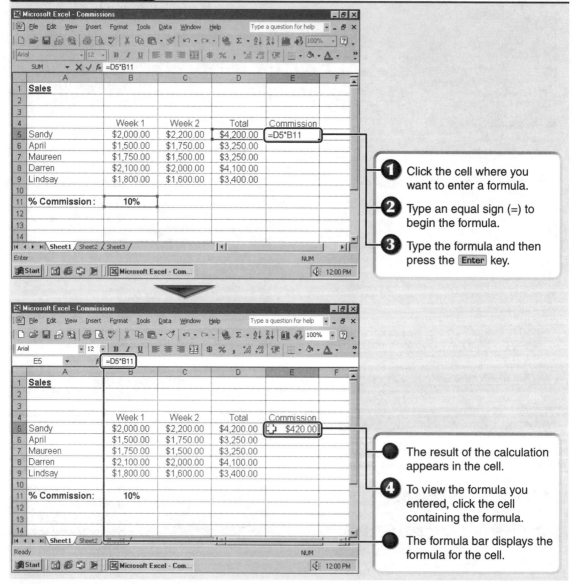

1 Click the cell where you want to enter a formula.

2 Type an equal sign (=) to begin the formula.

3 Type the formula and then press the Enter key.

■ The result of the calculation appears in the cell.

4 To view the formula you entered, click the cell containing the formula.

■ The formula bar displays the formula for the cell.

in an **instant**

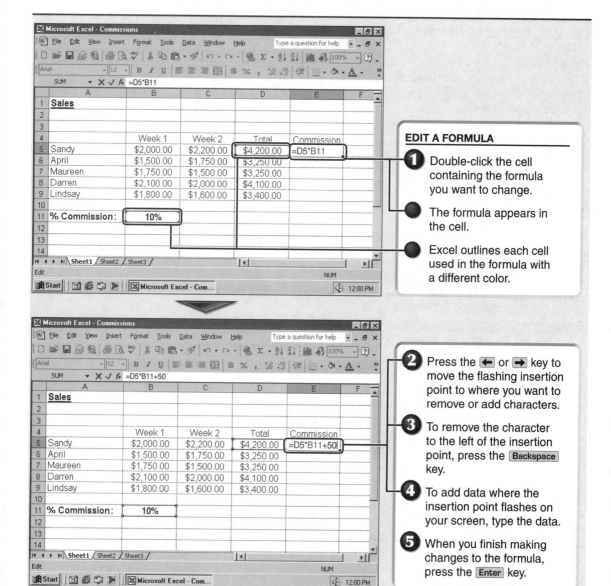

EDIT A FORMULA

1 Double-click the cell containing the formula you want to change.

The formula appears in the cell.

Excel outlines each cell used in the formula with a different color.

2 Press the ← or → key to move the flashing insertion point to where you want to remove or add characters.

3 To remove the character to the left of the insertion point, press the Backspace key.

4 To add data where the insertion point flashes on your screen, type the data.

5 When you finish making changes to the formula, press the Enter key.

121

ENTER A FUNCTION

Excel helps you enter functions into your worksheet. Functions allow you to perform calculations without typing long, complex formulas. Excel offers over 200 functions to help you analyze data in your worksheet. There are financial functions, date and time functions, math and trigonometry functions, statistical functions and many more.

ENTER A FUNCTION

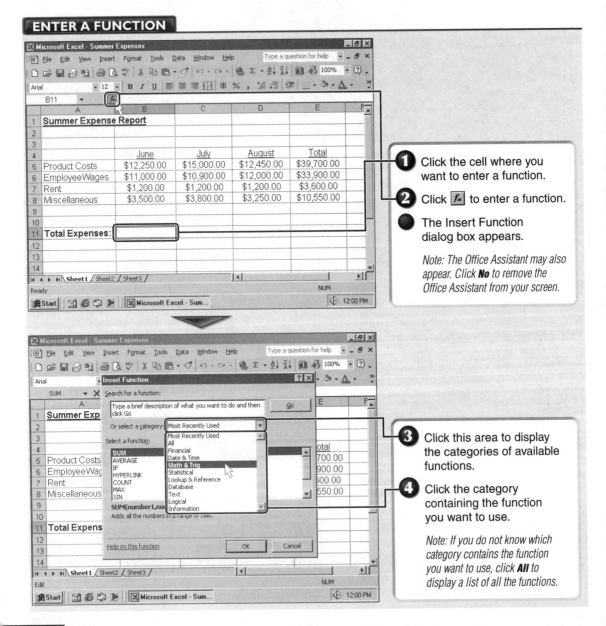

1 Click the cell where you want to enter a function.

2 Click f_x to enter a function.

● The Insert Function dialog box appears.

Note: The Office Assistant may also appear. Click No to remove the Office Assistant from your screen.

3 Click this area to display the categories of available functions.

4 Click the category containing the function you want to use.

Note: If you do not know which category contains the function you want to use, click All to display a list of all the functions.

in an *Instant*

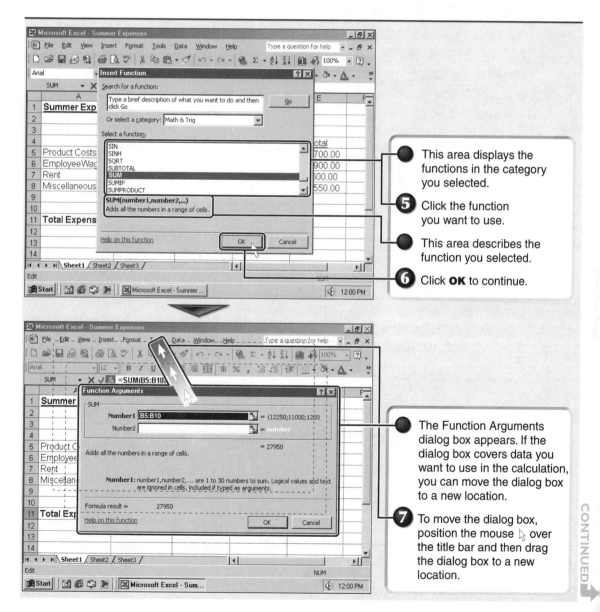

- This area displays the functions in the category you selected.

5 Click the function you want to use.

- This area describes the function you selected.

6 Click **OK** to continue.

- The Function Arguments dialog box appears. If the dialog box covers data you want to use in the calculation, you can move the dialog box to a new location.

7 To move the dialog box, position the mouse ⟨⟩ over the title bar and then drag the dialog box to a new location.

CONTINUED

123

ENTER A FUNCTION

When entering a function, you must specify which numbers you want to use in the calculation. Excel allows you to click the cells in your worksheet that contain the numbers you want to use in the calculation.

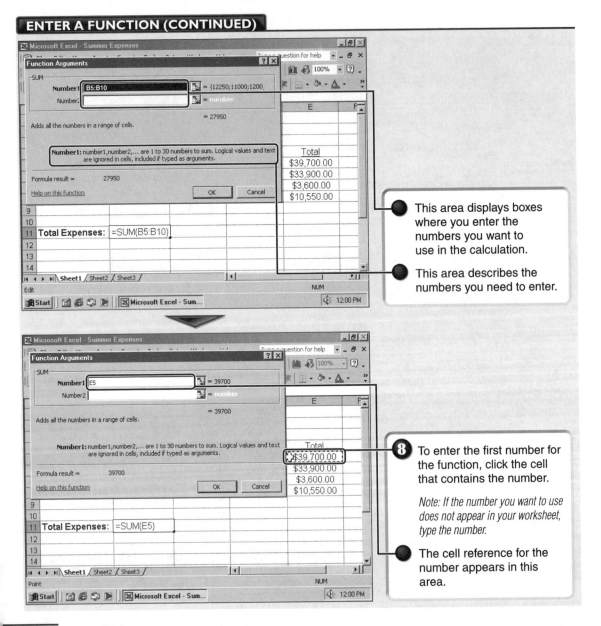

This area displays boxes where you enter the numbers you want to use in the calculation.

This area describes the numbers you need to enter.

8 To enter the first number for the function, click the cell that contains the number.

Note: If the number you want to use does not appear in your worksheet, type the number.

The cell reference for the number appears in this area.

in an instant

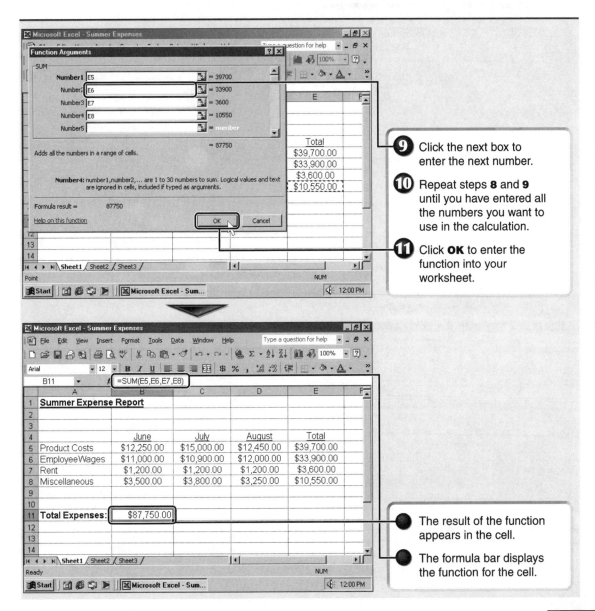

9 Click the next box to enter the next number.

10 Repeat steps **8** and **9** until you have entered all the numbers you want to use in the calculation.

11 Click **OK** to enter the function into your worksheet.

● The result of the function appears in the cell.

● The formula bar displays the function for the cell.

PERFORM COMMON CALCULATIONS

You can quickly perform common calculations on a list of numbers in your worksheet. For example, you can calculate the sum or the average value of a list of numbers. You can also count the number of values or find the largest or smallest value in a list of numbers.

PERFORM COMMON CALCULATIONS

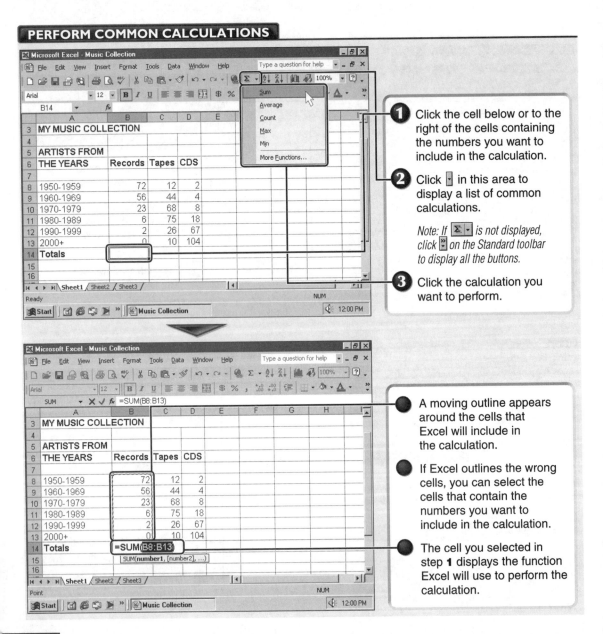

1 Click the cell below or to the right of the cells containing the numbers you want to include in the calculation.

2 Click ▪ in this area to display a list of common calculations.

Note: If Σ ▪ is not displayed, click ▪ on the Standard toolbar to display all the buttons.

3 Click the calculation you want to perform.

● A moving outline appears around the cells that Excel will include in the calculation.

● If Excel outlines the wrong cells, you can select the cells that contain the numbers you want to include in the calculation.

● The cell you selected in step 1 displays the function Excel will use to perform the calculation.

in an *Instant*

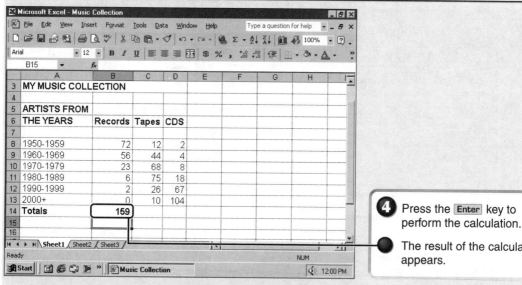

4 Press the Enter key to perform the calculation.

● The result of the calculation appears.

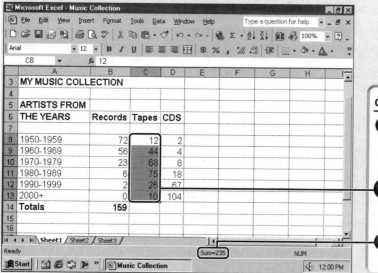

QUICKLY ADD NUMBERS

● You can quickly display the sum of a list of numbers without entering a formula into your worksheet.

1 Select the cells containing the numbers you want to add.

● This area displays the sum of the cells you selected.

COPY A FORMULA

If you want to use the same formula several times in your worksheet, you can save time by copying the formula. When you copy a formula to other cells in your worksheet, Excel automatically changes the cell references in the new formulas. A cell reference that changes when you copy a formula is called a relative reference.

COPY A FORMULA

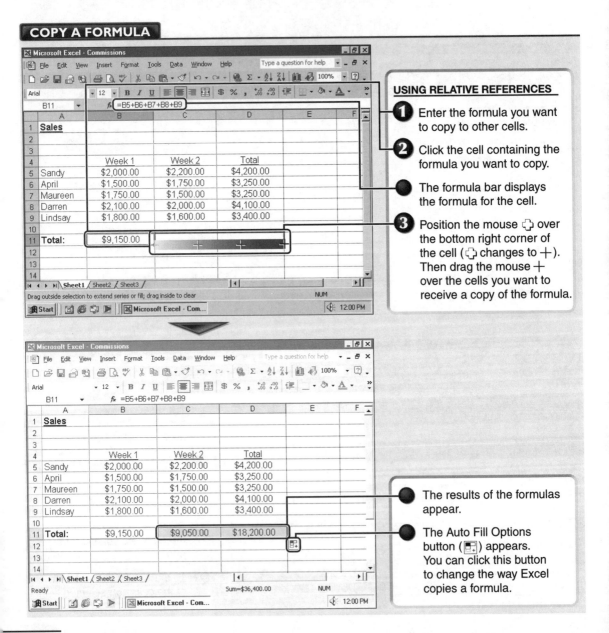

USING RELATIVE REFERENCES

1 Enter the formula you want to copy to other cells.

2 Click the cell containing the formula you want to copy.

■ The formula bar displays the formula for the cell.

3 Position the mouse ⬚ over the bottom right corner of the cell (⬚ changes to +). Then drag the mouse + over the cells you want to receive a copy of the formula.

■ The results of the formulas appear.

■ The Auto Fill Options button (▦) appears. You can click this button to change the way Excel copies a formula.

in an Instant

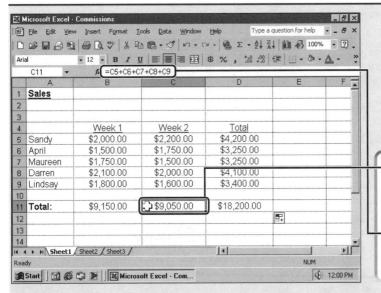

4 To view one of the new formulas, click a cell that received a copy of the formula.

● The formula bar displays the formula with the new cell references.

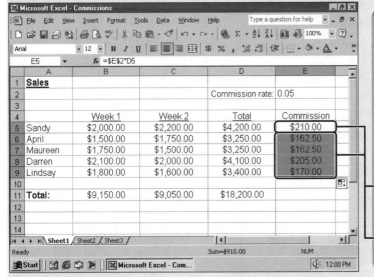

USING ABSOLUTE REFERENCES

● You can use an absolute reference to prevent Excel from changing a cell reference when you copy a formula. To make a cell reference absolute, type a dollar sign ($) before both the column letter and row number.

1 Enter the formula you want to copy to other cells (example: =E2*D5).

2 Perform steps **2** and **3** on page 128 to copy the formula.

CHANGE COLUMN WIDTH

You can change the width of columns to improve the appearance of your worksheet and display any hidden data. The text in a cell may be hidden if the text spills into a neighboring cell that contains data. You can increase the column width to display all the text in the cell.

CHANGE COLUMN WIDTH

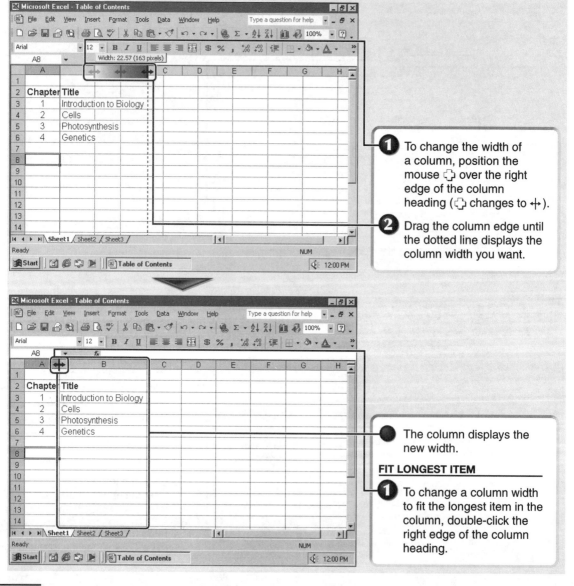

1 To change the width of a column, position the mouse ⊕ over the right edge of the column heading (⊕ changes to ↔).

2 Drag the column edge until the dotted line displays the column width you want.

● The column displays the new width.

FIT LONGEST ITEM

1 To change a column width to fit the longest item in the column, double-click the right edge of the column heading.

130

CHANGE ROW HEIGHT

You can change the height of rows to add space between the rows of data in your worksheet. Changing the height of rows can help improve the layout of data in your worksheet and make the data easier to read.

CHANGE ROW HEIGHT

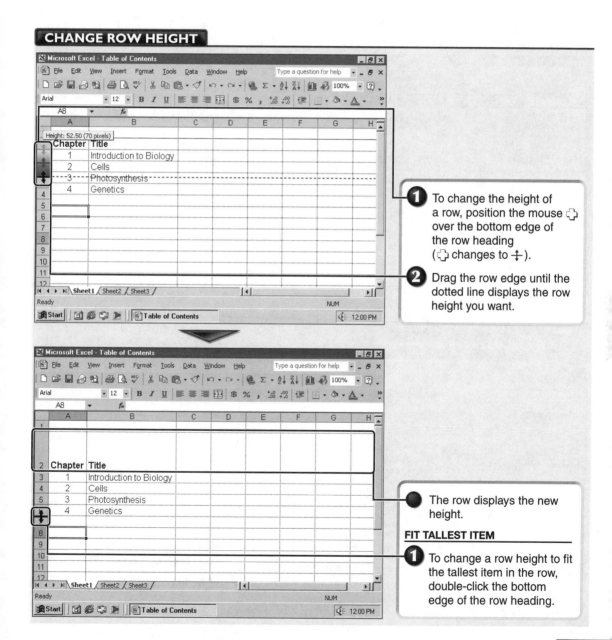

1 To change the height of a row, position the mouse ⬚ over the bottom edge of the row heading (⬚ changes to ✛).

2 Drag the row edge until the dotted line displays the row height you want.

■ The row displays the new height.

FIT TALLEST ITEM

1 To change a row height to fit the tallest item in the row, double-click the bottom edge of the row heading.

131

CHANGE FONT OF DATA

You can change the font of data to enhance the appearance of your worksheet. Excel provides a list of fonts for you to choose from. The fonts appear in the list as they will appear in your worksheet. This allows you to preview a font before you select the font.

CHANGE FONT OF DATA

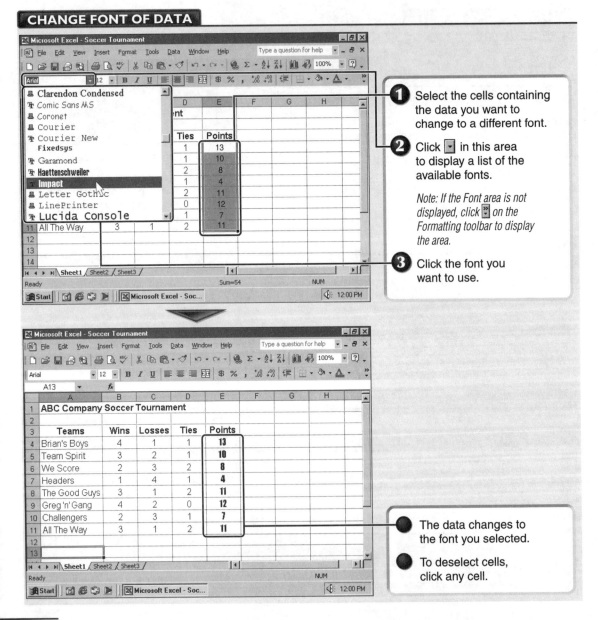

1 Select the cells containing the data you want to change to a different font.

2 Click ▼ in this area to display a list of the available fonts.

Note: If the Font area is not displayed, click ⁑ on the Formatting toolbar to display the area.

3 Click the font you want to use.

● The data changes to the font you selected.

● To deselect cells, click any cell.

You can increase or decrease the size of data in your worksheet. Larger data is easier to read, but smaller data allows you to fit more information on a page. Excel measures the size of data in points. There are approximately 72 points in an inch.

CHANGE SIZE OF DATA

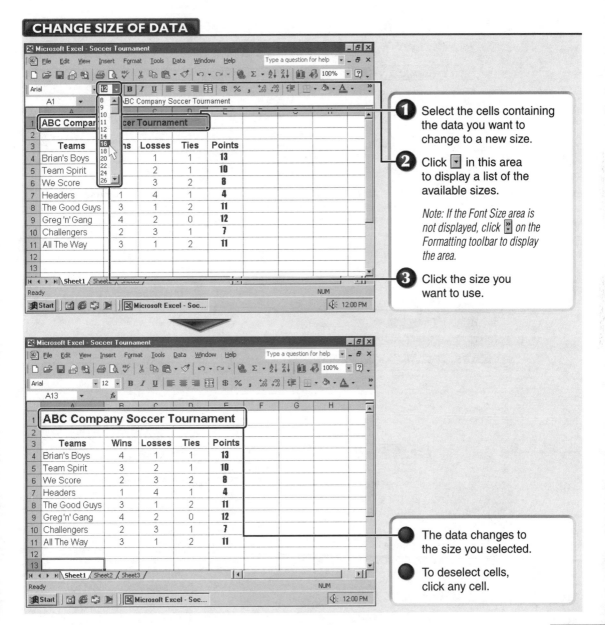

1 Select the cells containing the data you want to change to a new size.

2 Click 🔽 in this area to display a list of the available sizes.

Note: If the Font Size area is not displayed, click 🔄 on the Formatting toolbar to display the area.

3 Click the size you want to use.

● The data changes to the size you selected.

● To deselect cells, click any cell.

CHANGE NUMBER FORMAT

You can change the appearance of numbers in your worksheet without retyping the numbers. Excel offers several number format categories for you to choose from, including Currency, Date, Time, Percentage and Scientific. When you change the format of numbers, you do not change the value of the numbers.

CHANGE NUMBER FORMAT

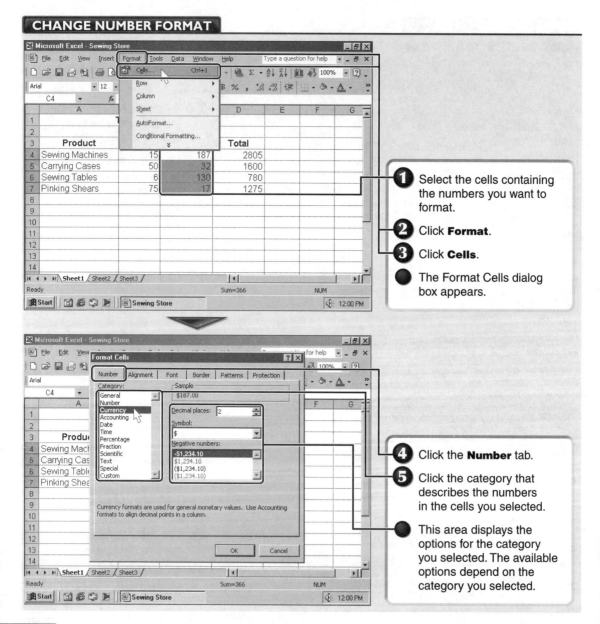

1 Select the cells containing the numbers you want to format.

2 Click **Format**.

3 Click **Cells**.

● The Format Cells dialog box appears.

4 Click the **Number** tab.

5 Click the category that describes the numbers in the cells you selected.

● This area displays the options for the category you selected. The available options depend on the category you selected.

in an *Instant*

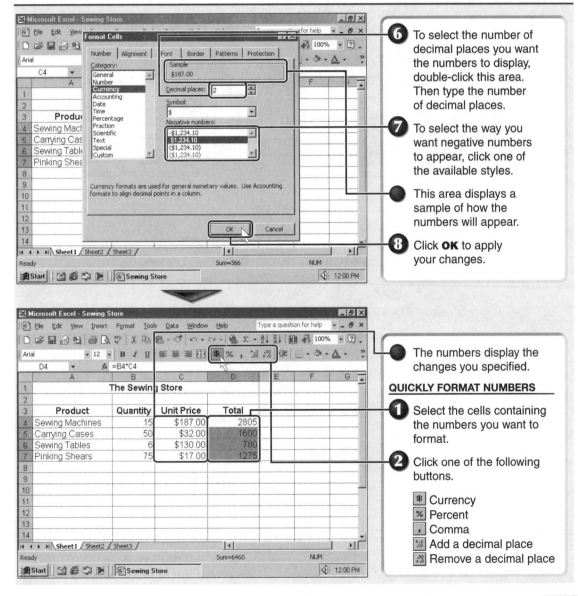

6 To select the number of decimal places you want the numbers to display, double-click this area. Then type the number of decimal places.

7 To select the way you want negative numbers to appear, click one of the available styles.

● This area displays a sample of how the numbers will appear.

8 Click **OK** to apply your changes.

● The numbers display the changes you specified.

QUICKLY FORMAT NUMBERS

1 Select the cells containing the numbers you want to format.

2 Click one of the following buttons.

$	Currency
%	Percent
,	Comma
+.0	Add a decimal place
.00	Remove a decimal place

CHANGE DATA COLOR

You can change the color of data in your worksheet to draw attention to important information. When changing the color of data, you should choose a color that works well with the color of the cells. For example, red data in blue cells can be difficult to read.

CHANGE DATA COLOR

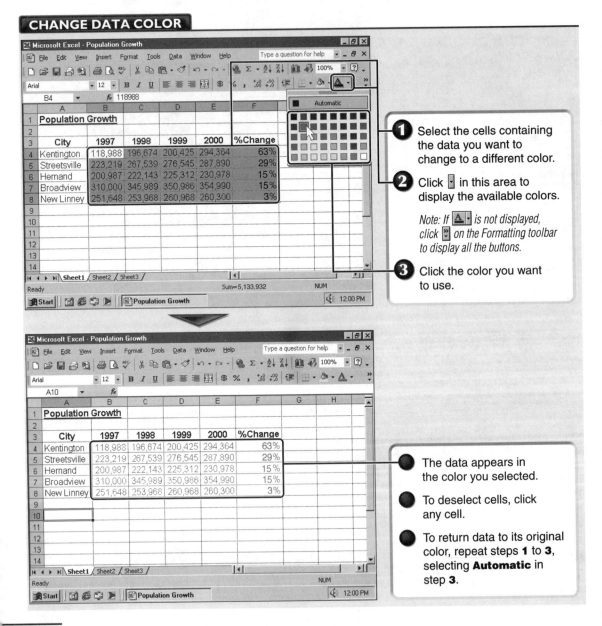

1 Select the cells containing the data you want to change to a different color.

2 Click ⬝ in this area to display the available colors.

Note: If ▲▾ *is not displayed, click* ▾ *on the Formatting toolbar to display all the buttons.*

3 Click the color you want to use.

■ The data appears in the color you selected.

■ To deselect cells, click any cell.

■ To return data to its original color, repeat steps **1** to **3**, selecting **Automatic** in step **3**.

You can add color to cells to make the cells stand out in your worksheet. Adding color to cells is useful when you want to distinguish between different types of information in your worksheet. For example, you may want to add color to cells containing headings.

CHANGE CELL COLOR

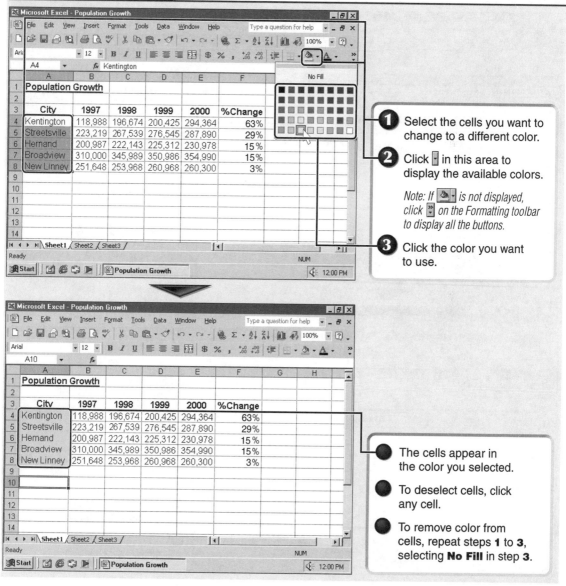

1 Select the cells you want to change to a different color.

2 Click ⬝ in this area to display the available colors.

Note: If ⬝ is not displayed, click ⬝ on the Formatting toolbar to display all the buttons.

3 Click the color you want to use.

● The cells appear in the color you selected.

● To deselect cells, click any cell.

● To remove color from cells, repeat steps **1** to **3**, selecting **No Fill** in step **3**.

CHANGE ALIGNMENT OF DATA

You can change the alignment of data in the cells of your worksheet. Changing the alignment of data can help enhance the appearance of your worksheet. When you enter data into cells, Excel automatically left aligns text and right aligns numbers and dates.

CHANGE ALIGNMENT OF DATA

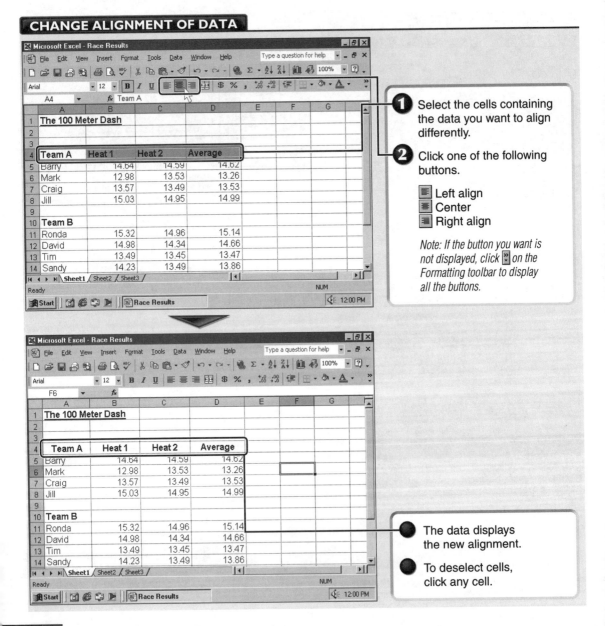

1 Select the cells containing the data you want to align differently.

2 Click one of the following buttons.

▤ Left align
▤ Center
▤ Right align

Note: If the button you want is not displayed, click ▸ on the Formatting toolbar to display all the buttons.

● The data displays the new alignment.

● To deselect cells, click any cell.

You can center data across several columns in your worksheet. This is useful for centering titles over your data. When centering data across several columns, the first cell you select should contain the data you want to center.

CENTER DATA ACROSS COLUMNS

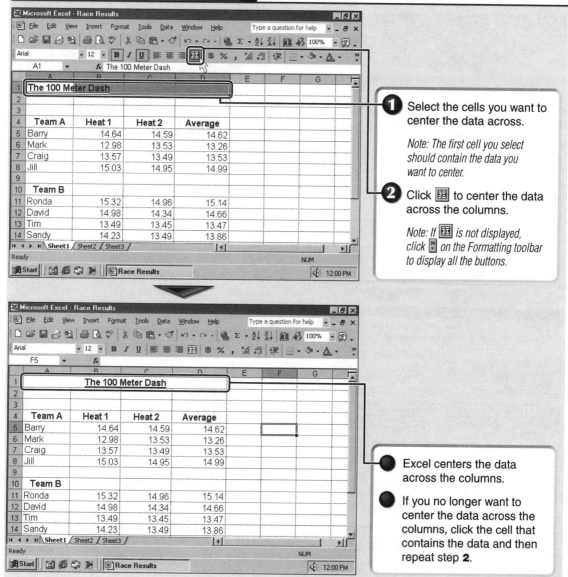

1 Select the cells you want to center the data across.

Note: The first cell you select should contain the data you want to center.

2 Click 🔳 to center the data across the columns.

Note: If 🔳 is not displayed, click ⏵ on the Formatting toolbar to display all the buttons.

● Excel centers the data across the columns.

● If you no longer want to center the data across the columns, click the cell that contains the data and then repeat step **2**.

BOLD, ITALICIZE OR UNDERLINE DATA

You can bold, italicize or underline data to emphasize data in your worksheet. For example, you can bold headings to make them stand out from the rest of the data in your worksheet. You can also underline important data in your worksheet, such as subtotals and totals.

BOLD, ITALICIZE OR UNDERLINE DATA

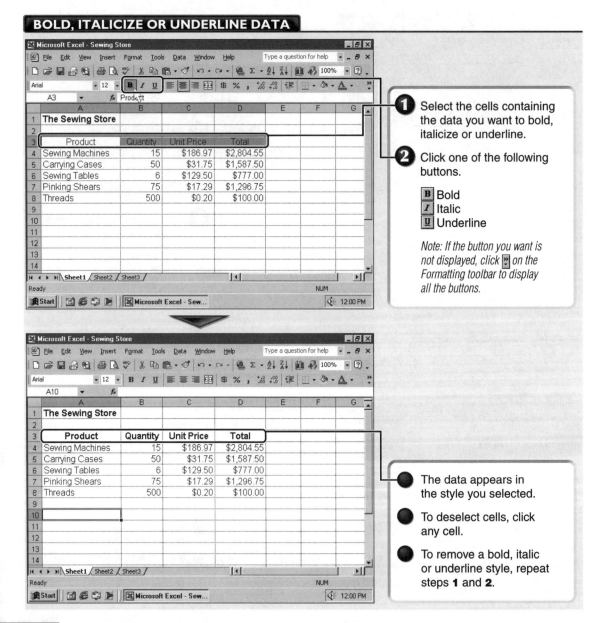

1 Select the cells containing the data you want to bold, italicize or underline.

2 Click one of the following buttons.

B Bold
I Italic
U Underline

Note: If the button you want is not displayed, click ⊠ on the Formatting toolbar to display all the buttons.

● The data appears in the style you selected.

● To deselect cells, click any cell.

● To remove a bold, italic or underline style, repeat steps **1** and **2**.

You can copy the formatting of a cell to make other cells in your worksheet look exactly the same. You may want to copy the formatting of cells to make all the titles in your worksheet look the same. This will give the information in your worksheet a consistent appearance.

COPY FORMATTING

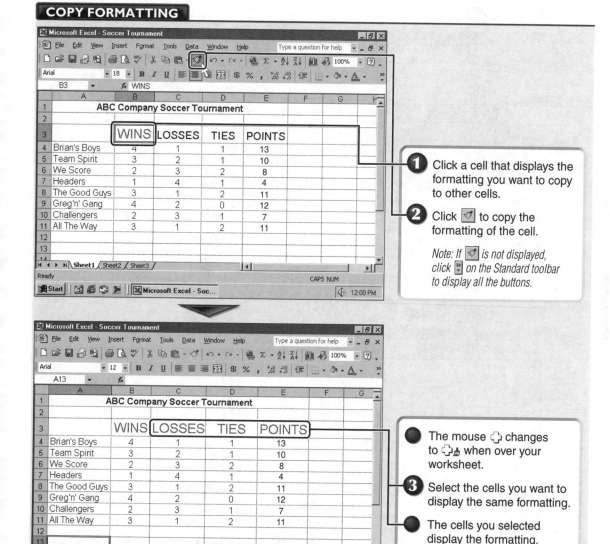

1 Click a cell that displays the formatting you want to copy to other cells.

2 Click 🖌 to copy the formatting of the cell.

Note: If 🖌 is not displayed, click 》 on the Standard toolbar to display all the buttons.

■ The mouse ⊕ changes to ⊕🖌 when over your worksheet.

3 Select the cells you want to display the same formatting.

■ The cells you selected display the formatting.

■ To deselect cells, click any cell.

APPLY AN AUTOFORMAT

Excel offers many ready-to-use designs, called autoformats, which you can choose from to give your worksheet a professional appearance. Each autoformat includes a combination of formats, such as fonts, colors, borders, alignments and number styles. When you apply an autoformat, Excel may also adjust the column width and row height of the cells to best fit the data in the cells.

APPLY AN AUTOFORMAT

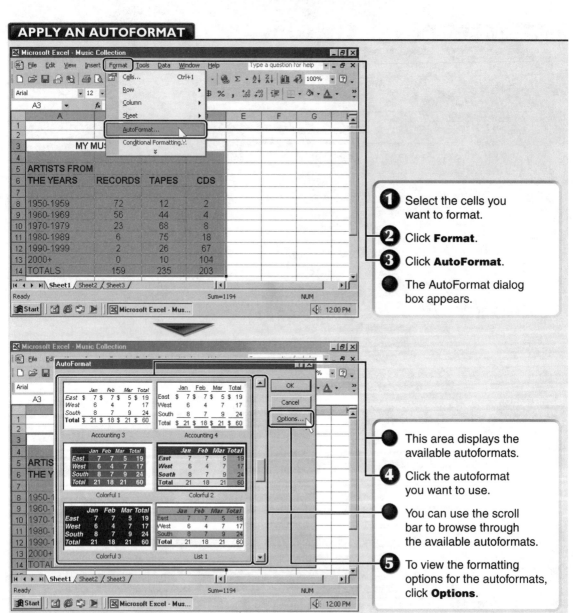

1 Select the cells you want to format.

2 Click **Format**.

3 Click **AutoFormat**.

● The AutoFormat dialog box appears.

● This area displays the available autoformats.

4 Click the autoformat you want to use.

● You can use the scroll bar to browse through the available autoformats.

5 To view the formatting options for the autoformats, click **Options**.

in an *instant*

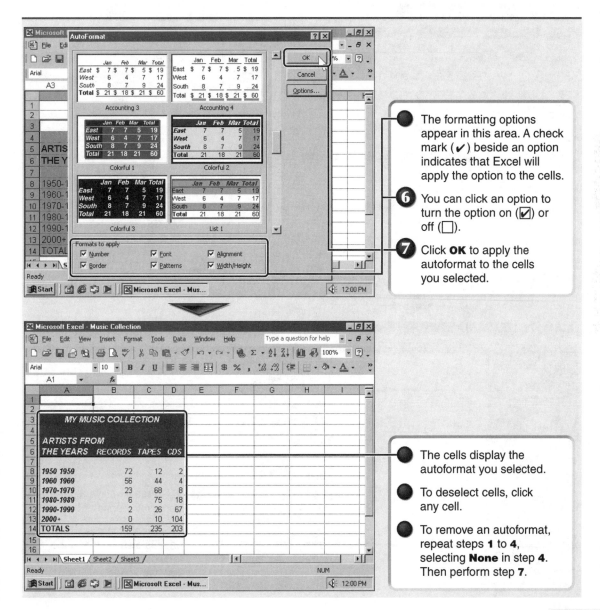

The formatting options appear in this area. A check mark (✔) beside an option indicates that Excel will apply the option to the cells.

6 You can click an option to turn the option on (☑) or off (☐).

7 Click **OK** to apply the autoformat to the cells you selected.

The cells display the autoformat you selected.

To deselect cells, click any cell.

To remove an autoformat, repeat steps **1** to **4**, selecting **None** in step **4**. Then perform step **7**.

PREVIEW A WORKSHEET

You can use the Print Preview feature to see how your worksheet will look when printed. This allows you to confirm that the worksheet will print the way you expect. If you are using a black-and-white printer, your worksheet appears in black and white in the Print Preview window. If you are using a color printer, your worksheet will appear in color.

PREVIEW A WORKSHEET

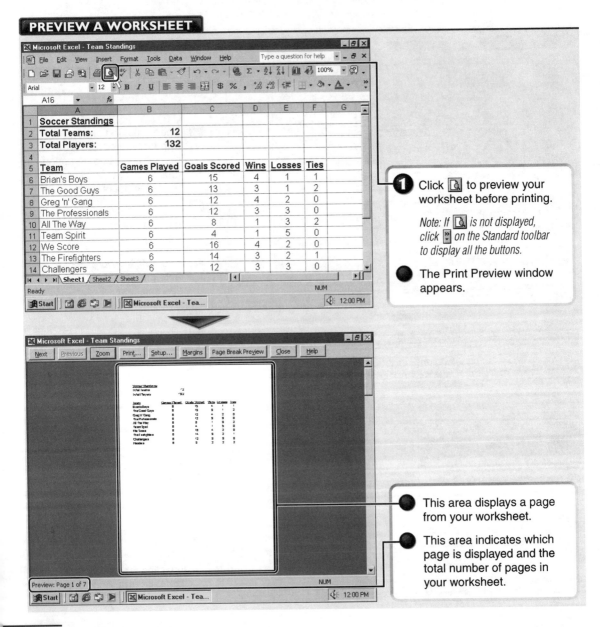

1 Click 🔍 to preview your worksheet before printing.

Note: If 🔍 is not displayed, click 🔽 on the Standard toolbar to display all the buttons.

● The Print Preview window appears.

● This area displays a page from your worksheet.

● This area indicates which page is displayed and the total number of pages in your worksheet.

in an *instant*

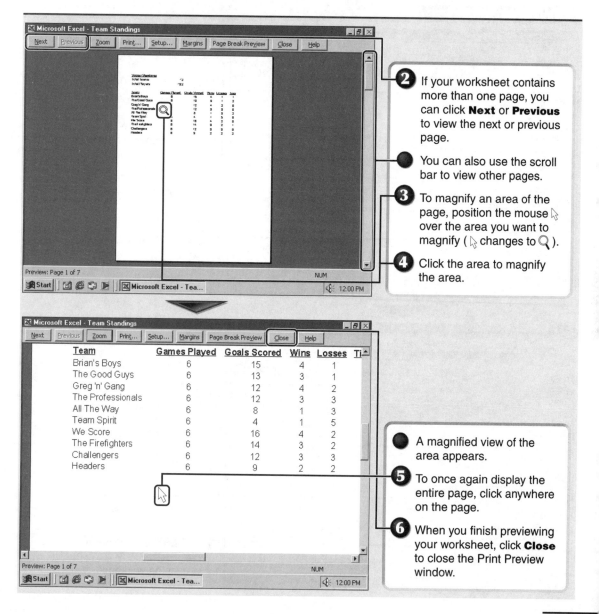

2 If your worksheet contains more than one page, you can click **Next** or **Previous** to view the next or previous page.

● You can also use the scroll bar to view other pages.

3 To magnify an area of the page, position the mouse over the area you want to magnify (changes to Q).

4 Click the area to magnify the area.

● A magnified view of the area appears.

5 To once again display the entire page, click anywhere on the page.

6 When you finish previewing your worksheet, click **Close** to close the Print Preview window.

PRINT A WORKSHEET

You can produce a paper copy of the worksheet displayed on your screen. Excel also allows you to print only specific cells in the worksheet or all the worksheets in your workbook. Before printing, you should make sure your printer is turned on and contains paper.

PRINT A WORKSHEET

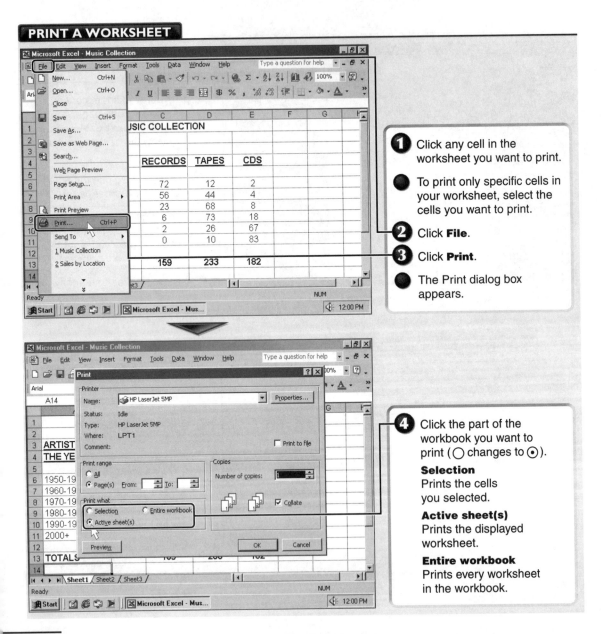

1 Click any cell in the worksheet you want to print.

● To print only specific cells in your worksheet, select the cells you want to print.

2 Click **File**.

3 Click **Print**.

● The Print dialog box appears.

4 Click the part of the workbook you want to print (○ changes to ⊙).

Selection
Prints the cells you selected.

Active sheet(s)
Prints the displayed worksheet.

Entire workbook
Prints every worksheet in the workbook.

in an instant

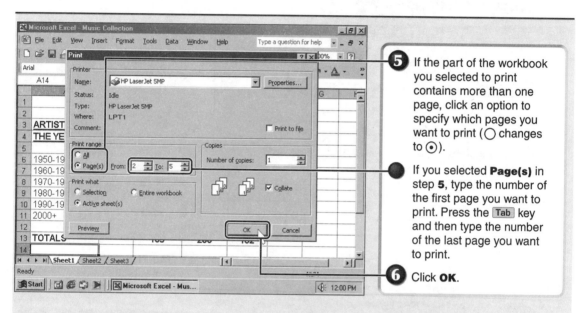

5 If the part of the workbook you selected to print contains more than one page, click an option to specify which pages you want to print (○ changes to ⊙).

● If you selected **Page(s)** in step **5**, type the number of the first page you want to print. Press the Tab key and then type the number of the last page you want to print.

6 Click **OK**.

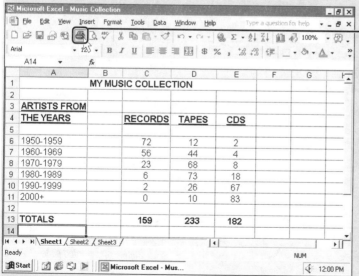

QUICKLY PRINT DISPLAYED WORKSHEET

1 Click 🖨 to quickly print the worksheet displayed on your screen.

Note: If 🖨 is not displayed, click ⋙ on the Standard toolbar to display all the buttons.

147

CHANGE PAGE ORIENTATION

You can change the page orientation to change the way your worksheet appears on a printed page. Excel automatically prints your worksheets in the portrait orientation. The landscape orientation is useful when you want a wide worksheet to fit on one printed page. Changing the page orientation will not affect the way your worksheet appears on your screen.

CHANGE PAGE ORIENTATION

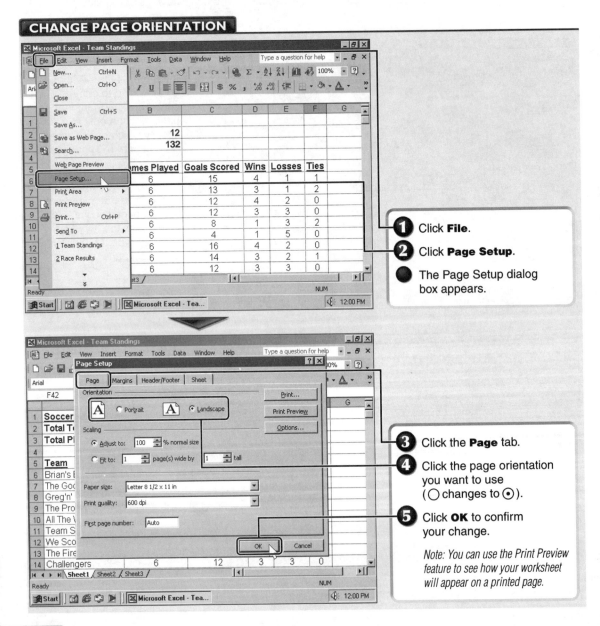

1 Click **File**.

2 Click **Page Setup**.

● The Page Setup dialog box appears.

3 Click the **Page** tab.

4 Click the page orientation you want to use (○ changes to ⊙).

5 Click **OK** to confirm your change.

Note: You can use the Print Preview feature to see how your worksheet will appear on a printed page.

CHANGE MARGINS

You can change the margins in your worksheet. A margin is the amount of space between the data on a page and the edge of your paper. Excel automatically sets the top and bottom margins to 1 inch and the left and right margins to 0.75 inches. Changing the margins allows you to adjust the amount of information that can fit on a page.

CHANGE MARGINS

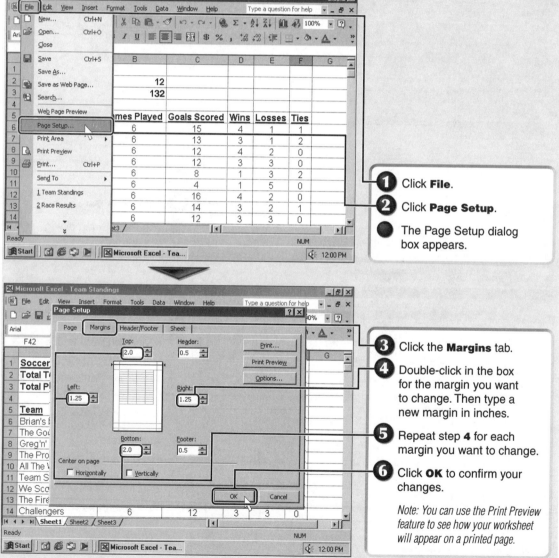

1 Click **File**.

2 Click **Page Setup**.

● The Page Setup dialog box appears.

3 Click the **Margins** tab.

4 Double-click in the box for the margin you want to change. Then type a new margin in inches.

5 Repeat step **4** for each margin you want to change.

6 Click **OK** to confirm your changes.

Note: You can use the Print Preview feature to see how your worksheet will appear on a printed page.

CHANGE PRINT OPTIONS

You can use the print options that Excel offers to change the way your worksheet appears on a printed page. For example, you can print a colored worksheet in black and white. This is useful when you want to print a colored worksheet on a black-and-white printer. Changing the print options will not affect the way your worksheet appears on your screen.

CHANGE PRINT OPTIONS

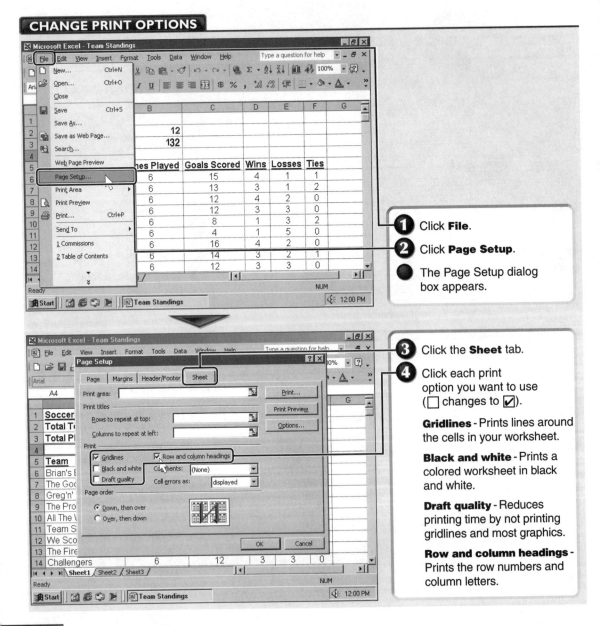

1 Click **File**.

2 Click **Page Setup**.

● The Page Setup dialog box appears.

3 Click the **Sheet** tab.

4 Click each print option you want to use (☐ changes to ☑).

Gridlines - Prints lines around the cells in your worksheet.

Black and white - Prints a colored worksheet in black and white.

Draft quality - Reduces printing time by not printing gridlines and most graphics.

Row and column headings - Prints the row numbers and column letters.

in an instant

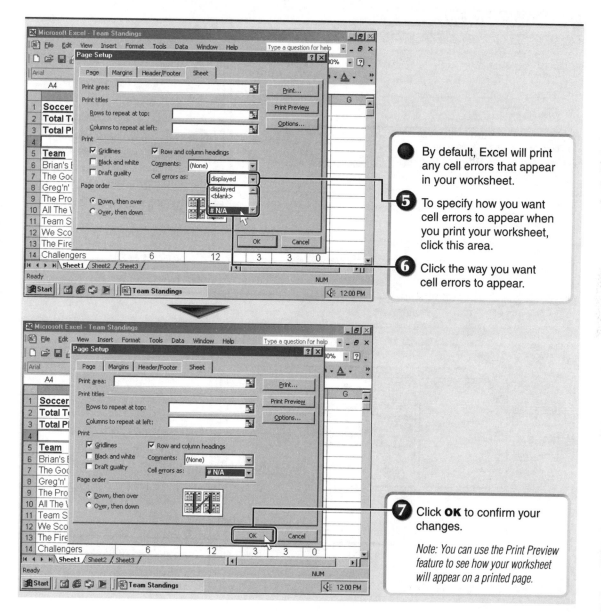

By default, Excel will print any cell errors that appear in your worksheet.

5 To specify how you want cell errors to appear when you print your worksheet, click this area.

6 Click the way you want cell errors to appear.

7 Click **OK** to confirm your changes.

Note: You can use the Print Preview feature to see how your worksheet will appear on a printed page.

151

CREATE A CHART

You can create a chart to graphically display your worksheet data. Charts allow you to easily compare data and view patterns and trends. When creating a chart, you select the data in your worksheet you want the chart to display. If you later change the data in your worksheet, Excel will update the chart to display the changes.

CREATE A CHART

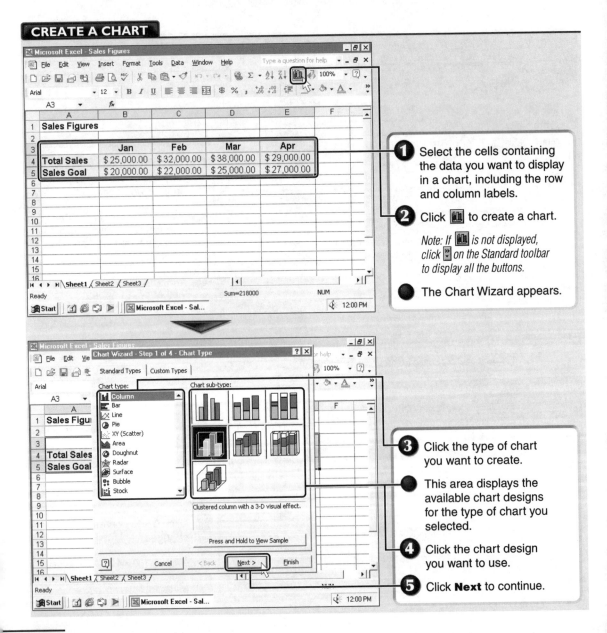

1 Select the cells containing the data you want to display in a chart, including the row and column labels.

2 Click 📊 to create a chart.

Note: If 📊 is not displayed, click 🔽 on the Standard toolbar to display all the buttons.

● The Chart Wizard appears.

3 Click the type of chart you want to create.

● This area displays the available chart designs for the type of chart you selected.

4 Click the chart design you want to use.

5 Click **Next** to continue.

in an *instant*

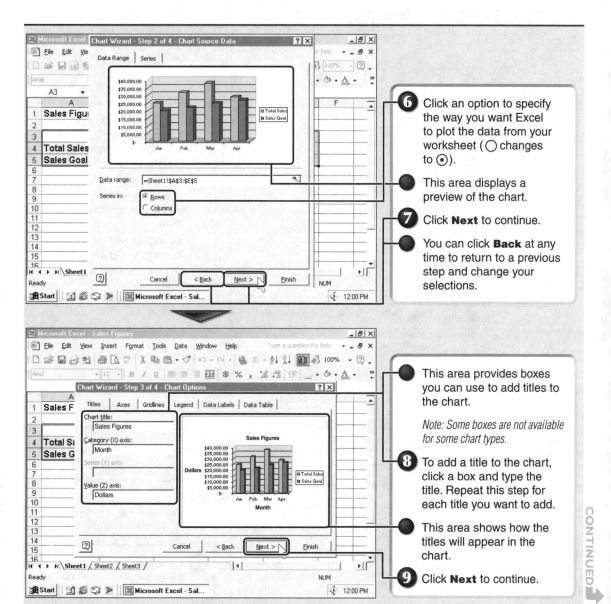

6 Click an option to specify the way you want Excel to plot the data from your worksheet (○ changes to ⊙).

● This area displays a preview of the chart.

7 Click **Next** to continue.

● You can click **Back** at any time to return to a previous step and change your selections.

● This area provides boxes you can use to add titles to the chart.

Note: Some boxes are not available for some chart types.

8 To add a title to the chart, click a box and type the title. Repeat this step for each title you want to add.

● This area shows how the titles will appear in the chart.

9 Click **Next** to continue.

CONTINUED

CREATE A CHART

You can display a chart you create on the same worksheet as the data or on its own sheet, called a chart sheet. Displaying a chart with your worksheet data is useful when you want to print the chart and data on the same page. Displaying a chart on a chart sheet is ideal when you want to view the chart separately from your worksheet data.

CREATE A CHART (CONTINUED)

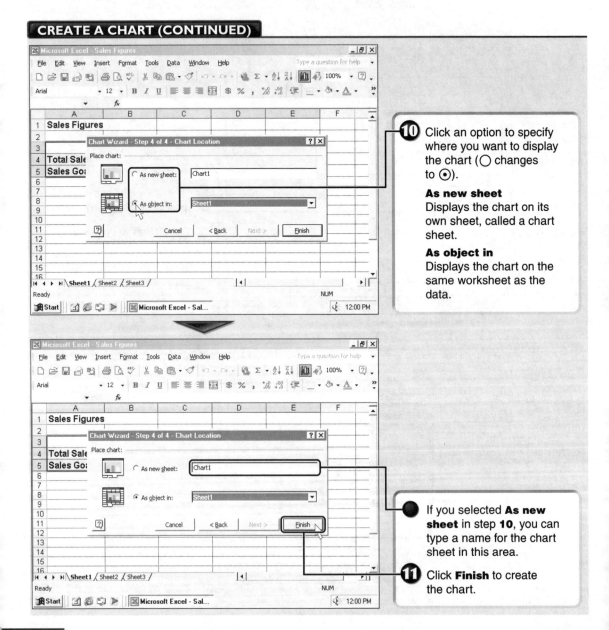

10 Click an option to specify where you want to display the chart (○ changes to ⊙).

As new sheet
Displays the chart on its own sheet, called a chart sheet.

As object in
Displays the chart on the same worksheet as the data.

If you selected **As new sheet** in step **10**, you can type a name for the chart sheet in this area.

11 Click **Finish** to create the chart.

in an *Instant*

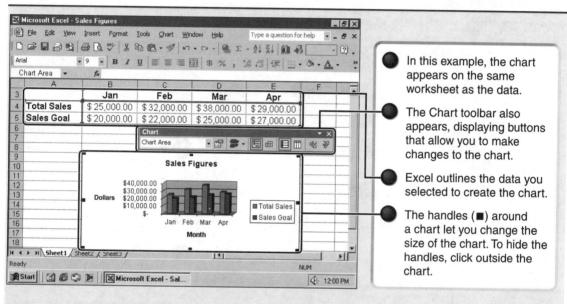

- In this example, the chart appears on the same worksheet as the data.

- The Chart toolbar also appears, displaying buttons that allow you to make changes to the chart.

- Excel outlines the data you selected to create the chart.

- The handles (■) around a chart let you change the size of the chart. To hide the handles, click outside the chart.

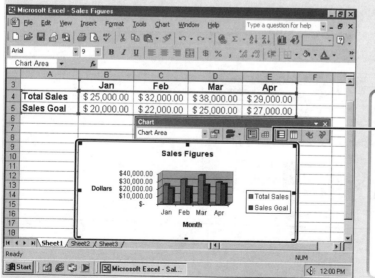

DELETE A CHART

1 Click a blank area in the chart you want to delete. Handles (■) appear around the chart.

2 Press the Delete key to delete the chart.

Note: To delete a chart displayed on a chart sheet, you must delete the sheet.

MOVE OR RESIZE A CHART

You can change the location and size of a chart displayed on your worksheet. Moving a chart is useful when the chart covers worksheet data. Increasing the size of a chart can help you view the information in the chart more clearly.

MOVE A CHART

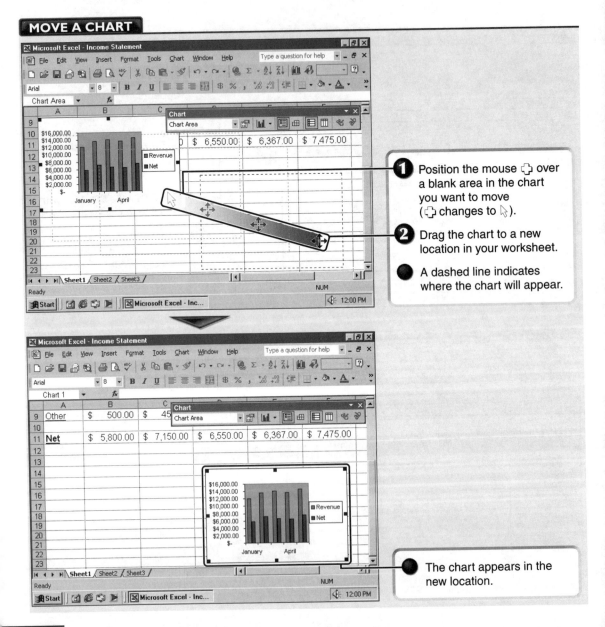

1 Position the mouse ⊕ over a blank area in the chart you want to move (⊕ changes to ⇖).

2 Drag the chart to a new location in your worksheet.

● A dashed line indicates where the chart will appear.

● The chart appears in the new location.

in an Instant

RESIZE A CHART

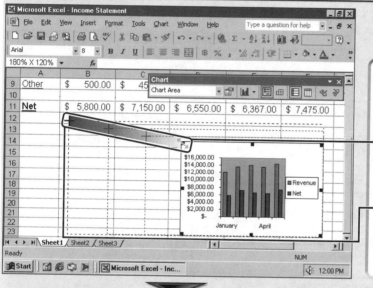

1 Click a blank area in the chart you want to resize. Handles (■) appear around the chart.

2 Position the mouse ⌖ over one of the handles (⌖ changes to ↘, ↗, ↔ or ↕).

3 Drag the handle until the chart is the size you want.

● A dashed line shows the new size.

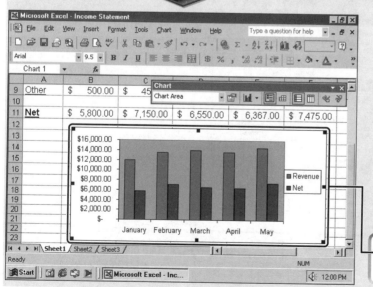

● The chart appears in the new size.

CHANGE THE CHART TYPE

After you create a chart, you can change the chart type to present your data more effectively. The type of chart you should use depends on your data. For example, area, column and line charts are ideal for showing changes to values over time. Pie charts are ideal for showing percentages.

CHANGE THE CHART TYPE

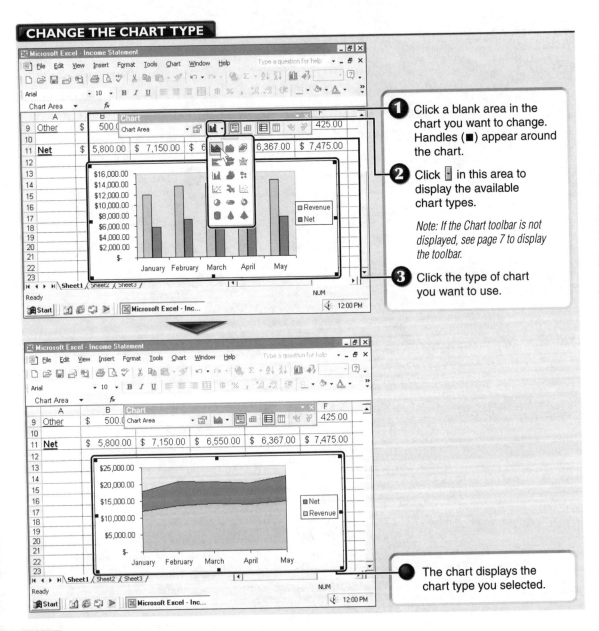

1 Click a blank area in the chart you want to change. Handles (■) appear around the chart.

2 Click ⊡ in this area to display the available chart types.

Note: If the Chart toolbar is not displayed, see page 7 to display the toolbar.

3 Click the type of chart you want to use.

● The chart displays the chart type you selected.

PRINT A CHART

You can print your chart with the worksheet data or on its own page. Printing a chart with the worksheet data is useful when you want the chart and the data to appear on the same page. When you print a chart on its own page, the chart will expand to fill the page.

PRINT A CHART

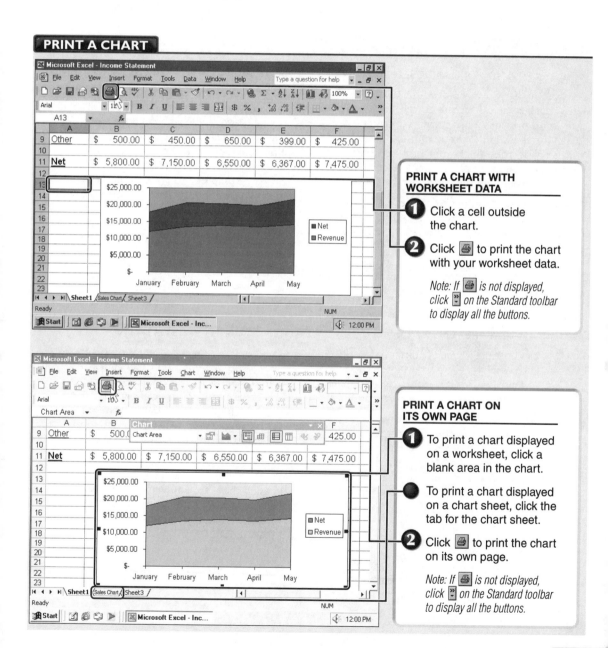

PRINT A CHART WITH WORKSHEET DATA

1 Click a cell outside the chart.

2 Click 🖨 to print the chart with your worksheet data.

Note: If 🖨 is not displayed, click ⏩ on the Standard toolbar to display all the buttons.

PRINT A CHART ON ITS OWN PAGE

1 To print a chart displayed on a worksheet, click a blank area in the chart.

● To print a chart displayed on a chart sheet, click the tab for the chart sheet.

2 Click 🖨 to print the chart on its own page.

Note: If 🖨 is not displayed, click ⏩ on the Standard toolbar to display all the buttons.

159

INTRODUCTION TO POWERPOINT

PowerPoint helps you plan, organize, design and deliver professional presentations.

INTRODUCTION TO POWERPOINT

CREATE AND EDIT A PRESENTATION

You can use PowerPoint's AutoContent Wizard to quickly create a presentation. The wizard provides a design and sample text for all the slides in the presentation. PowerPoint also allows you to create a blank presentation, which is useful when you want to create a presentation one slide at a time.

You can add new text to a slide in a presentation or remove text you no longer need. PowerPoint also allows you to move text in a presentation so you can quickly re-organize ideas. To include an additional topic in a presentation, you can easily add a new slide to the presentation.

ADD OBJECTS TO A PRESENTATION

You can add objects, such as pictures, clip art images, charts and diagrams, to the slides in a presentation. Adding professionally-designed clip art images to slides can help make a presentation more interesting and entertaining. You can add a picture stored on your computer to a slide. This is useful when you want to include a company logo or picture of a product in a presentation. Adding a chart to a slide is ideal for displaying trends and comparing data. You can add a diagram to a slide to illustrate a concept or idea.

ENHANCE A PRESENTATION

You can bold, italicize or underline text on a slide to emphasize important information. You can also change the font, size, alignment and color of text to make the text stand out.

PowerPoint provides many ready-to-use designs that you can choose from to give the slides in a presentation a new appearance. You can change the design of a single slide or an entire presentation. You can also change the color scheme of a single slide or an entire presentation.

FINE-TUNE A PRESENTATION

You can fine-tune a presentation before you deliver the presentation to an audience. If you plan to deliver a presentation on a computer screen, you can add special effects called transitions to help you move from one slide to the next. You can also re-organize the slides in a presentation and delete slides you no longer need.

PowerPoint allows you to create notes that contain the ideas you want to discuss for each slide in a presentation. You can use these notes as a guide when delivering the presentation.

THE POWERPOINT WINDOW

The PowerPoint window displays many items you can use to create and work with your presentations, such as menus, toolbars and panes.

THE POWERPOINT WINDOW

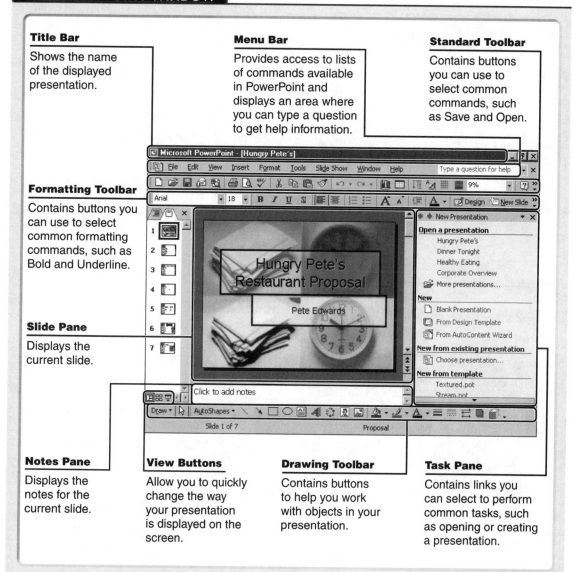

Title Bar

Shows the name of the displayed presentation.

Menu Bar

Provides access to lists of commands available in PowerPoint and displays an area where you can type a question to get help information.

Standard Toolbar

Contains buttons you can use to select common commands, such as Save and Open.

Formatting Toolbar

Contains buttons you can use to select common formatting commands, such as Bold and Underline.

Slide Pane

Displays the current slide.

Notes Pane

Displays the notes for the current slide.

View Buttons

Allow you to quickly change the way your presentation is displayed on the screen.

Drawing Toolbar

Contains buttons to help you work with objects in your presentation.

Task Pane

Contains links you can select to perform common tasks, such as opening or creating a presentation.

CREATE A PRESENTATION USING THE AUTOCONTENT WIZARD

You can use the AutoContent Wizard to create a presentation. The wizard asks you a series of questions and then sets up a presentation based on your answers. The AutoContent Wizard provides a design and sample text for the slides in your presentation.

USING THE AUTOCONTENT WIZARD

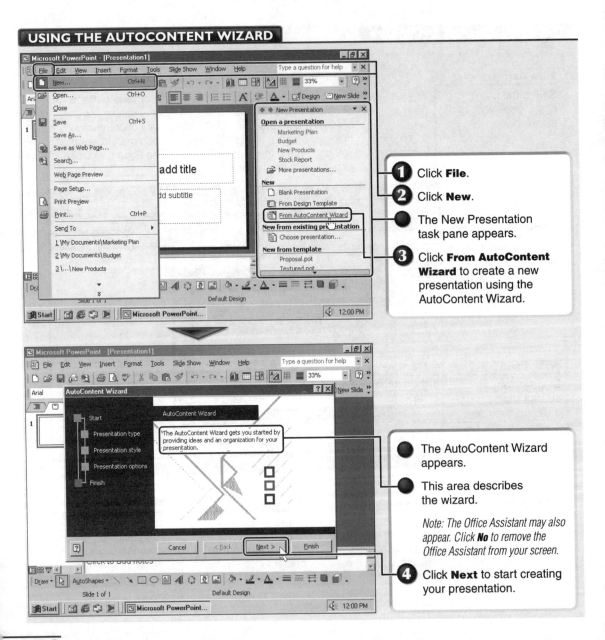

1 Click **File**.

2 Click **New**.

The New Presentation task pane appears.

3 Click **From AutoContent Wizard** to create a new presentation using the AutoContent Wizard.

The AutoContent Wizard appears.

This area describes the wizard.

Note: The Office Assistant may also appear. Click No to remove the Office Assistant from your screen.

4 Click **Next** to start creating your presentation.

in an *instant*

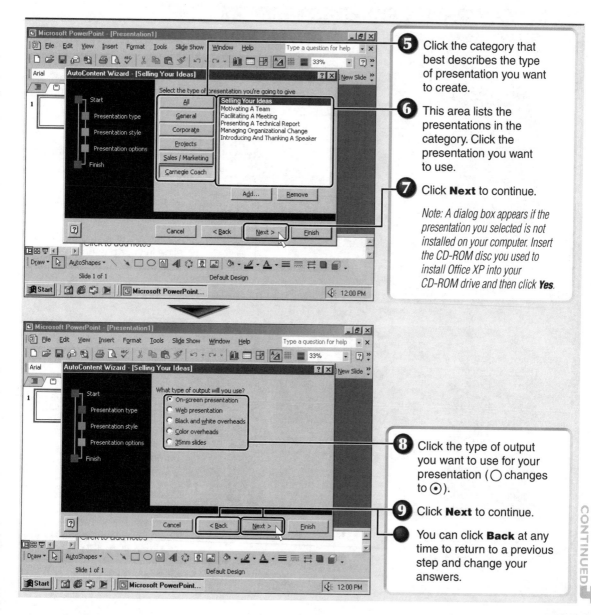

5 Click the category that best describes the type of presentation you want to create.

6 This area lists the presentations in the category. Click the presentation you want to use.

7 Click **Next** to continue.

*Note: A dialog box appears if the presentation you selected is not installed on your computer. Insert the CD-ROM disc you used to install Office XP into your CD-ROM drive and then click **Yes**.*

8 Click the type of output you want to use for your presentation (○ changes to ⊙).

9 Click **Next** to continue.

● You can click **Back** at any time to return to a previous step and change your answers.

CONTINUED▶

CREATE A PRESENTATION USING THE AUTOCONTENT WIZARD

The AutoContent Wizard allows you to specify a title for the first slide in your presentation. You can also specify information you want to include on each slide, such as footer text, the date and the slide number. If you include the date, PowerPoint will automatically update the date each time you open your presentation.

USING THE AUTOCONTENT WIZARD (CONTINUED)

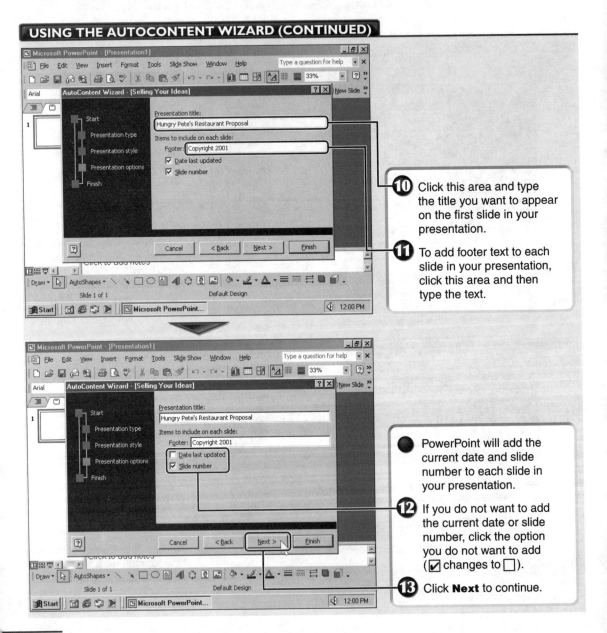

➓ Click this area and type the title you want to appear on the first slide in your presentation.

⓫ To add footer text to each slide in your presentation, click this area and then type the text.

● PowerPoint will add the current date and slide number to each slide in your presentation.

⓬ If you do not want to add the current date or slide number, click the option you do not want to add (☑ changes to ☐).

⓭ Click **Next** to continue.

in an *instant*

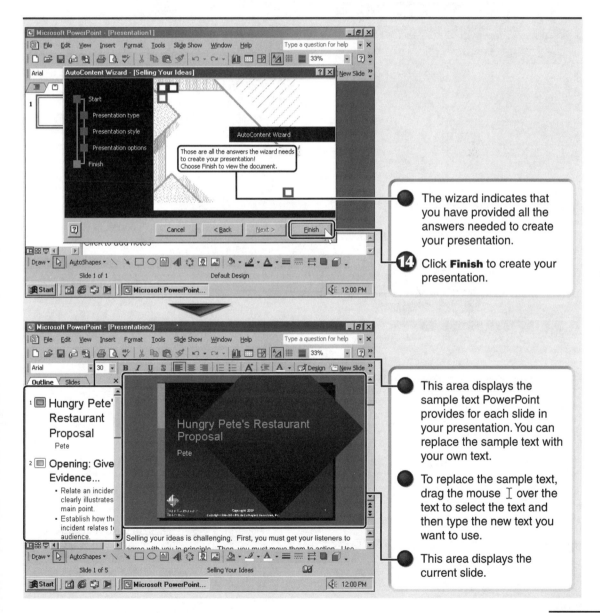

The wizard indicates that you have provided all the answers needed to create your presentation.

14 Click **Finish** to create your presentation.

This area displays the sample text PowerPoint provides for each slide in your presentation. You can replace the sample text with your own text.

To replace the sample text, drag the mouse I over the text to select the text and then type the new text you want to use.

This area displays the current slide.

CREATE A BLANK PRESENTATION

You can use PowerPoint to create a blank presentation. Blank presentations are useful when you want to create your own content and design for the slides. When you create a blank presentation, PowerPoint creates only the first slide. You can add additional slides to your presentation as you need them.

CREATE A BLANK PRESENTATION

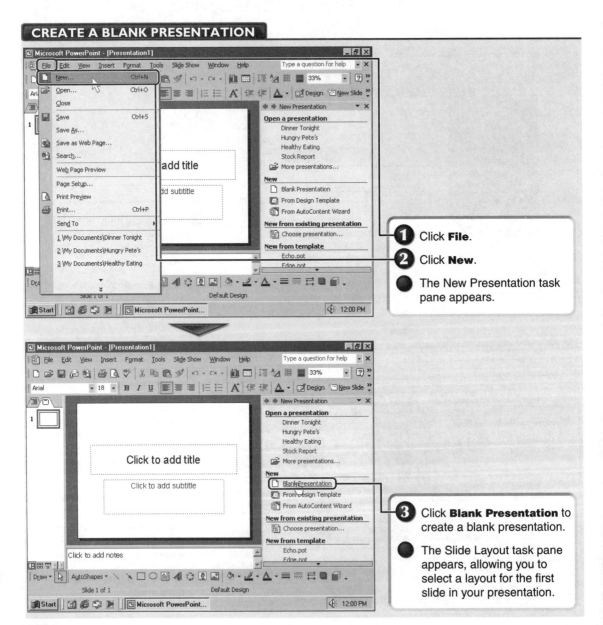

1 Click **File**.

2 Click **New**.

■ The New Presentation task pane appears.

3 Click **Blank Presentation** to create a blank presentation.

■ The Slide Layout task pane appears, allowing you to select a layout for the first slide in your presentation.

in an *instant*

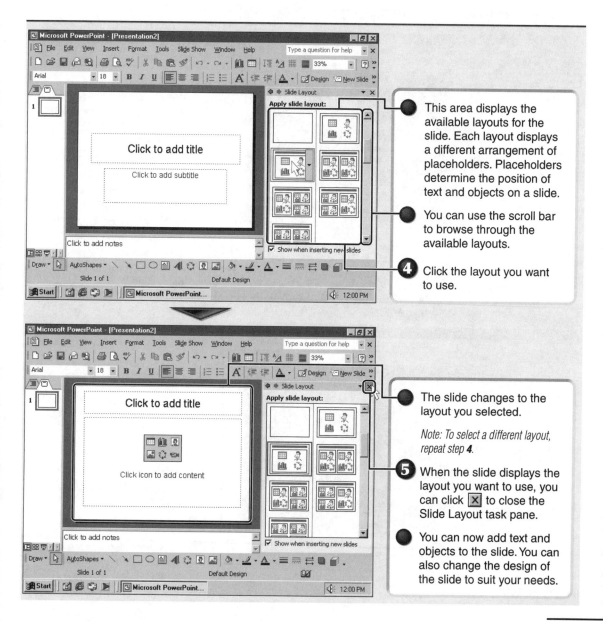

This area displays the available layouts for the slide. Each layout displays a different arrangement of placeholders. Placeholders determine the position of text and objects on a slide.

You can use the scroll bar to browse through the available layouts.

4 Click the layout you want to use.

The slide changes to the layout you selected.

*Note: To select a different layout, repeat step **4**.*

5 When the slide displays the layout you want to use, you can click ⊠ to close the Slide Layout task pane.

You can now add text and objects to the slide. You can also change the design of the slide to suit your needs.

CHANGE VIEW OF PRESENTATION

PowerPoint offers several ways that you can view a presentation on your screen. Each view displays the same presentation. If you make changes to your presentation in one view, the other views will also display the changes.

CHANGE VIEW OF PRESENTATION

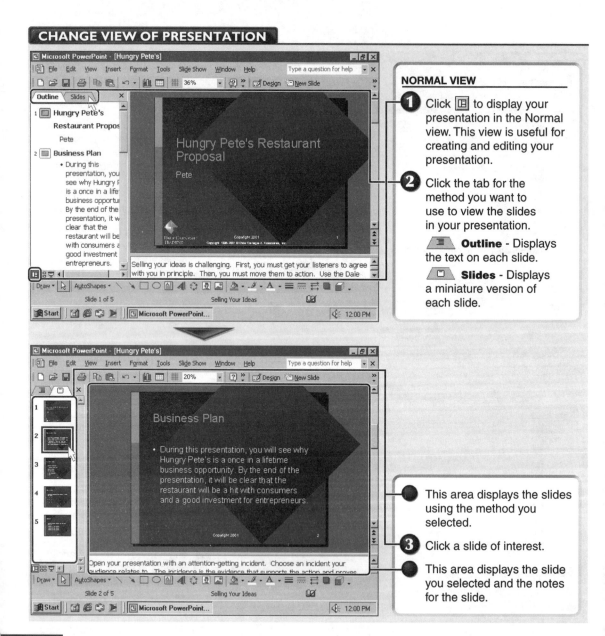

NORMAL VIEW

1 Click ▣ to display your presentation in the Normal view. This view is useful for creating and editing your presentation.

2 Click the tab for the method you want to use to view the slides in your presentation.

▤ **Outline** - Displays the text on each slide.

▢ **Slides** - Displays a miniature version of each slide.

● This area displays the slides using the method you selected.

3 Click a slide of interest.

● This area displays the slide you selected and the notes for the slide.

in an *instant*

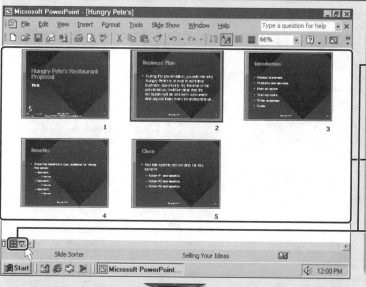

SLIDE SORTER VIEW

1 Click ⊞ to display your presentation in the Slide Sorter view. This view allows you to see the overall organization of your presentation.

● This area displays a miniature version of each slide in your presentation.

SLIDE SHOW VIEW

1 Click 🖵 to display your presentation in the Slide Show view.

Business Plan

- During this presentation, you will see why Hungry Pete's is a once in a lifetime business opportunity. By the end of the presentation, it will be clear that the restaurant will be a hit with consumers and a good investment for entrepreneurs.

Copyright 2001   2

● The Slide Show view is useful for previewing your presentation. This view allows you to see how your audience will view your presentation.

● A full-screen version of the current slide appears on your screen. You can click anywhere on the current slide to move through the slides in your presentation and view your entire slide show.

BROWSE THROUGH A PRESENTATION

Your computer screen cannot display your entire presentation at once. To view other areas of your presentation, you must browse through the presentation. You can browse through the text or the slides in your presentation. You can also browse through the notes for a slide.

BROWSE THROUGH A PRESENTATION

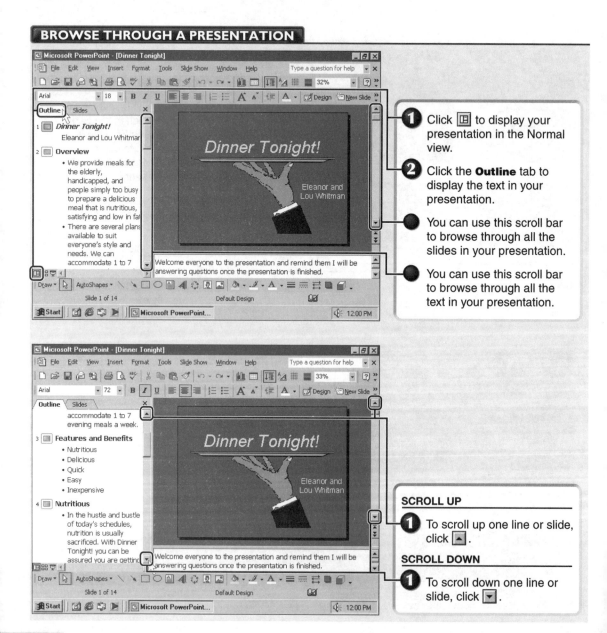

1 Click ▣ to display your presentation in the Normal view.

2 Click the **Outline** tab to display the text in your presentation.

● You can use this scroll bar to browse through all the slides in your presentation.

● You can use this scroll bar to browse through all the text in your presentation.

SCROLL UP

1 To scroll up one line or slide, click ▲ .

SCROLL DOWN

1 To scroll down one line or slide, click ▼ .

in an *instant*

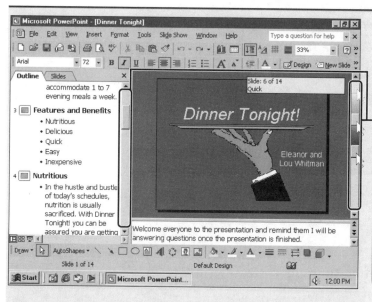

QUICKLY SCROLL

1 To quickly scroll through your presentation, drag the scroll box along the scroll bar.

● The location of the scroll box indicates which part of your presentation you are viewing. To view the middle of your presentation, drag the scroll box halfway down the scroll bar.

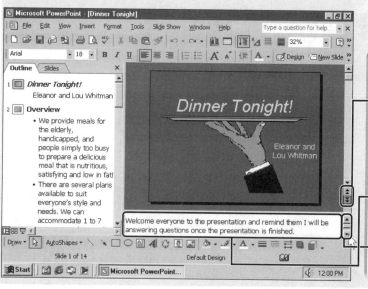

DISPLAY PREVIOUS OR NEXT SLIDE

1 Click one of the following buttons.

▲ Display previous slide
▼ Display next slide

BROWSE THROUGH NOTES

● Any notes you have created for the current slide appear in the Notes pane.

1 To browse through the notes, click ▲ or ▼.

SAVE A PRESENTATION

You can save your presentation to store the presentation for future use. Saving a presentation allows you to later review and edit the presentation. You should regularly save changes you make to a presentation to avoid losing your work.

SAVE A PRESENTATION

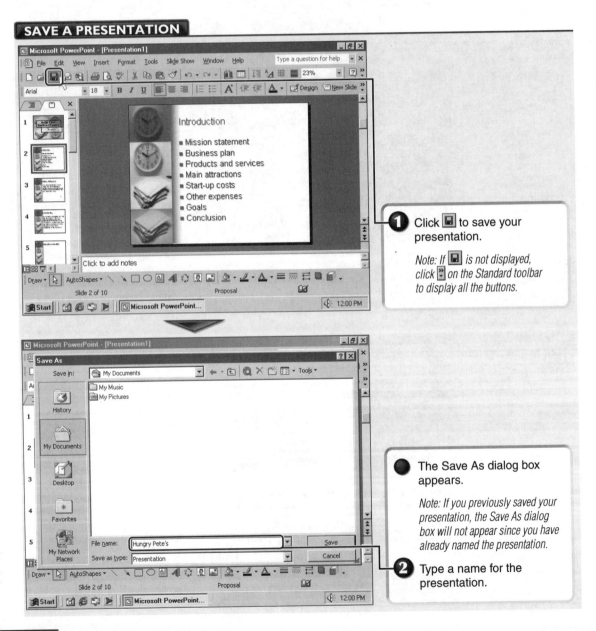

1 Click 🖫 to save your presentation.

Note: If 🖫 is not displayed, click 🔃 on the Standard toolbar to display all the buttons.

● The Save As dialog box appears.

Note: If you previously saved your presentation, the Save As dialog box will not appear since you have already named the presentation.

2 Type a name for the presentation.

172

in an instant

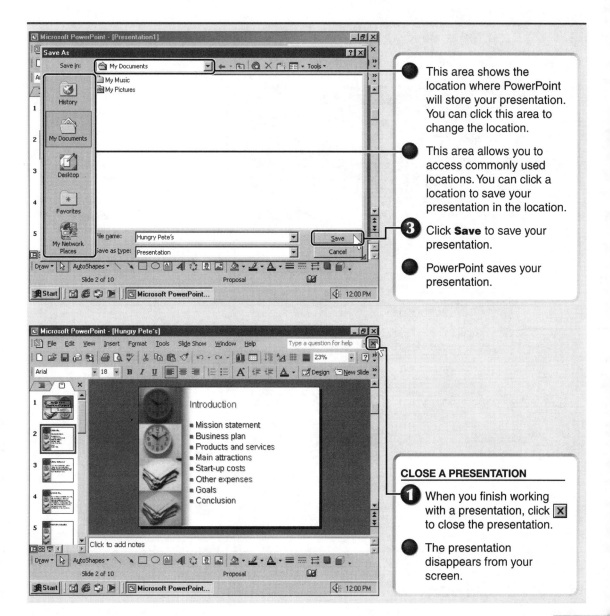

This area shows the location where PowerPoint will store your presentation. You can click this area to change the location.

This area allows you to access commonly used locations. You can click a location to save your presentation in the location.

3 Click **Save** to save your presentation.

PowerPoint saves your presentation.

CLOSE A PRESENTATION

1 When you finish working with a presentation, click ☒ to close the presentation.

The presentation disappears from your screen.

OPEN A PRESENTATION

You can open a saved presentation to view the presentation on your screen. This allows you to review and make changes to the presentation. You can have more than one presentation open at a time.

OPEN A PRESENTATION

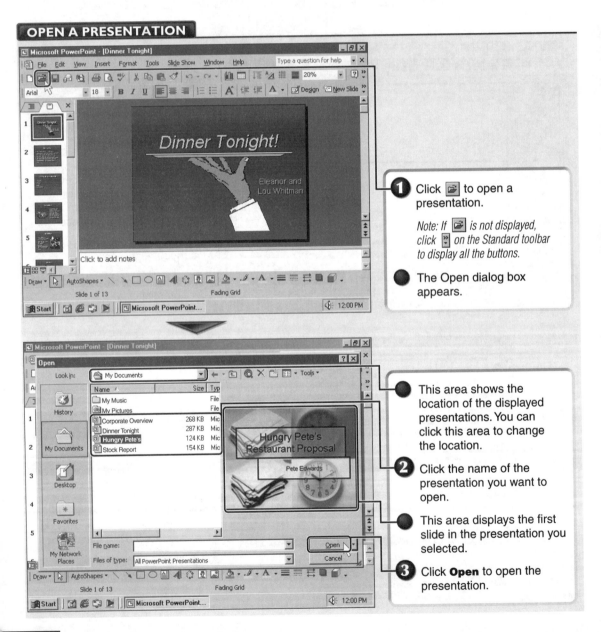

1 Click 📂 to open a presentation.

Note: If 📂 is not displayed, click ≫ on the Standard toolbar to display all the buttons.

● The Open dialog box appears.

● This area shows the location of the displayed presentations. You can click this area to change the location.

2 Click the name of the presentation you want to open.

● This area displays the first slide in the presentation you selected.

3 Click **Open** to open the presentation.

in an instant

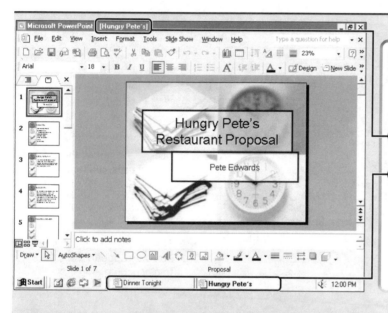

- The presentation opens and appears on your screen. You can now review and make changes to the presentation.

- This area displays the name of the open presentation.

- If you already had a presentation open, the new presentation appears in a new Microsoft PowerPoint window. You can click the buttons on the taskbar to switch between the open presentations.

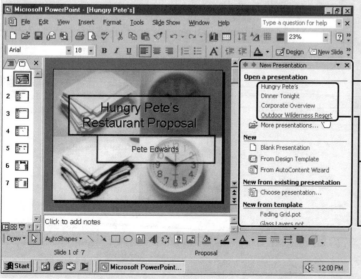

QUICKLY OPEN A PRESENTATION

- The New Presentation task pane appears each time you start PowerPoint. To display the New Presentation task pane, see page 8.

- This area displays the names of the last four presentations you worked with.

1 Click the name of the presentation you want to open.

E-MAIL A PRESENTATION

You can e-mail a presentation to a friend, family member or colleague. When sending an e-mail message, you must specify the e-mail address of each person you want to receive the message. You can also send a copy of the message to people who are not directly involved but would be interested in the message.

E-MAIL A PRESENTATION

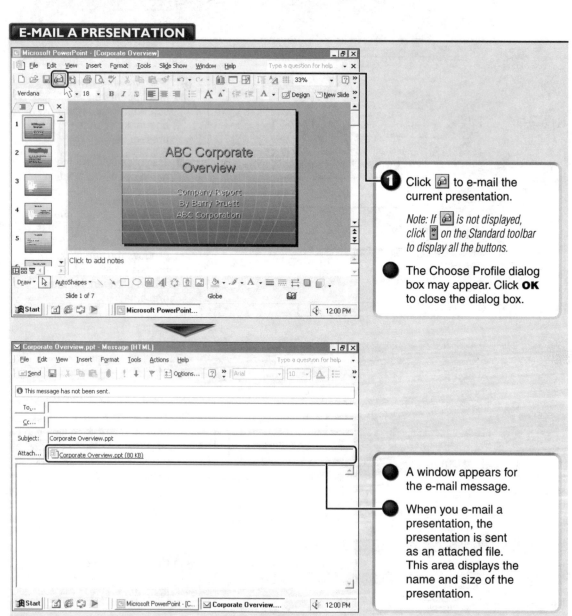

1 Click 🖃 to e-mail the current presentation.

Note: If 🖃 is not displayed, click 🔽 on the Standard toolbar to display all the buttons.

● The Choose Profile dialog box may appear. Click **OK** to close the dialog box.

● A window appears for the e-mail message.

● When you e-mail a presentation, the presentation is sent as an attached file. This area displays the name and size of the presentation.

in an instant

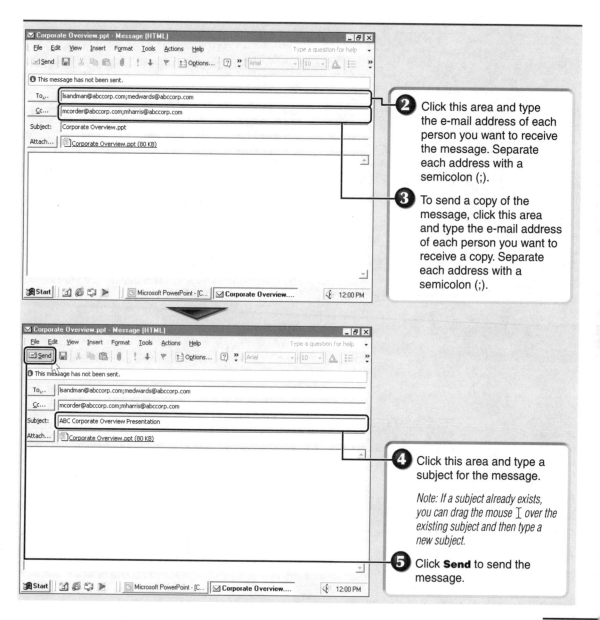

2 Click this area and type the e-mail address of each person you want to receive the message. Separate each address with a semicolon (;).

3 To send a copy of the message, click this area and type the e-mail address of each person you want to receive a copy. Separate each address with a semicolon (;).

4 Click this area and type a subject for the message.

Note: If a subject already exists, you can drag the mouse I over the existing subject and then type a new subject.

5 Click **Send** to send the message.

SELECT TEXT

Before making changes to text in your presentation, you will often need to select the text you want to work with. You can select a word, sentence, point or any amount of text on a slide. Selected text appears highlighted on your screen.

SELECT TEXT

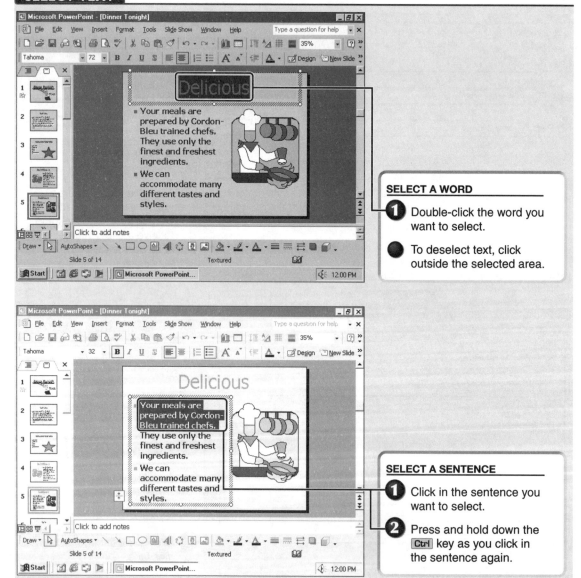

SELECT A WORD

1 Double-click the word you want to select.

● To deselect text, click outside the selected area.

SELECT A SENTENCE

1 Click in the sentence you want to select.

2 Press and hold down the Ctrl key as you click in the sentence again.

in an *instant*

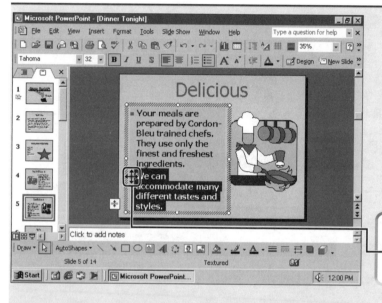

SELECT A POINT

1 Click the bullet (■) beside the point you want to select.

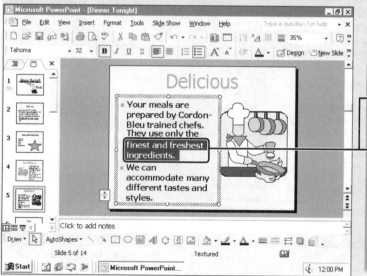

SELECT ANY AMOUNT OF TEXT

1 Position the mouse I over the first word you want to select.

2 Drag the mouse I over the text until you highlight all the text you want to select.

Note: You can also perform these steps to select text on the Outline tab in the Normal view. The Outline tab displays the text for all the slides in your presentation.

INSERT TEXT

You can add new text to a slide in your presentation quickly and easily. For example, you can add characters, a word or a new point to a slide. Adding a new point allows you to include another idea on the slide.

INSERT TEXT

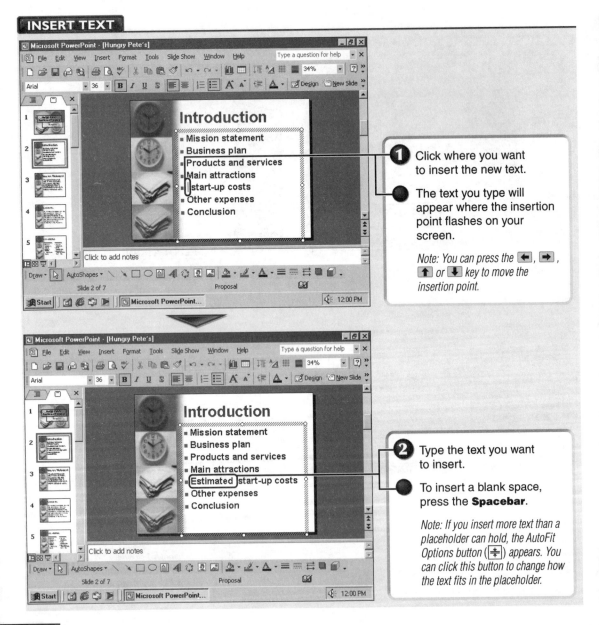

1 Click where you want to insert the new text.

The text you type will appear where the insertion point flashes on your screen.

Note: You can press the ← *,* → *,* ↑ *or* ↓ *key to move the insertion point.*

2 Type the text you want to insert.

To insert a blank space, press the **Spacebar**.

Note: If you insert more text than a placeholder can hold, the AutoFit Options button (⬍) appears. You can click this button to change how the text fits in the placeholder.

in an *instant*

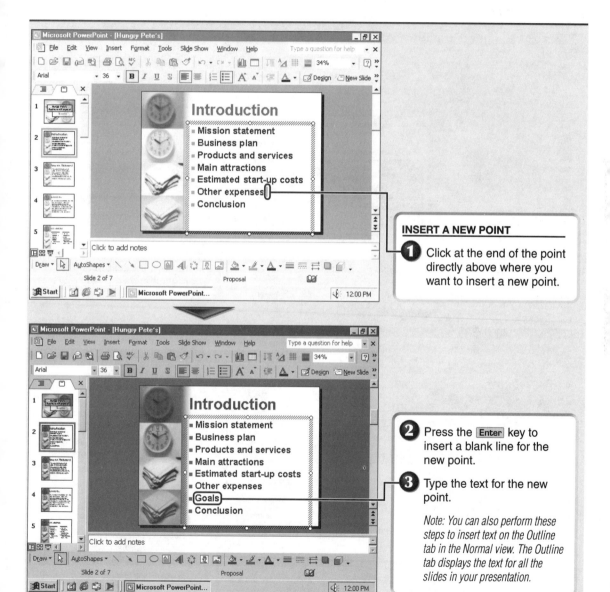

INSERT A NEW POINT

1 Click at the end of the point directly above where you want to insert a new point.

2 Press the Enter key to insert a blank line for the new point.

3 Type the text for the new point.

Note: You can also perform these steps to insert text on the Outline tab in the Normal view. The Outline tab displays the text for all the slides in your presentation.

DELETE TEXT

You can delete text from a slide to remove information you no longer need in your presentation. You can delete any amount of text, such as a word, sentence or point. You can also delete a single character. When deleting a single character, PowerPoint deletes the character to the left of the flashing insertion point.

DELETE TEXT

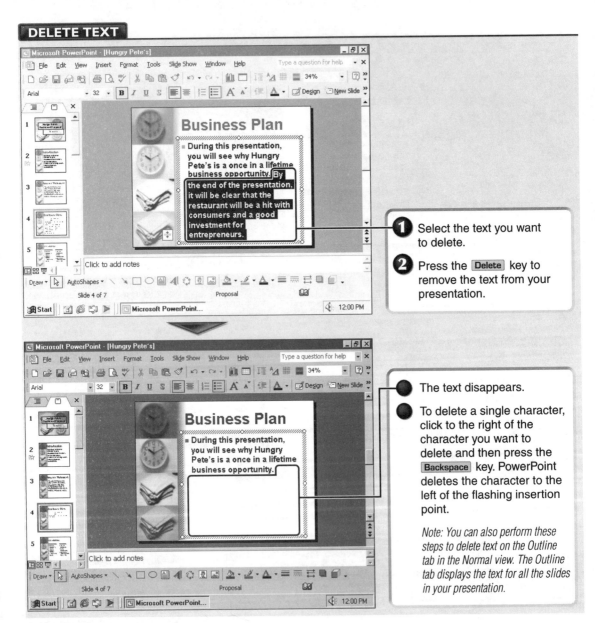

1 Select the text you want to delete.

2 Press the Delete key to remove the text from your presentation.

The text disappears.

To delete a single character, click to the right of the character you want to delete and then press the Backspace key. PowerPoint deletes the character to the left of the flashing insertion point.

Note: You can also perform these steps to delete text on the Outline tab in the Normal view. The Outline tab displays the text for all the slides in your presentation.

182

UNDO CHANGES

PowerPoint remembers the last changes you made to
your presentation. If you regret these changes, you can
cancel them by using the Undo feature. The Undo feature
can cancel your last editing and formatting changes.

UNDO CHANGES

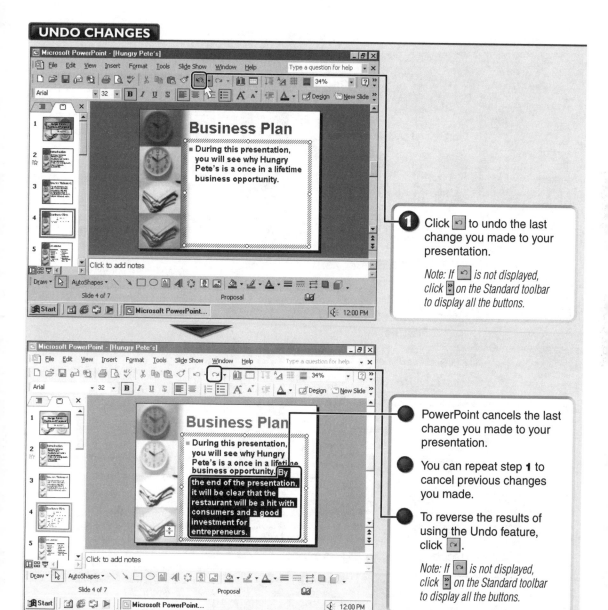

1 Click 🔄 to undo the last
change you made to your
presentation.

*Note: If 🔄 is not displayed,
click ⚹ on the Standard toolbar
to display all the buttons.*

● PowerPoint cancels the last
change you made to your
presentation.

● You can repeat step **1** to
cancel previous changes
you made.

● To reverse the results of
using the Undo feature,
click 🔁.

*Note: If 🔁 is not displayed,
click ⚹ on the Standard toolbar
to display all the buttons.*

You can move text in your presentation to re-organize your ideas. Dragging and dropping text is useful when moving text short distances, such as re-arranging points on a slide. Using the toolbar buttons to move text is ideal when moving text long distances, such as moving a point to a new slide in your presentation.

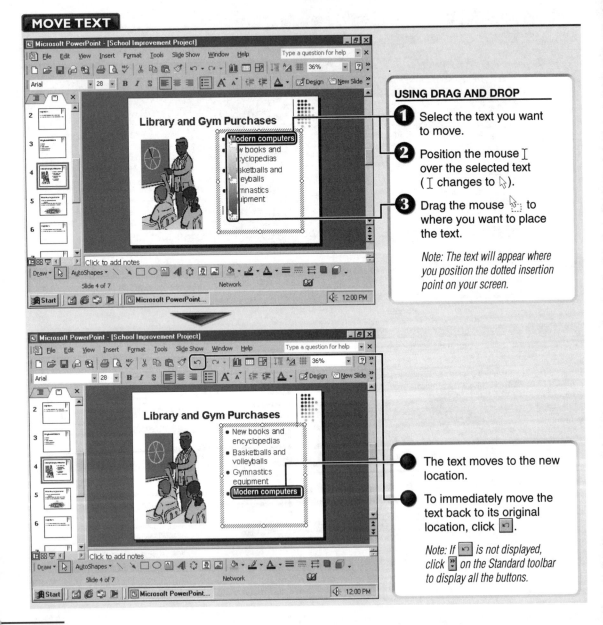

USING DRAG AND DROP

1 Select the text you want to move.

2 Position the mouse I over the selected text (I changes to).

3 Drag the mouse to where you want to place the text.

Note: The text will appear where you position the dotted insertion point on your screen.

- The text moves to the new location.

- To immediately move the text back to its original location, click.

Note: If is not displayed, click on the Standard toolbar to display all the buttons.

in an *instant*

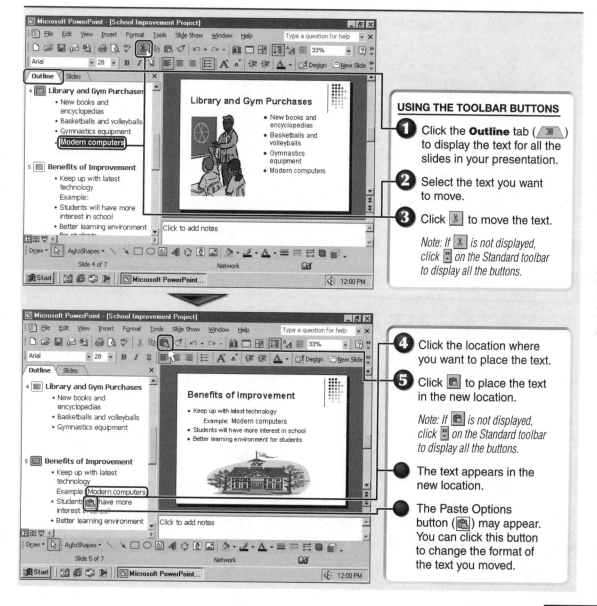

USING THE TOOLBAR BUTTONS

1 Click the **Outline** tab ( ) to display the text for all the slides in your presentation.

2 Select the text you want to move.

3 Click to move the text.

Note: If is not displayed, click on the Standard toolbar to display all the buttons.

4 Click the location where you want to place the text.

5 Click to place the text in the new location.

Note: If is not displayed, click on the Standard toolbar to display all the buttons.

● The text appears in the new location.

● The Paste Options button ( ) may appear. You can click this button to change the format of the text you moved.

CHECK SPELLING

You can find and correct all the spelling errors in your presentation. PowerPoint compares every word in your presentation to words in its dictionary. If a word in your presentation does not exist in the dictionary, the word is considered misspelled. PowerPoint automatically underlines misspelled words in red. The underlines will not appear when you print your presentation or view the slide show.

CHECK SPELLING

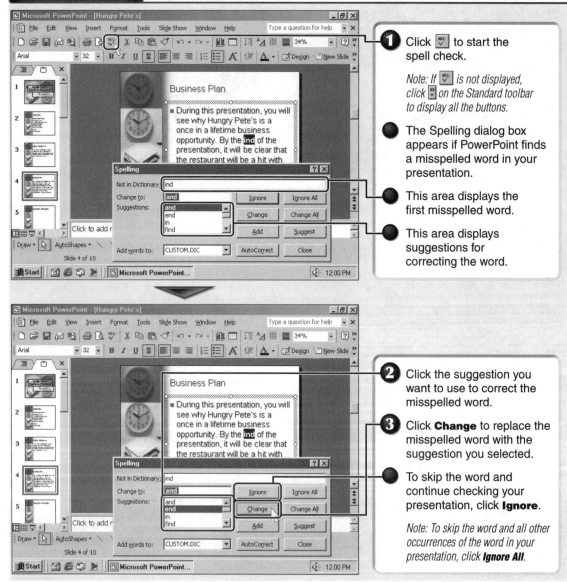

1 Click  to start the spell check.

Note: If  is not displayed, click  on the Standard toolbar to display all the buttons.

● The Spelling dialog box appears if PowerPoint finds a misspelled word in your presentation.

● This area displays the first misspelled word.

● This area displays suggestions for correcting the word.

2 Click the suggestion you want to use to correct the misspelled word.

3 Click **Change** to replace the misspelled word with the suggestion you selected.

● To skip the word and continue checking your presentation, click **Ignore**.

*Note: To skip the word and all other occurrences of the word in your presentation, click **Ignore All**.*

in an *instant*

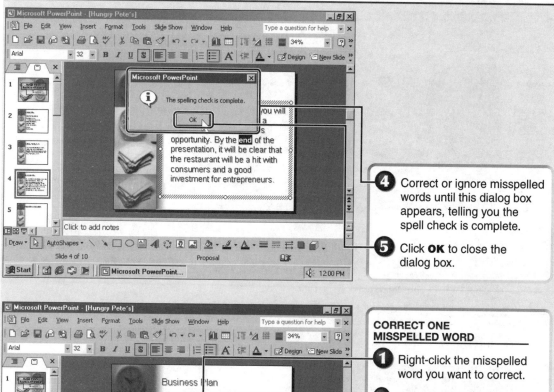

4 Correct or ignore misspelled words until this dialog box appears, telling you the spell check is complete.

5 Click **OK** to close the dialog box.

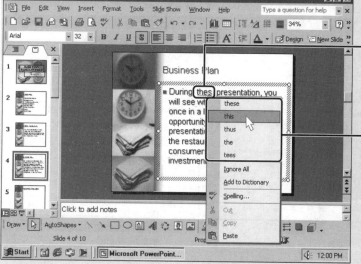

CORRECT ONE MISSPELLED WORD

1 Right-click the misspelled word you want to correct.

● A menu appears with suggestions to correct the word.

2 To replace the misspelled word with one of the suggestions, click the suggestion.

Note: If you do not want to use any of the suggestions to correct the word, click outside the menu to close the menu.

ADD A NEW SLIDE

You can insert a new slide into your presentation to add a new topic you want to discuss. If a slide in your presentation contains too much text, you may also want to add a new slide to accommodate some of the text. A slide containing too much text may be difficult to read and the impact of important ideas may be minimized.

ADD A NEW SLIDE

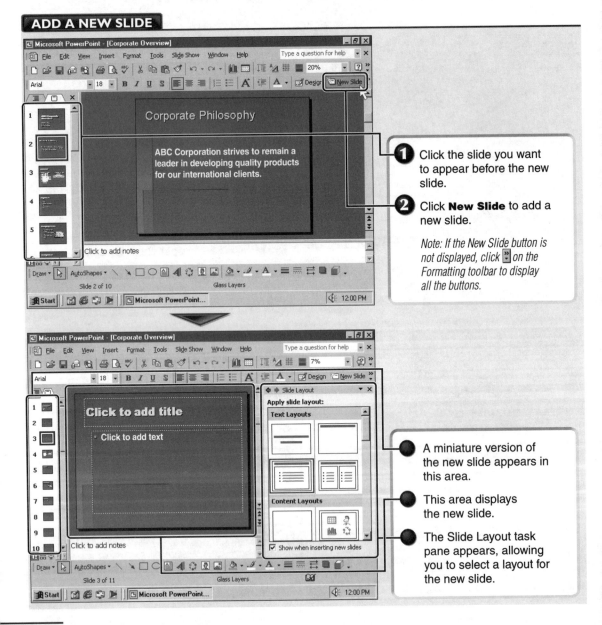

1 Click the slide you want to appear before the new slide.

2 Click **New Slide** to add a new slide.

Note: If the New Slide button is not displayed, click » on the Formatting toolbar to display all the buttons.

■ A miniature version of the new slide appears in this area.

■ This area displays the new slide.

■ The Slide Layout task pane appears, allowing you to select a layout for the new slide.

in an *instant*

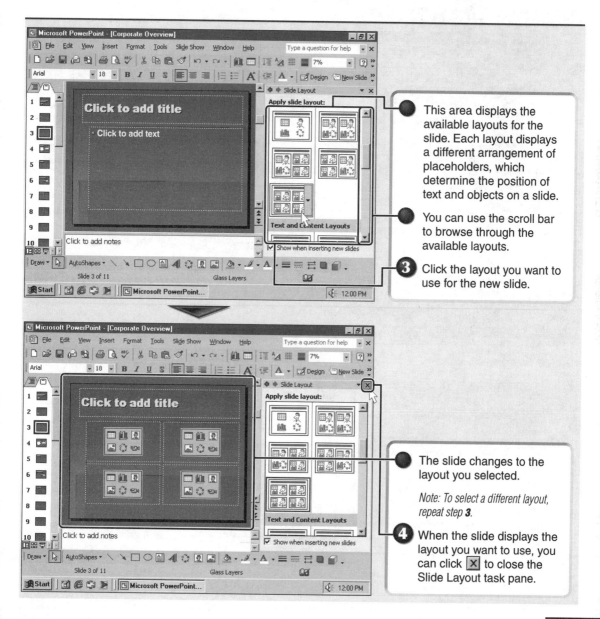

This area displays the available layouts for the slide. Each layout displays a different arrangement of placeholders, which determine the position of text and objects on a slide.

You can use the scroll bar to browse through the available layouts.

3 Click the layout you want to use for the new slide.

The slide changes to the layout you selected.

Note: To select a different layout, repeat step 3.

4 When the slide displays the layout you want to use, you can click ☒ to close the Slide Layout task pane.

CHANGE THE SLIDE LAYOUT

You can change the layout of a slide in your presentation to accommodate text and objects you want to add. Each slide layout displays a different arrangement of placeholders. Placeholders allow you to easily add objects you want to appear on a slide, such as a clip art image or chart.

CHANGE THE SLIDE LAYOUT

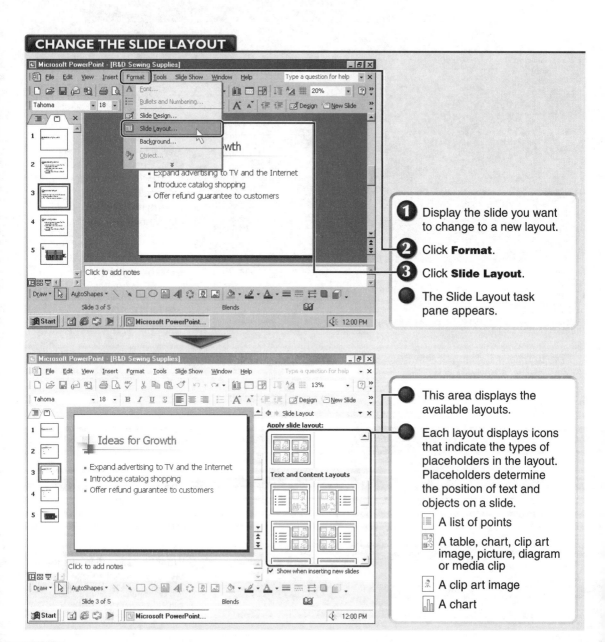

1 Display the slide you want to change to a new layout.

2 Click **Format**.

3 Click **Slide Layout**.

■ The Slide Layout task pane appears.

■ This area displays the available layouts.

■ Each layout displays icons that indicate the types of placeholders in the layout. Placeholders determine the position of text and objects on a slide.

≣ A list of points

▦ A table, chart, clip art image, picture, diagram or media clip

▨ A clip art image

▥ A chart

in an *Instant*

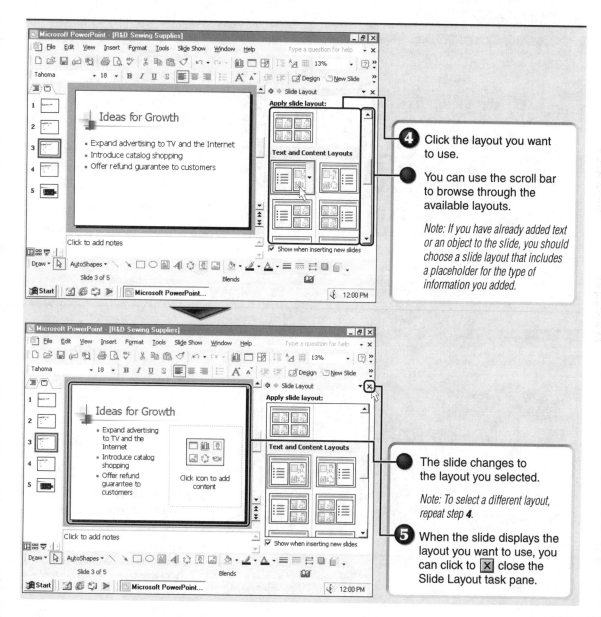

4 Click the layout you want to use.

You can use the scroll bar to browse through the available layouts.

Note: If you have already added text or an object to the slide, you should choose a slide layout that includes a placeholder for the type of information you added.

The slide changes to the layout you selected.

Note: To select a different layout, repeat step 4.

5 When the slide displays the layout you want to use, you can click to ☒ close the Slide Layout task pane.

ADD AN AUTOSHAPE

PowerPoint provides many ready-made shapes, called AutoShapes, that you can add to your slides. PowerPoint offers several types of AutoShapes, including lines, arrows and stars. You can add text to AutoShapes such as banners and callouts. AutoShapes containing text are ideal for adding interest and information to your slides.

ADD AN AUTOSHAPE

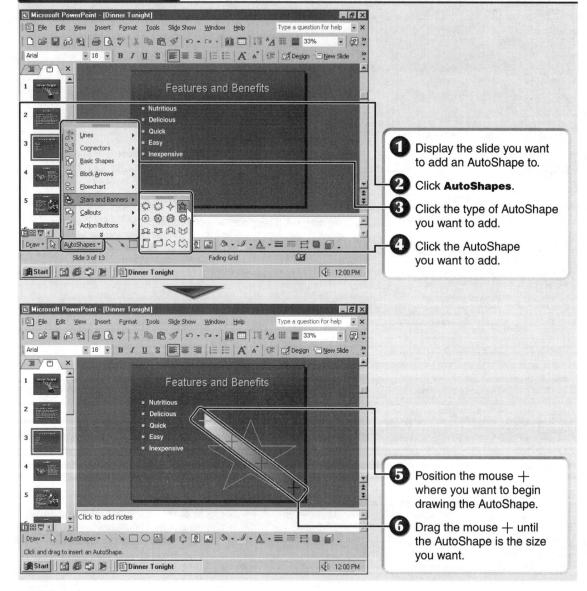

1 Display the slide you want to add an AutoShape to.

2 Click **AutoShapes**.

3 Click the type of AutoShape you want to add.

4 Click the AutoShape you want to add.

5 Position the mouse + where you want to begin drawing the AutoShape.

6 Drag the mouse + until the AutoShape is the size you want.

in an *instant*

● The AutoShape appears on the slide.

● To deselect an AutoShape, click outside the AutoShape.

● You can add text to most AutoShapes. To add text to an AutoShape, click the AutoShape and then type the text you want the AutoShape to display. To change the size of the text, see page 209.

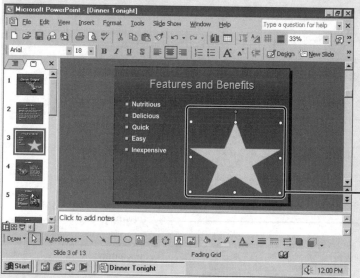

DELETE AN AUTOSHAPE

1 Click the AutoShape you want to delete.

2 Press the Delete key to remove the AutoShape from the slide.

ADD WORDART

You can add WordArt to a slide in your presentation to enhance the appearance of a title or draw attention to an important point. WordArt allows you to add eye-catching text effects to your slides quickly and easily.

ADD WORDART

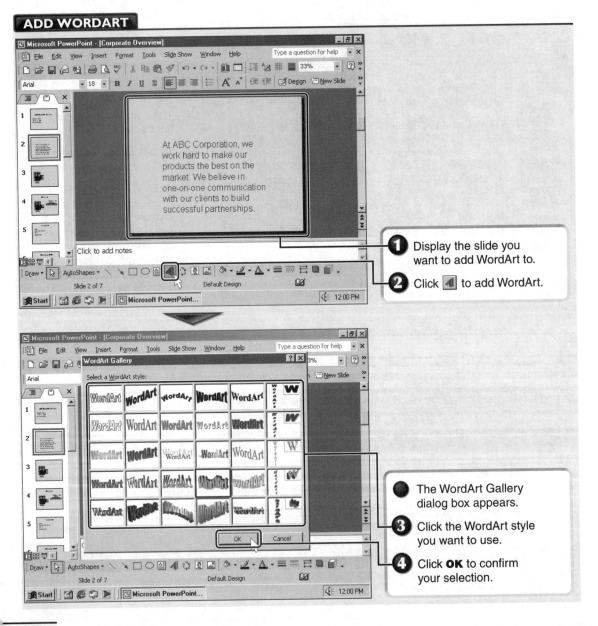

1 Display the slide you want to add WordArt to.

2 Click ▲ to add WordArt.

■ The WordArt Gallery dialog box appears.

3 Click the WordArt style you want to use.

4 Click **OK** to confirm your selection.

in an *instant*

The Edit WordArt Text dialog box appears.

5 Type the text you want the WordArt to display.

6 Click **OK** to add the WordArt to the slide.

The WordArt appears on the slide.

To deselect WordArt, click outside the WordArt.

To edit WordArt text, double-click the WordArt to display the Edit WordArt Text dialog box. Then perform steps **5** and **6**.

DELETE WORDART

1 Click the WordArt you want to delete and then press the Delete key.

ADD A PICTURE

You can add a picture stored on your computer to a slide in your presentation. Adding a picture is useful when you want to display your company logo or a picture of your products on a slide.

ADD A PICTURE

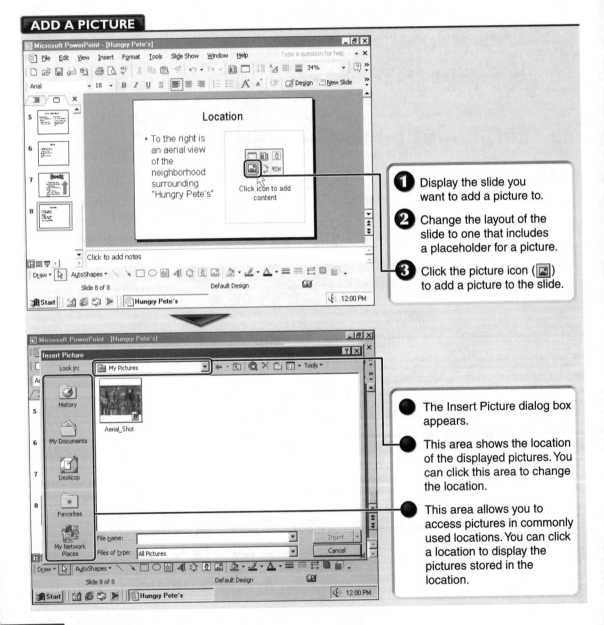

1 Display the slide you want to add a picture to.

2 Change the layout of the slide to one that includes a placeholder for a picture.

3 Click the picture icon (🖾) to add a picture to the slide.

● The Insert Picture dialog box appears.

● This area shows the location of the displayed pictures. You can click this area to change the location.

● This area allows you to access pictures in commonly used locations. You can click a location to display the pictures stored in the location.

in an *Instant*

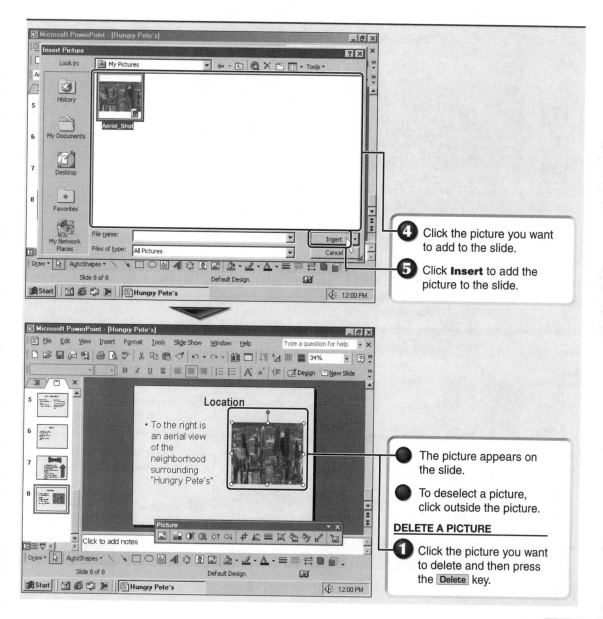

4 Click the picture you want to add to the slide.

5 Click **Insert** to add the picture to the slide.

■ The picture appears on the slide.

■ To deselect a picture, click outside the picture.

DELETE A PICTURE

1 Click the picture you want to delete and then press the Delete key.

ADD A CLIP ART IMAGE

You can add a clip art image to a slide to make your presentation more interesting and entertaining. You can browse through all the available clip art images to find the clip art image you want to add. You can also search for clip art images by specifying a word of interest.

ADD A CLIP ART IMAGE

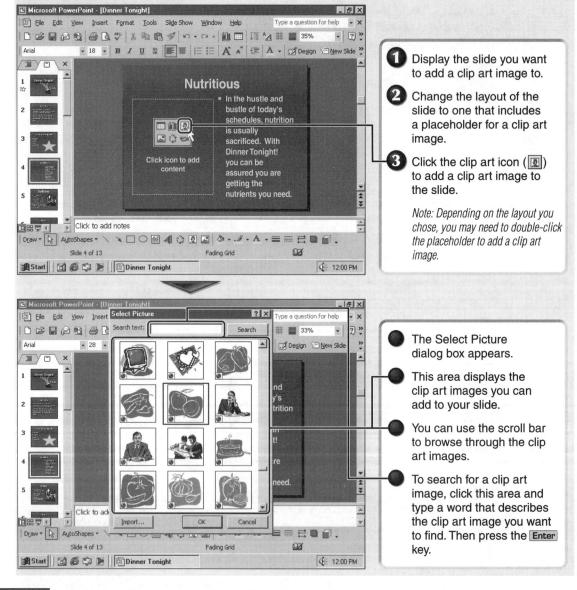

1 Display the slide you want to add a clip art image to.

2 Change the layout of the slide to one that includes a placeholder for a clip art image.

3 Click the clip art icon (📷) to add a clip art image to the slide.

Note: Depending on the layout you chose, you may need to double-click the placeholder to add a clip art image.

● The Select Picture dialog box appears.

● This area displays the clip art images you can add to your slide.

● You can use the scroll bar to browse through the clip art images.

● To search for a clip art image, click this area and type a word that describes the clip art image you want to find. Then press the `Enter` key.

in an *instant*

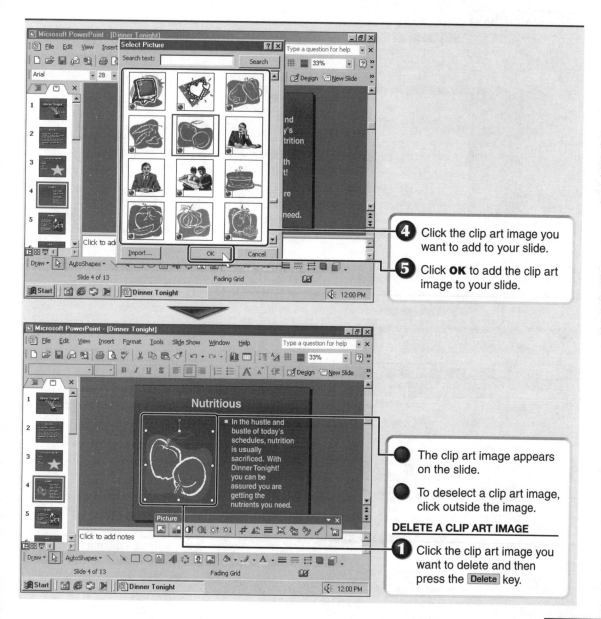

4 Click the clip art image you want to add to your slide.

5 Click **OK** to add the clip art image to your slide.

● The clip art image appears on the slide.

● To deselect a clip art image, click outside the image.

DELETE A CLIP ART IMAGE

1 Click the clip art image you want to delete and then press the Delete key.

ADD A CHART

You can add a chart to a slide to show trends and compare data. Adding a chart is useful when a slide in your presentation contains numerical data. A chart is more appealing and often easier to understand than a list of numbers.

ADD A CHART

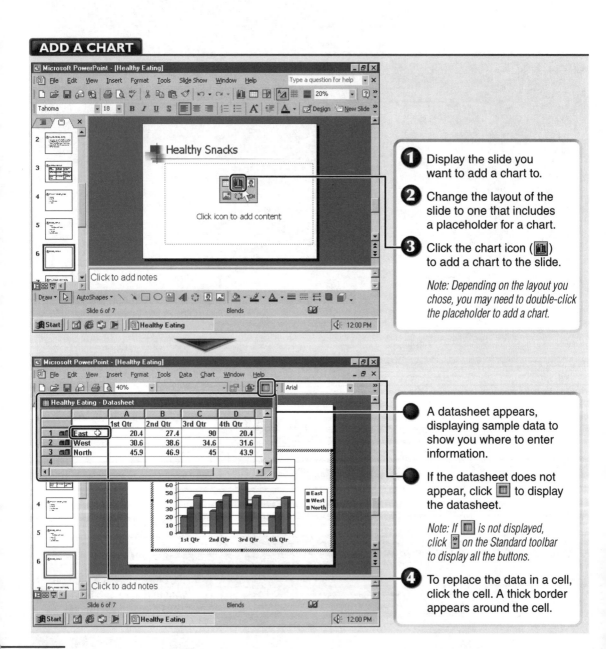

1 Display the slide you want to add a chart to.

2 Change the layout of the slide to one that includes a placeholder for a chart.

3 Click the chart icon ([icon]) to add a chart to the slide.

Note: Depending on the layout you chose, you may need to double-click the placeholder to add a chart.

■ A datasheet appears, displaying sample data to show you where to enter information.

■ If the datasheet does not appear, click [icon] to display the datasheet.

Note: If [icon] is not displayed, click [icon] on the Standard toolbar to display all the buttons.

4 To replace the data in a cell, click the cell. A thick border appears around the cell.

in an instant

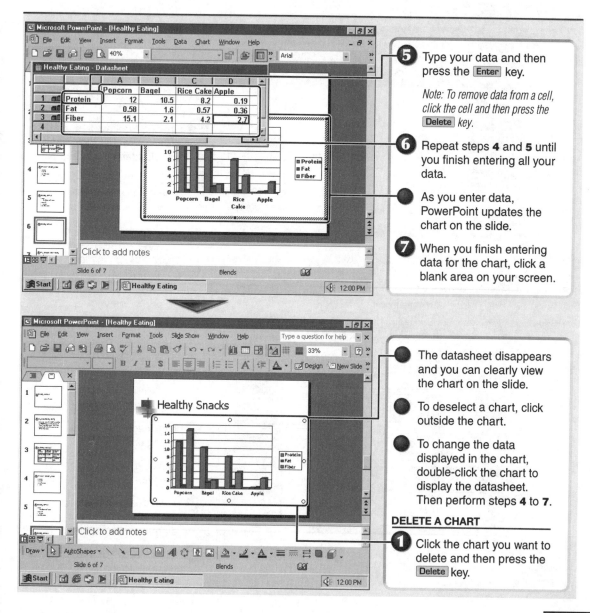

5 Type your data and then press the [Enter] key.

Note: To remove data from a cell, click the cell and then press the [Delete] key.

6 Repeat steps **4** and **5** until you finish entering all your data.

● As you enter data, PowerPoint updates the chart on the slide.

7 When you finish entering data for the chart, click a blank area on your screen.

● The datasheet disappears and you can clearly view the chart on the slide.

● To deselect a chart, click outside the chart.

● To change the data displayed in the chart, double-click the chart to display the datasheet. Then perform steps **4** to **7**.

DELETE A CHART

1 Click the chart you want to delete and then press the [Delete] key.

ADD A DIAGRAM

You can add a diagram to a slide to illustrate a concept or idea. PowerPoint offers several types of diagrams for you to choose from, including Cycle, Radial, Pyramid, Venn and Target. You can also add an organization chart to a slide. Organization charts are useful for showing how a group of people or things are related.

ADD A DIAGRAM

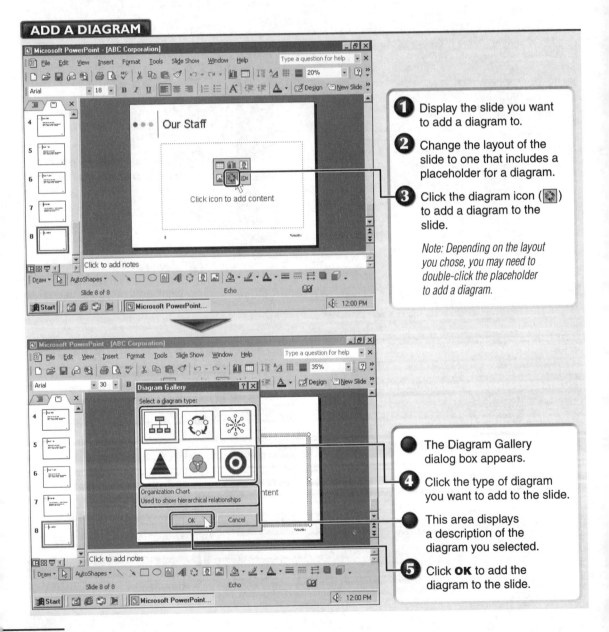

1 Display the slide you want to add a diagram to.

2 Change the layout of the slide to one that includes a placeholder for a diagram.

3 Click the diagram icon (⊞) to add a diagram to the slide.

Note: Depending on the layout you chose, you may need to double-click the placeholder to add a diagram.

■ The Diagram Gallery dialog box appears.

4 Click the type of diagram you want to add to the slide.

■ This area displays a description of the diagram you selected.

5 Click **OK** to add the diagram to the slide.

in an *Instant*

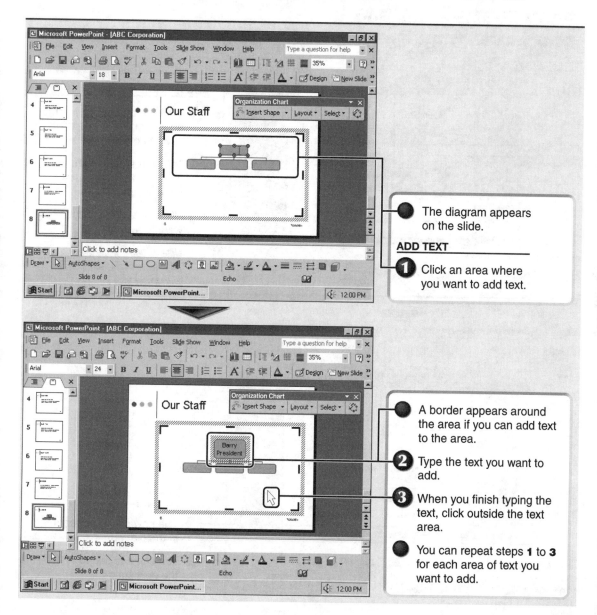

The diagram appears
on the slide.

ADD TEXT

1 Click an area where
you want to add text.

A border appears around
the area if you can add text
to the area.

2 Type the text you want to
add.

3 When you finish typing the
text, click outside the text
area.

You can repeat steps **1** to **3**
for each area of text you
want to add.

ADD A DIAGRAM

You can add a new shape to a diagram to include additional information in the diagram. When adding a new shape to an organization chart, you can choose the type of shape you want to add. You can also delete a shape or a diagram you no longer need.

ADD A DIAGRAM (CONTINUED)

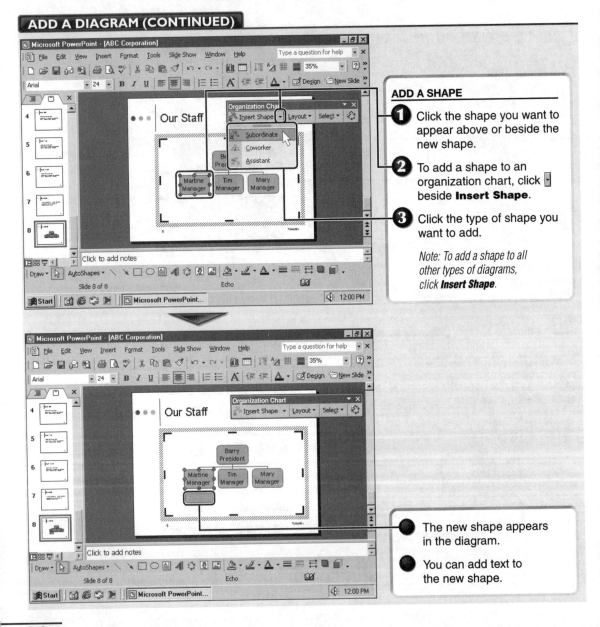

ADD A SHAPE

1. Click the shape you want to appear above or beside the new shape.

2. To add a shape to an organization chart, click ⬗ beside **Insert Shape**.

3. Click the type of shape you want to add.

   Note: To add a shape to all other types of diagrams, click **Insert Shape**.

● The new shape appears in the diagram.

● You can add text to the new shape.

204

in an *instant*

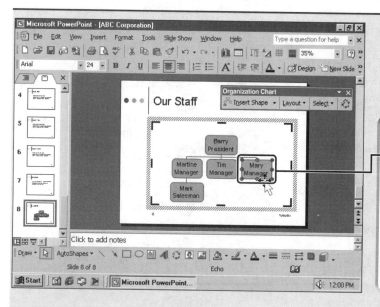

DELETE A SHAPE

1 Click a border of the shape you want to delete. Handles (⊗) appear around the shape.

2 Press the Delete key to delete the shape.

● The shape disappears from the diagram.

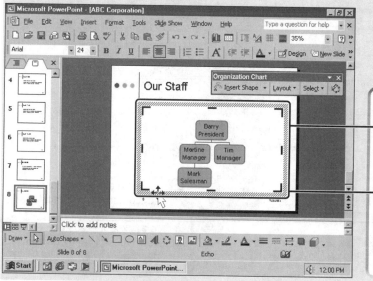

DELETE A DIAGRAM

1 Click in the diagram you want to delete. A border appears around the diagram.

2 Click the border and then press the Delete key to delete the diagram.

● The diagram disappears from the slide.

MOVE OR RESIZE AN OBJECT

You can change the location and size of an object on a slide in your presentation. PowerPoint allows you to move and resize objects such as AutoShapes, WordArt, pictures, clip art images and charts.

MOVE AN OBJECT

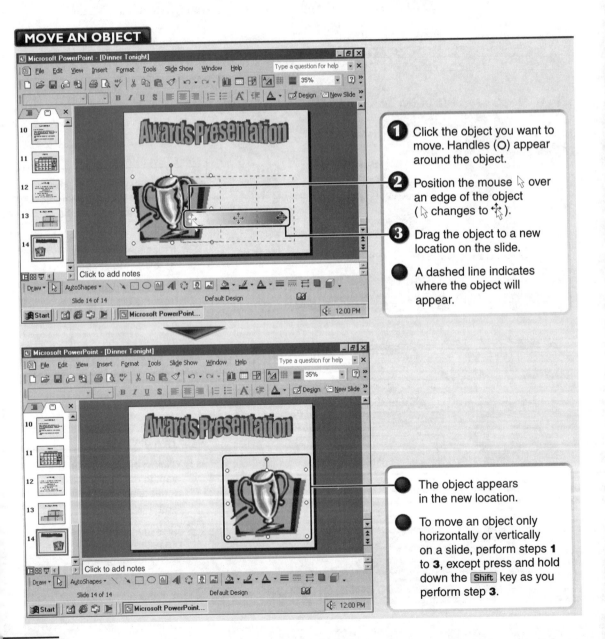

1 Click the object you want to move. Handles (O) appear around the object.

2 Position the mouse ⮂ over an edge of the object (⮂ changes to ✛).

3 Drag the object to a new location on the slide.

● A dashed line indicates where the object will appear.

● The object appears in the new location.

● To move an object only horizontally or vertically on a slide, perform steps **1** to **3**, except press and hold down the Shift key as you perform step **3**.

in an *instant*

RESIZE AN OBJECT

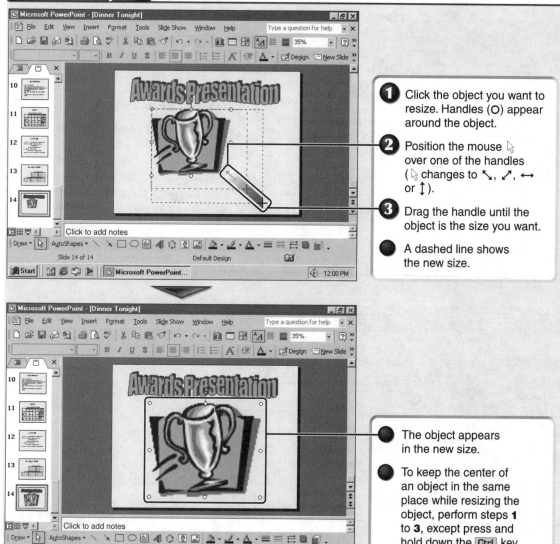

1. Click the object you want to resize. Handles (O) appear around the object.

2. Position the mouse over one of the handles (changes to ↘, ↗, ↔ or ↕).

3. Drag the handle until the object is the size you want.

● A dashed line shows the new size.

● The object appears in the new size.

● To keep the center of an object in the same place while resizing the object, perform steps **1** to **3**, except press and hold down the **Ctrl** key as you perform step **3**.

CHANGE FONT OF TEXT

You can change the font of text to enhance the appearance of a slide. When choosing a font, you should consider your audience. For example, choose an informal font, such as Comic Sans MS, for a presentation to your co-workers and a conservative font, such as Times New Roman, for a presentation to your clients.

CHANGE FONT OF TEXT

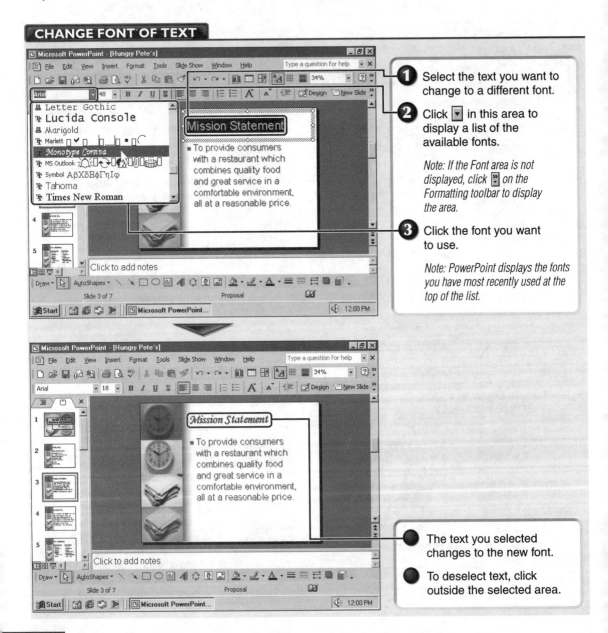

1 Select the text you want to change to a different font.

2 Click ▼ in this area to display a list of the available fonts.

Note: If the Font area is not displayed, click » on the Formatting toolbar to display the area.

3 Click the font you want to use.

Note: PowerPoint displays the fonts you have most recently used at the top of the list.

● The text you selected changes to the new font.

● To deselect text, click outside the selected area.

You can increase or decrease the size of text on a slide. Larger text is easier to read, but smaller text allows you to fit more information on a slide. PowerPoint measures the size of text in points. There are approximately 72 points in an inch.

CHANGE SIZE OF TEXT

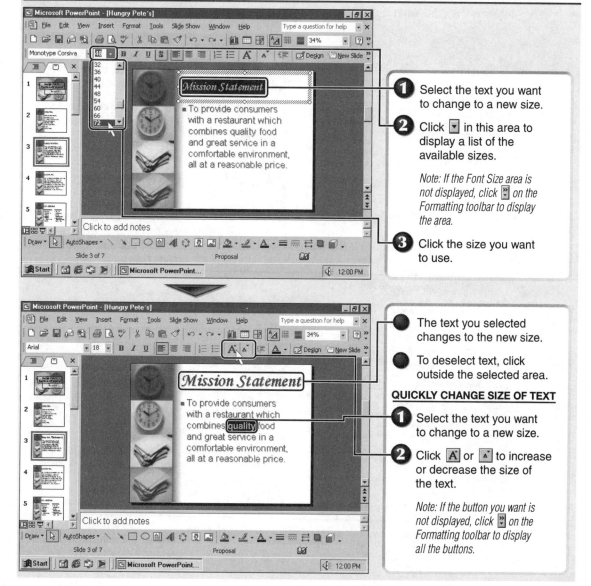

1 Select the text you want to change to a new size.

2 Click ☑ in this area to display a list of the available sizes.

Note: If the Font Size area is not displayed, click ☒ on the Formatting toolbar to display the area.

3 Click the size you want to use.

● The text you selected changes to the new size.

● To deselect text, click outside the selected area.

QUICKLY CHANGE SIZE OF TEXT

1 Select the text you want to change to a new size.

2 Click A or A to increase or decrease the size of the text.

Note: If the button you want is not displayed, click ☒ on the Formatting toolbar to display all the buttons.

CHANGE STYLE OF TEXT

You can bold, italicize, underline or add a shadow to text to emphasize information on a slide. For example, you can underline important words or phrases to make them stand out from the rest of the text on a slide.

CHANGE STYLE OF TEXT

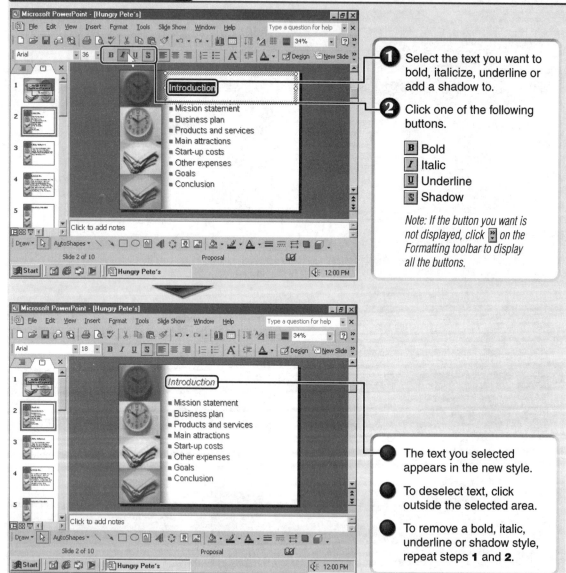

1 Select the text you want to bold, italicize, underline or add a shadow to.

2 Click one of the following buttons.

B Bold
I Italic
U Underline
S Shadow

Note: If the button you want is not displayed, click ⤼ on the Formatting toolbar to display all the buttons.

● The text you selected appears in the new style.

● To deselect text, click outside the selected area.

● To remove a bold, italic, underline or shadow style, repeat steps **1** and **2**.

CHANGE ALIGNMENT OF TEXT

You can change the alignment of text on a slide. Changing the alignment of text can help your audience distinguish between different types of information. For example, you may want to left align the main points on a slide and center the heading.

CHANGE ALIGNMENT OF TEXT

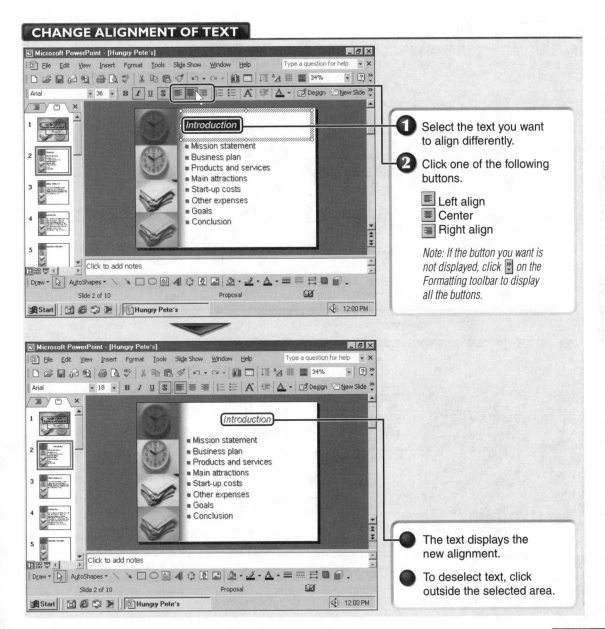

1 Select the text you want to align differently.

2 Click one of the following buttons.

▤ Left align
▤ Center
▤ Right align

Note: If the button you want is not displayed, click ≫ on the Formatting toolbar to display all the buttons.

● The text displays the new alignment.

● To deselect text, click outside the selected area.

211

CHANGE TEXT COLOR

You can change the color of text on a slide to enhance the appearance of the slide and draw attention to important information. The available colors for a slide depend on the color scheme of the slide.

CHANGE TEXT COLOR

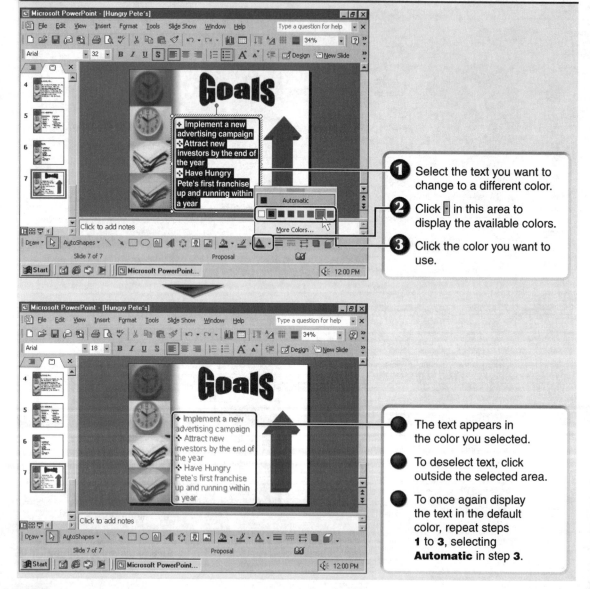

1 Select the text you want to change to a different color.

2 Click ⏷ in this area to display the available colors.

3 Click the color you want to use.

● The text appears in the color you selected.

● To deselect text, click outside the selected area.

● To once again display the text in the default color, repeat steps **1** to **3**, selecting **Automatic** in step **3**.

CHANGE OBJECT COLOR

You can change the color of an object on a slide to better suit the design of the slide. PowerPoint allows you to change the color of objects such as AutoShapes, WordArt, clip art images and charts. The available colors for a slide depend on the color scheme of the slide.

CHANGE OBJECT COLOR

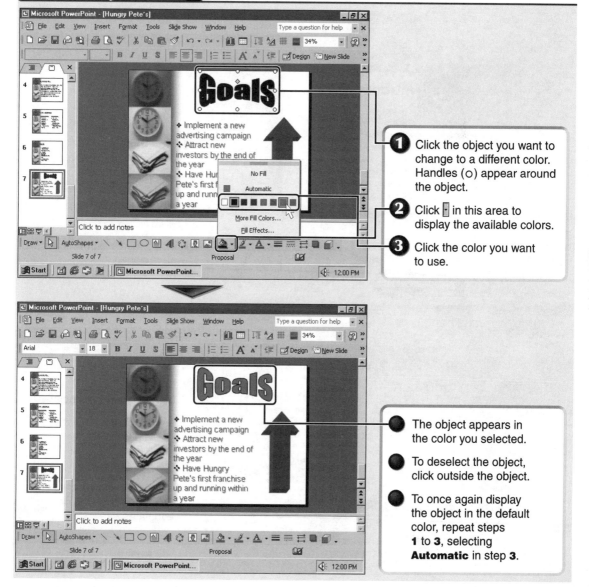

1 Click the object you want to change to a different color. Handles (o) appear around the object.

2 Click ▪ in this area to display the available colors.

3 Click the color you want to use.

● The object appears in the color you selected.

● To deselect the object, click outside the object.

● To once again display the object in the default color, repeat steps **1** to **3**, selecting **Automatic** in step **3**.

CHANGE THE DESIGN TEMPLATE

PowerPoint offers many design templates that you can choose from to give the slides in your presentation a professional look. You can change the design template for your entire presentation or for a single slide. Changing the design template for a single slide can make the slide stand out from the rest of your presentation.

CHANGE THE DESIGN TEMPLATE

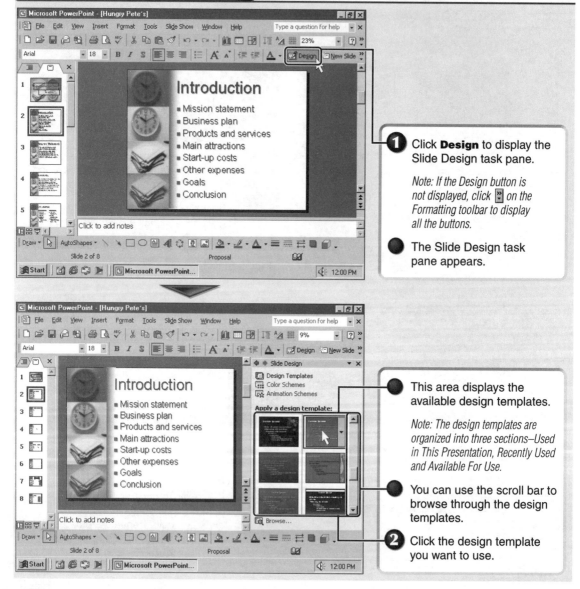

1 Click **Design** to display the Slide Design task pane.

Note: If the Design button is not displayed, click 》 on the Formatting toolbar to display all the buttons.

The Slide Design task pane appears.

This area displays the available design templates.

Note: The design templates are organized into three sections—Used in This Presentation, Recently Used and Available For Use.

You can use the scroll bar to browse through the design templates.

2 Click the design template you want to use.

in an instant

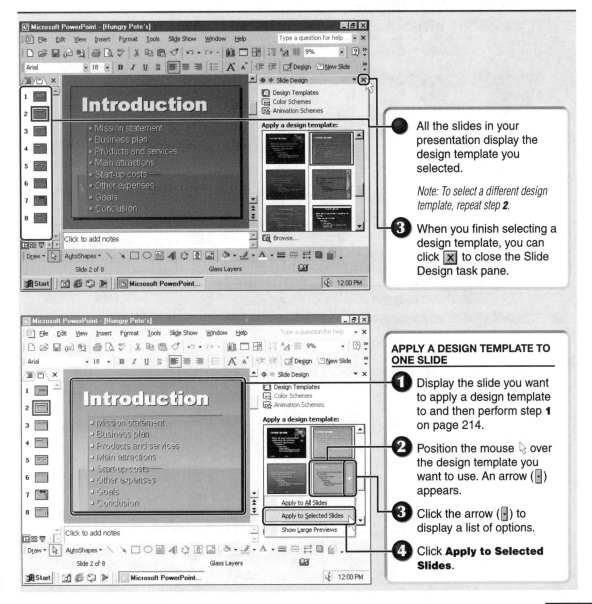

All the slides in your presentation display the design template you selected.

Note: To select a different design template, repeat step 2.

3 When you finish selecting a design template, you can click ⊠ to close the Slide Design task pane.

APPLY A DESIGN TEMPLATE TO ONE SLIDE

1 Display the slide you want to apply a design template to and then perform step 1 on page 214.

2 Position the mouse ⤺ over the design template you want to use. An arrow (▾) appears.

3 Click the arrow (▾) to display a list of options.

4 Click **Apply to Selected Slides**.

CHANGE THE COLOR SCHEME

You can change the color scheme of all the slides in your presentation. You can also change the color scheme of a single slide to make the slide stand out from the rest of your presentation. Each color scheme contains a set of eight coordinated colors, including colors for the background, text, lines, shadows, titles and accents.

CHANGE THE COLOR SCHEME

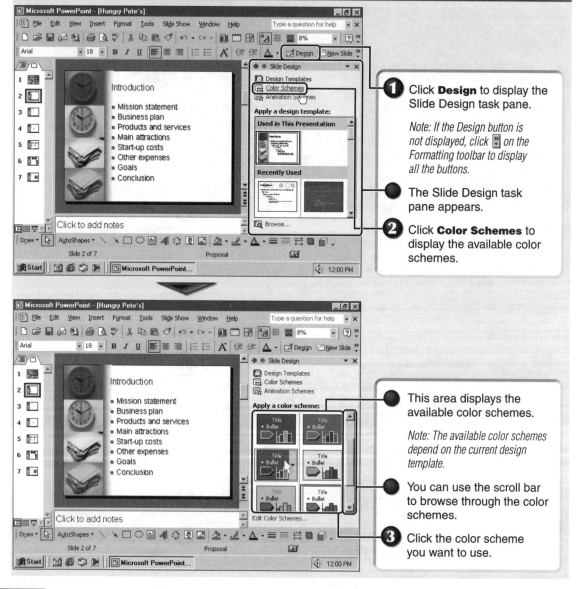

1 Click **Design** to display the Slide Design task pane.

Note: If the Design button is not displayed, click ⟨⟩ on the Formatting toolbar to display all the buttons.

● The Slide Design task pane appears.

2 Click **Color Schemes** to display the available color schemes.

● This area displays the available color schemes.

Note: The available color schemes depend on the current design template.

● You can use the scroll bar to browse through the color schemes.

3 Click the color scheme you want to use.

in an instant

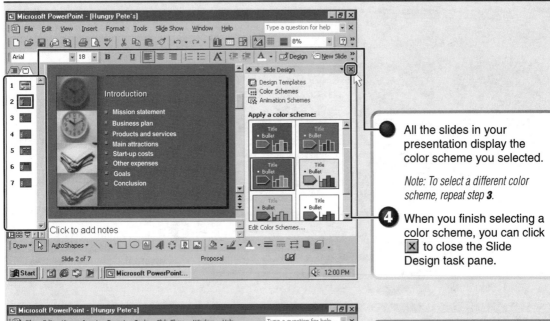

All the slides in your presentation display the color scheme you selected.

Note: To select a different color scheme, repeat step 3.

4 When you finish selecting a color scheme, you can click ☒ to close the Slide Design task pane.

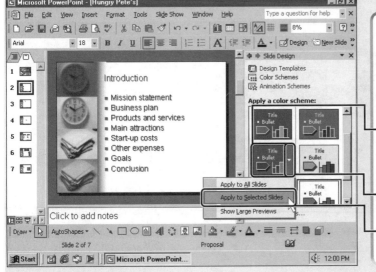

CHANGE THE COLOR SCHEME OF ONE SLIDE

1 Display the slide you want to use a different color scheme and then perform steps **1** and **2** on page 216.

2 Position the mouse ⬚ over the color scheme you want to use. An arrow (⬚) appears.

3 Click the arrow (⬚) to display a list of options.

4 Click **Apply to Selected Slides**.

REORDER SLIDES

You can change the order of the slides in your presentation to reorganize your ideas. The Slide Sorter view displays miniature versions of all your slides so you can see the overall organization of your presentation. This view allows you to easily reorder the slides in your presentation.

REORDER SLIDES

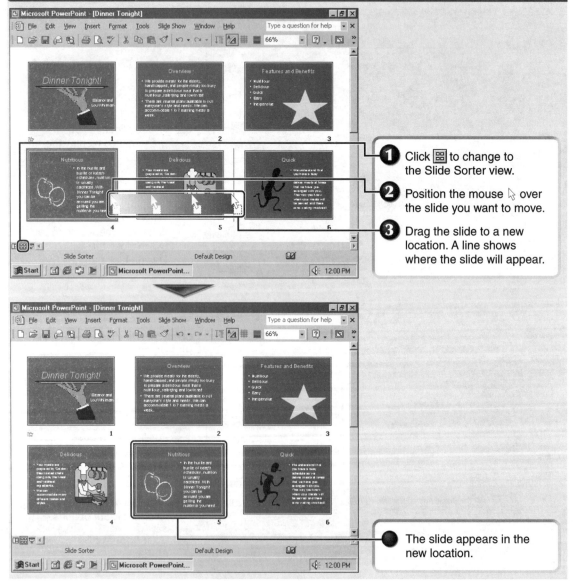

1. Click 🔠 to change to the Slide Sorter view.

2. Position the mouse ⇱ over the slide you want to move.

3. Drag the slide to a new location. A line shows where the slide will appear.

■ The slide appears in the new location.

You can remove a slide you no longer need from your presentation. This is useful if a slide contains incorrect or outdated information. The Slide Sorter view displays miniature versions of all your slides so you can see the overall organization of your presentation. This view allows you to remove a slide quickly and easily.

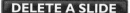

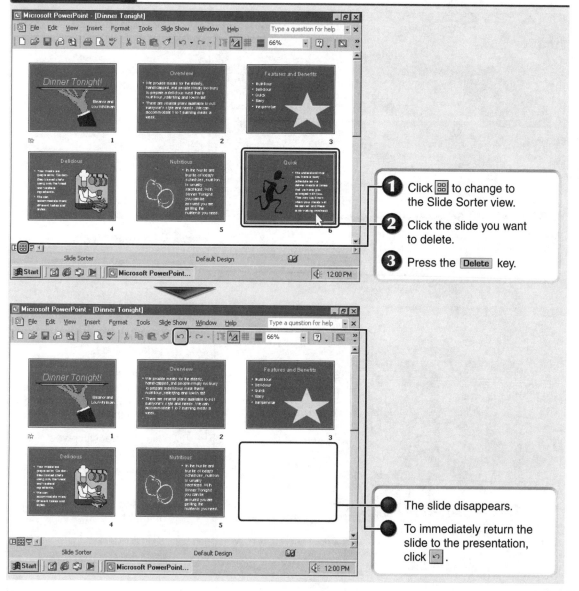

1 Click 🔲 to change to the Slide Sorter view.

2 Click the slide you want to delete.

3 Press the Delete key.

● The slide disappears.

● To immediately return the slide to the presentation, click ↺.

ADD SLIDE TRANSITIONS

You can add transitions to slides in your presentation. A transition is a visual effect that appears when you move from one slide to the next. Using transitions can help you introduce each slide during a slide show and signal your audience that new information is appearing.

ADD SLIDE TRANSITIONS

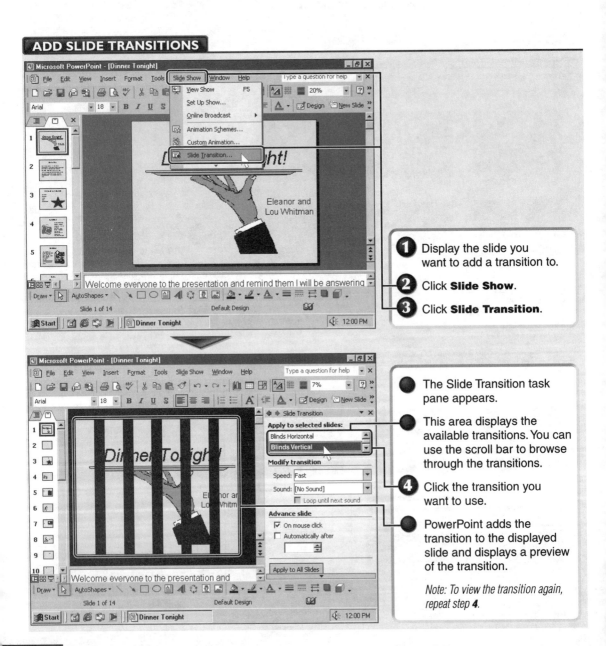

1 Display the slide you want to add a transition to.

2 Click **Slide Show**.

3 Click **Slide Transition**.

● The Slide Transition task pane appears.

● This area displays the available transitions. You can use the scroll bar to browse through the transitions.

4 Click the transition you want to use.

● PowerPoint adds the transition to the displayed slide and displays a preview of the transition.

Note: To view the transition again, repeat step 4.

in an *instant*

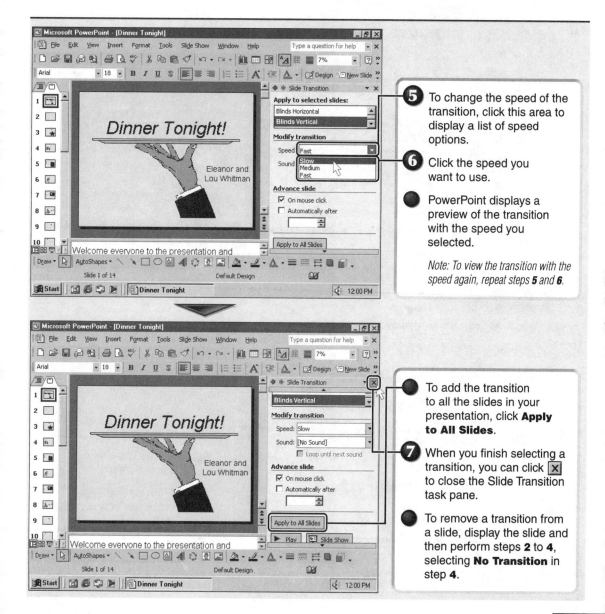

5 To change the speed of the transition, click this area to display a list of speed options.

6 Click the speed you want to use.

● PowerPoint displays a preview of the transition with the speed you selected.

Note: To view the transition with the speed again, repeat steps 5 and 6.

● To add the transition to all the slides in your presentation, click **Apply to All Slides**.

7 When you finish selecting a transition, you can click ☒ to close the Slide Transition task pane.

● To remove a transition from a slide, display the slide and then perform steps **2** to **4**, selecting **No Transition** in step **4**.

VIEW A SLIDE SHOW

You can view a slide show of your presentation on a computer screen. A slide show displays one slide at a time using the entire screen. Before presenting a slide show to an audience, you can view the slide show to rehearse your presentation.

VIEW A SLIDE SHOW

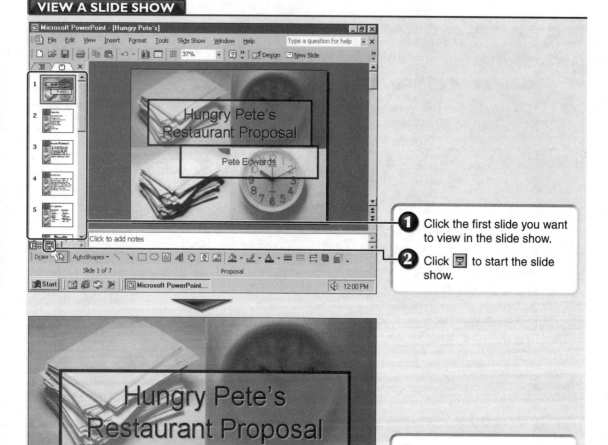

① Click the first slide you want to view in the slide show.

② Click 🖵 to start the slide show.

● The slide you selected fills your screen.

Note: You can press the Esc *key to end the slide show at any time.*

③ To display the next slide, click anywhere on the current slide or press the **Spacebar**.

in an *instant*

Introduction

- Mission statement
- Business plan
- Products and services
- Main attractions
- Start-up costs
- Other expenses
- Goals
- Conclusion

● The next slide appears.

● To return to the previous slide, press the Backspace key.

● To display any slide, type the number of the slide and then press the Enter key.

End of slide show, click to exit.

4 Repeat step **3** until this screen appears, indicating you have reached the end of the slide show.

5 Click the screen to exit the slide show.

CREATE NOTES

You can create notes that contain the ideas you want to discuss for each slide in your presentation. You can use these notes as a guide when delivering your presentation. Notes can include statistics and information that you may need to answer questions from the audience.

CREATE NOTES

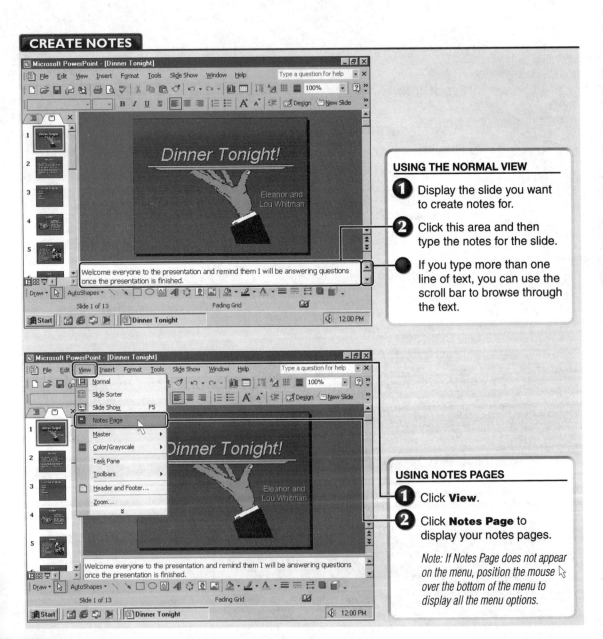

USING THE NORMAL VIEW

1 Display the slide you want to create notes for.

2 Click this area and then type the notes for the slide.

● If you type more than one line of text, you can use the scroll bar to browse through the text.

USING NOTES PAGES

1 Click **View**.

2 Click **Notes Page** to display your notes pages.

Note: If Notes Page does not appear on the menu, position the mouse ⌖ over the bottom of the menu to display all the menu options.

in an *instant*

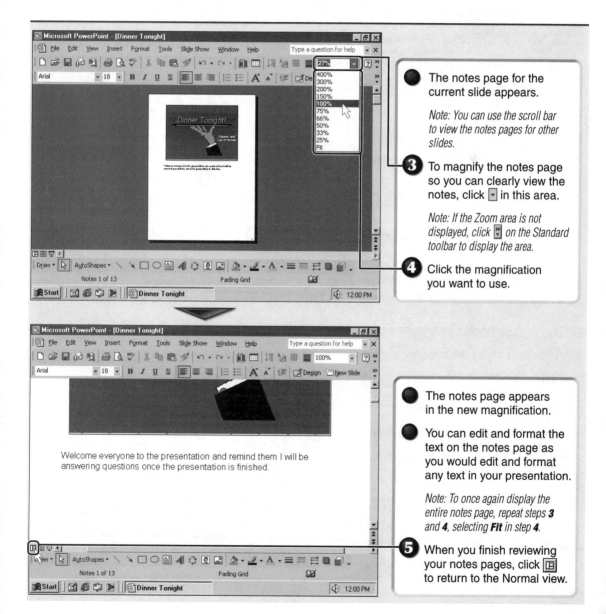

The notes page for the current slide appears.

Note: You can use the scroll bar to view the notes pages for other slides.

3 To magnify the notes page so you can clearly view the notes, click ⊡ in this area.

Note: If the Zoom area is not displayed, click » on the Standard toolbar to display the area.

4 Click the magnification you want to use.

The notes page appears in the new magnification.

You can edit and format the text on the notes page as you would edit and format any text in your presentation.

*Note: To once again display the entire notes page, repeat steps 3 and 4, selecting **Fit** in step 4.*

5 When you finish reviewing your notes pages, click 🔳 to return to the Normal view.

PREVIEW A PRESENTATION

You can use the Print Preview feature to see how your presentation will look when printed. This allows you to confirm that the presentation will print the way you want. You can preview the slides, handouts or notes pages in your presentation. You can also preview an outline of your presentation.

PREVIEW A PRESENTATION

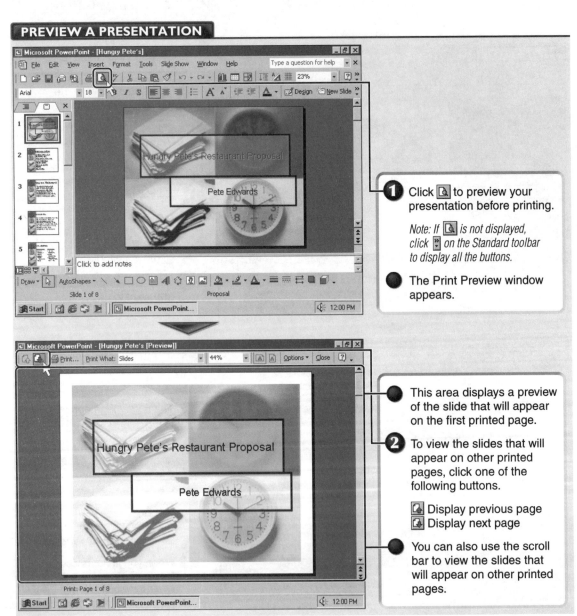

1 Click 🔍 to preview your presentation before printing.

Note: If 🔍 is not displayed, click » on the Standard toolbar to display all the buttons.

● The Print Preview window appears.

● This area displays a preview of the slide that will appear on the first printed page.

2 To view the slides that will appear on other printed pages, click one of the following buttons.

🔍 Display previous page
🔍 Display next page

● You can also use the scroll bar to view the slides that will appear on other printed pages.

in an *instant*

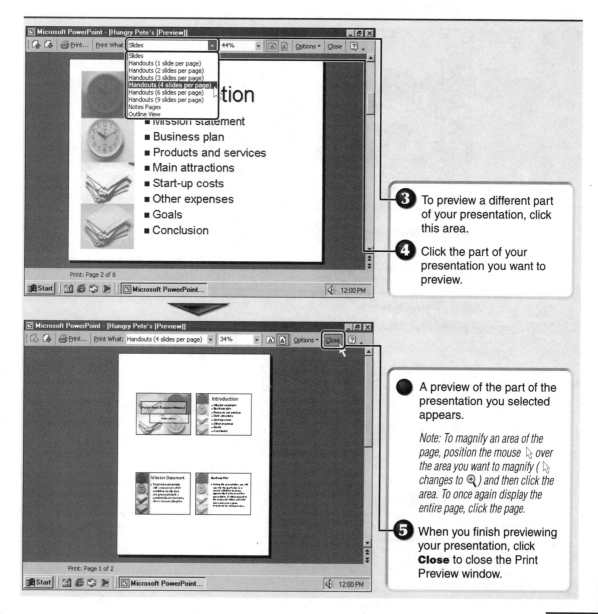

3 To preview a different part of your presentation, click this area.

4 Click the part of your presentation you want to preview.

● A preview of the part of the presentation you selected appears.

Note: To magnify an area of the page, position the mouse ⬉ over the area you want to magnify (⬉ changes to ⊕) and then click the area. To once again display the entire page, click the page.

5 When you finish previewing your presentation, click **Close** to close the Print Preview window.

PRINT A PRESENTATION

You can produce a paper copy of a presentation for your own use or to hand out to your audience. PowerPoint allows you to specify the part of your presentation you want to print. You can print the slides, handouts or notes pages in your presentation. You can also print an outline of your presentation.

PRINT A PRESENTATION

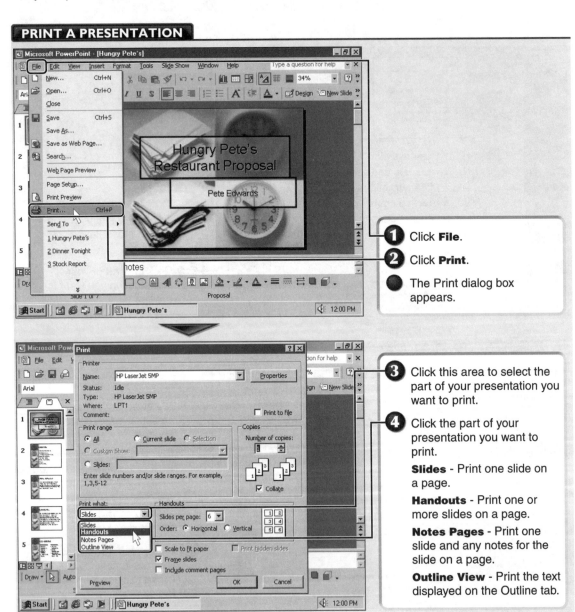

1 Click **File**.

2 Click **Print**.

● The Print dialog box appears.

3 Click this area to select the part of your presentation you want to print.

4 Click the part of your presentation you want to print.

Slides - Print one slide on a page.

Handouts - Print one or more slides on a page.

Notes Pages - Print one slide and any notes for the slide on a page.

Outline View - Print the text displayed on the Outline tab.

in an *instant*

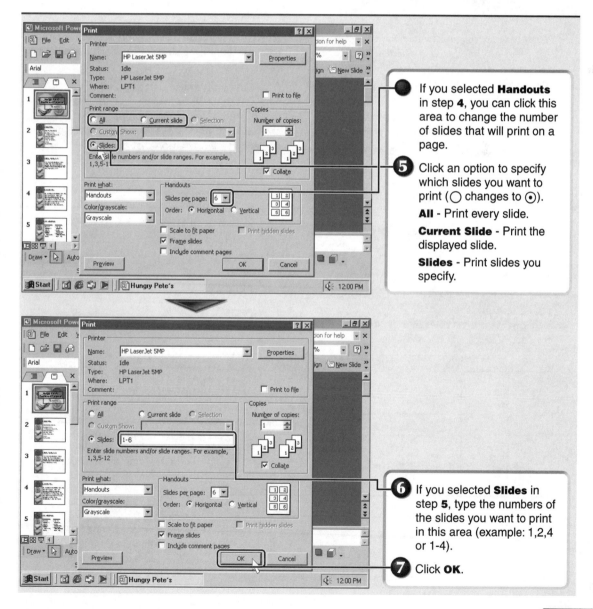

● If you selected **Handouts** in step **4**, you can click this area to change the number of slides that will print on a page.

❺ Click an option to specify which slides you want to print (◯ changes to ◉).

All - Print every slide.

Current Slide - Print the displayed slide.

Slides - Print slides you specify.

❻ If you selected **Slides** in step **5**, type the numbers of the slides you want to print in this area (example: 1,2,4 or 1-4).

❼ Click **OK**.

INTRODUCTION TO ACCESS

Access is a database program that allows you to store and manage large collections of information. Access provides you with all the tools you need to create an efficient and effective database.

DATABASE USES

A database stores and manages a collection of information related to a particular subject or purpose. Access allows you to efficiently add, edit, view and organize the information stored in a database.

Many people use databases to store personal information, such as addresses, recipes, music collections and wine lists. Using a database to store and organize information is much more efficient than using sheets of paper or index cards.

Companies often use databases to store information such as mailing lists, inventory, payroll and expense information. A database can help a company effectively review, update and analyze information that constantly changes.

PARTS OF A DATABASE

A database consists of objects such as tables, forms, queries and reports.

TABLES

A table stores a collection of information about a specific topic, such as a mailing list. You can have one or more tables in a database. A table consists of fields and records.

Address ID	First Name	Last Name	Address	City	State/Province	Postal Code
1	Jim	Schmith	258 Linton Ave.	New York	NY	10010
2	Brenda	Petterson	50 Tree Lane	Boston	MA	02117
3	Todd	Talbot	68 Cracker Ave.	San Francisco	CA	94110
4	Chuck	Dean	47 Crosby Ave.	Las Vegas	NV	89116
5	Melanie	Robinson	26 Arnold Cres.	Jacksonville	FL	32256
6	Susan	Hughes	401 Idon Dr.	Nashville	TN	37243
7	Allen	Toppins	10 Heldon St.	Atlanta	GA	30375
8	Greg	Kilkenny	36 Buzzard St.	Boston	MA	02118
9	Jason	Marcuson	15 Bizzo Pl.	New York	NY	10020
10	Jim	Martin	890 Apple St.	San Diego	CA	92121

Field Name

A field name identifies the information in a field.

Field

A field is a specific category of information in a table, such as the first names of all your customers.

Record

A record is a collection of information about one person, place or thing in a table, such as the name and address of one customer.

in an *instant*

PARTS OF A DATABASE (CONTINUED)

FORMS

Forms provide a quick way to view, enter and edit information in a database by presenting information in an attractive, easy-to-use format. A form displays boxes that clearly show you where to enter information. Forms usually display one record at a time.

QUERIES

Queries allow you to ask Access to find information of interest in a database. You can use criteria or conditions to specify the information you want to find. For example, you can create a query to find all customers who live in California.

REPORTS

Reports are professional-looking documents that summarize information from a database. You can perform calculations in a report to help you analyze the information. For example, you can create a report that displays the total sales for each product.

PLAN A DATABASE

You should take the time to plan a database. A well-planned database ensures that you will be able to perform tasks efficiently and accurately. When planning a database, you must decide what information you want the database to store and how you will use the information. If other people will be using the database, you should also consult with them to determine their needs.

DETERMINE THE TABLES YOU NEED

You should gather all the information you want to store in a database and then divide the information into separate tables. A table should contain information for only one subject. The same information should not appear in more than one table in a database. You can work more efficiently and reduce errors if you need to update information in only one table.

DETERMINE THE FIELDS YOU NEED

You should try to keep the number of fields in a table to a minimum. Each field should relate directly to the subject of the table. You should also break information down into its smallest parts. For example, break down names into two fields called First Name and Last Name.

CREATE A DATABASE USING A WIZARD

You can use the Database Wizard to quickly and easily create a database. The wizard saves you time by creating the tables, forms, queries and reports for your database. You can use the Database Wizard to create many types of databases, such as databases for contact management, expenses, inventory control and order entry.

CREATE A DATABASE USING A WIZARD

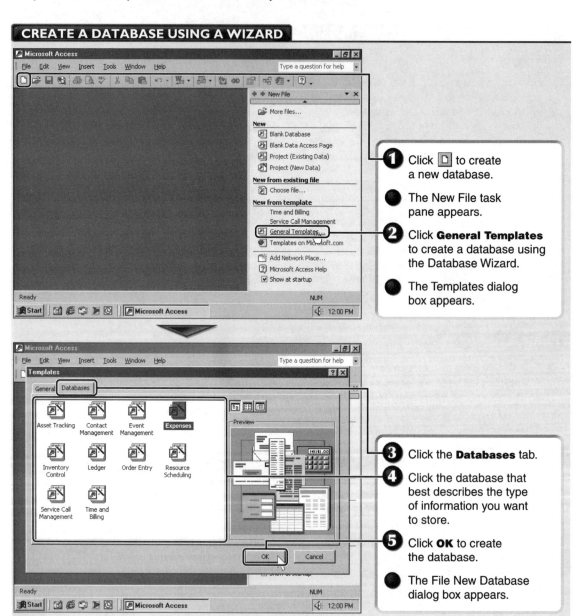

1 Click ⬜ to create a new database.

● The New File task pane appears.

2 Click **General Templates** to create a database using the Database Wizard.

● The Templates dialog box appears.

3 Click the **Databases** tab.

4 Click the database that best describes the type of information you want to store.

5 Click **OK** to create the database.

● The File New Database dialog box appears.

in an instant

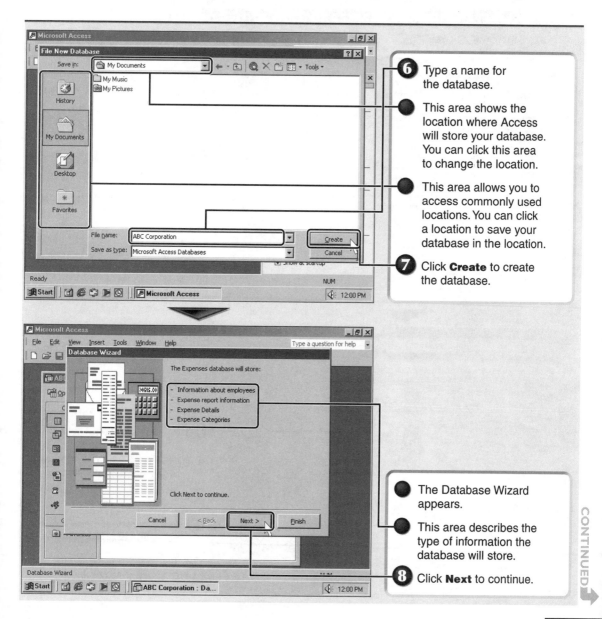

6 Type a name for the database.

This area shows the location where Access will store your database. You can click this area to change the location.

This area allows you to access commonly used locations. You can click a location to save your database in the location.

7 Click **Create** to create the database.

The Database Wizard appears.

This area describes the type of information the database will store.

8 Click **Next** to continue.

CONTINUED

CREATE A DATABASE USING A WIZARD

The Database Wizard displays the fields that are included in each table in your database. You can choose to include other optional fields. A field is a specific category of information in a table, such as the last names of all your customers.

CREATE A DATABASE USING A WIZARD (CONTINUED)

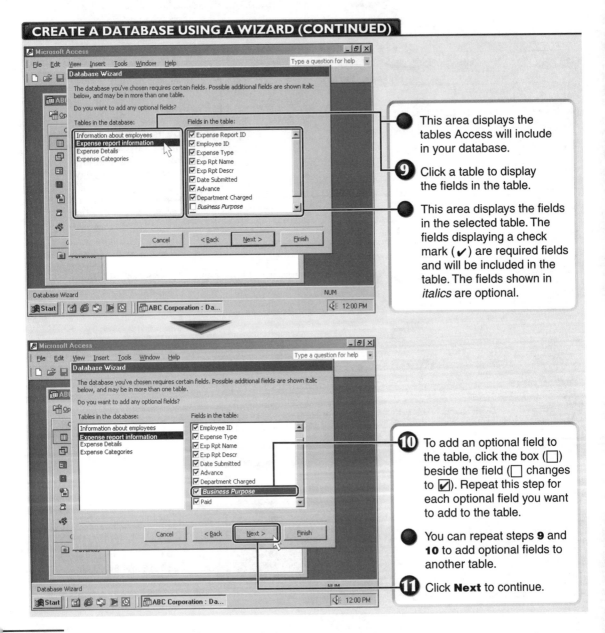

● This area displays the tables Access will include in your database.

⑨ Click a table to display the fields in the table.

● This area displays the fields in the selected table. The fields displaying a check mark (✔) are required fields and will be included in the table. The fields shown in *italics* are optional.

⑩ To add an optional field to the table, click the box (☐) beside the field (☐ changes to ☑). Repeat this step for each optional field you want to add to the table.

● You can repeat steps **9** and **10** to add optional fields to another table.

⑪ Click **Next** to continue.

in an instant

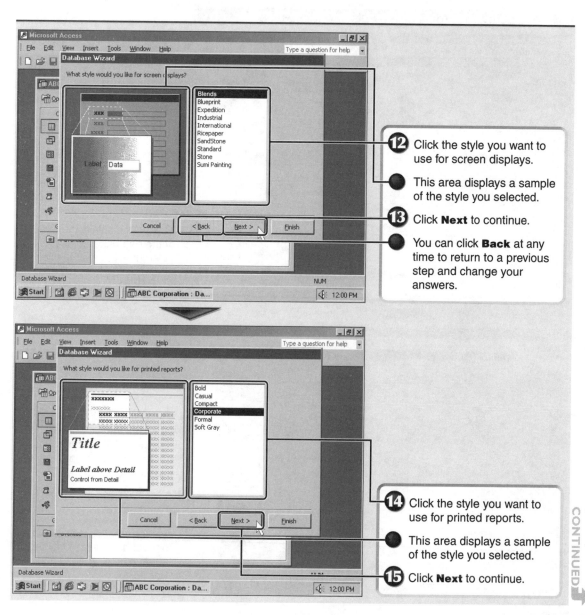

12 Click the style you want to use for screen displays.

This area displays a sample of the style you selected.

13 Click **Next** to continue.

You can click **Back** at any time to return to a previous step and change your answers.

14 Click the style you want to use for printed reports.

This area displays a sample of the style you selected.

15 Click **Next** to continue.

When you have provided all the information needed to create a database, Access creates the objects for the database. Access also displays a switchboard to help you perform common tasks in the database.

CREATE A DATABASE USING A WIZARD (CONTINUED)

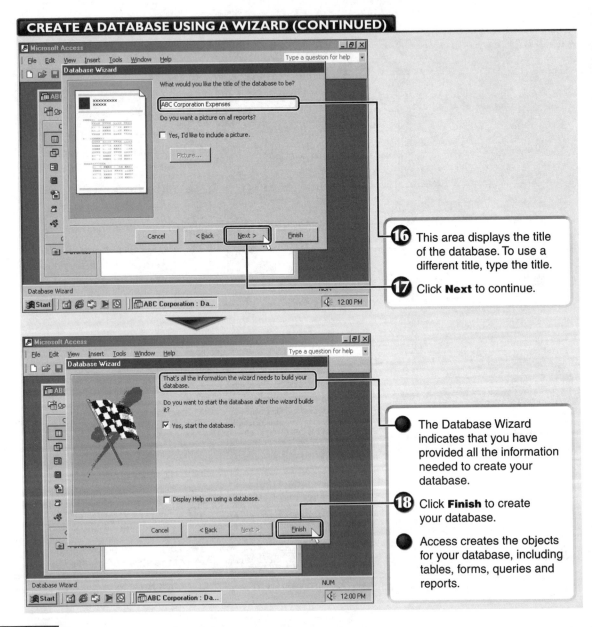

16 This area displays the title of the database. To use a different title, type the title.

17 Click **Next** to continue.

● The Database Wizard indicates that you have provided all the information needed to create your database.

18 Click **Finish** to create your database.

● Access creates the objects for your database, including tables, forms, queries and reports.

in an *instant*

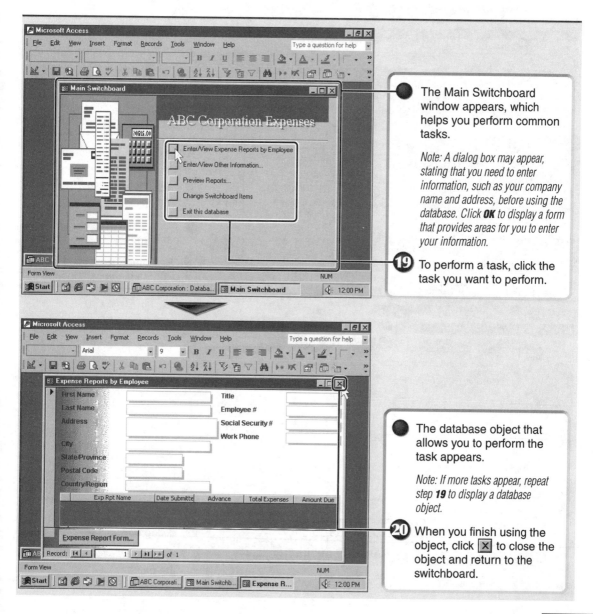

The Main Switchboard window appears, which helps you perform common tasks.

*Note: A dialog box may appear, stating that you need to enter information, such as your company name and address, before using the database. Click **OK** to display a form that provides areas for you to enter your information.*

⑲ To perform a task, click the task you want to perform.

The database object that allows you to perform the task appears.

*Note: If more tasks appear, repeat step **19** to display a database object.*

⑳ When you finish using the object, click ☒ to close the object and return to the switchboard.

237

CREATE A BLANK DATABASE

If you want to design your own database, you can create a blank database. Creating a blank database gives you the most flexibility and control. After creating a blank database, you can add objects, such as tables, forms, queries and reports, to the database.

CREATE A BLANK DATABASE

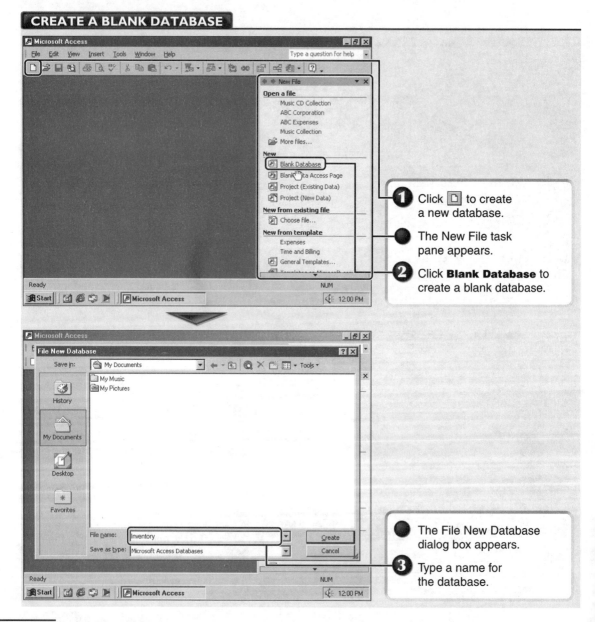

1 Click ☐ to create a new database.

● The New File task pane appears.

2 Click **Blank Database** to create a blank database.

● The File New Database dialog box appears.

3 Type a name for the database.

in an *instant*

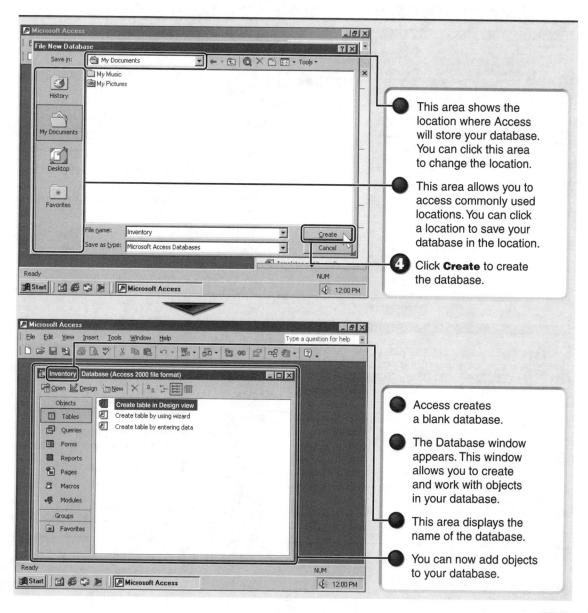

This area shows the location where Access will store your database. You can click this area to change the location.

This area allows you to access commonly used locations. You can click a location to save your database in the location.

④ Click **Create** to create the database.

● Access creates a blank database.

● The Database window appears. This window allows you to create and work with objects in your database.

● This area displays the name of the database.

● You can now add objects to your database.

OPEN A DATABASE OBJECT

You can use the Database window to open objects in your database, including tables, queries, forms and reports. You can also use the Database window to change the name of an object in your database.

OPEN A DATABASE OBJECT

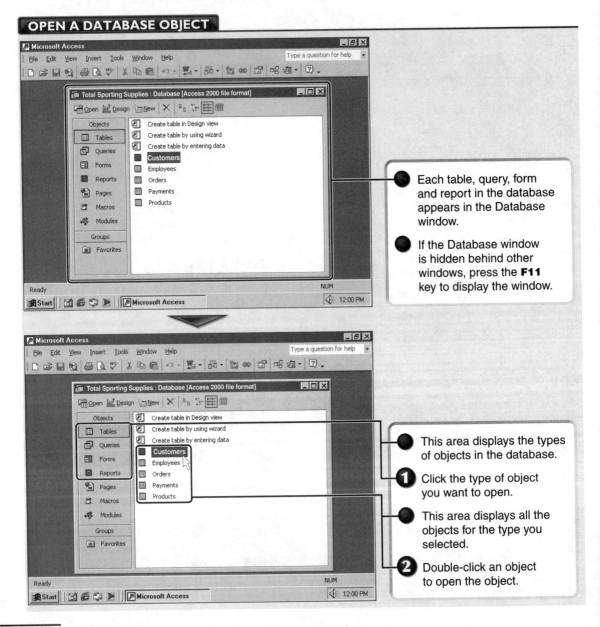

● Each table, query, form and report in the database appears in the Database window.

● If the Database window is hidden behind other windows, press the **F11** key to display the window.

● This area displays the types of objects in the database.

1 Click the type of object you want to open.

● This area displays all the objects for the type you selected.

2 Double-click an object to open the object.

in an Instant

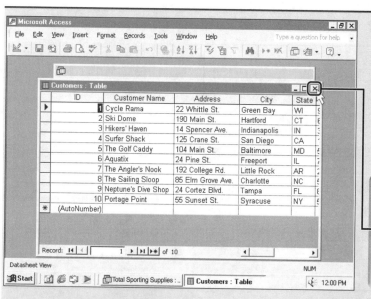

The object opens and appears on your screen.

3 When you finish working with the object, click ⊠ to close the object and return to the Database window.

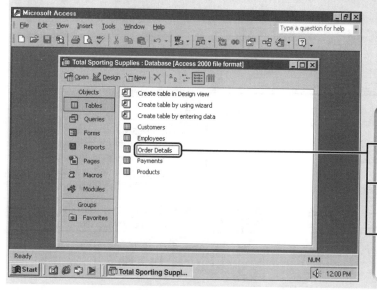

RENAME A DATABASE OBJECT

1 Click the name of the object you want to rename.

2 Press the F2 key. A black border appears around the name of the object.

3 Type a new name for the object and then press the Enter key.

OPEN A DATABASE

You can open a database to view the database on your screen. This allows you to review and make changes to the database. You can have only one database open at a time. Access will close a database displayed on your screen when you open another database.

OPEN A DATABASE

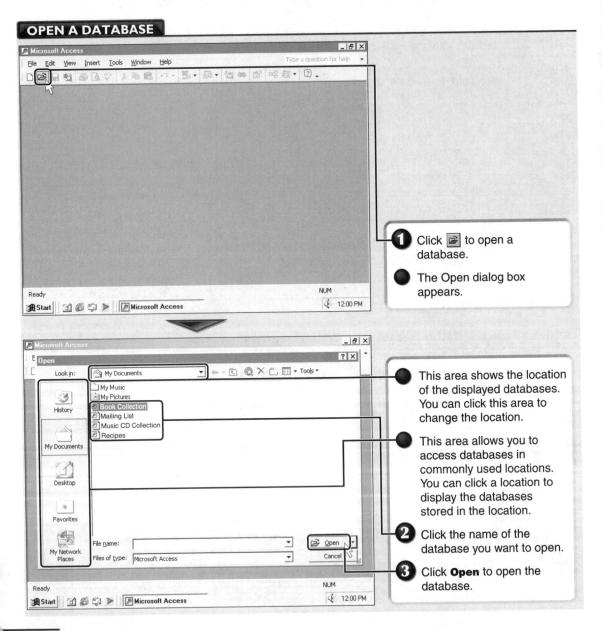

1 Click 📂 to open a database.

● The Open dialog box appears.

● This area shows the location of the displayed databases. You can click this area to change the location.

● This area allows you to access databases in commonly used locations. You can click a location to display the databases stored in the location.

2 Click the name of the database you want to open.

3 Click **Open** to open the database.

in an *Instant*

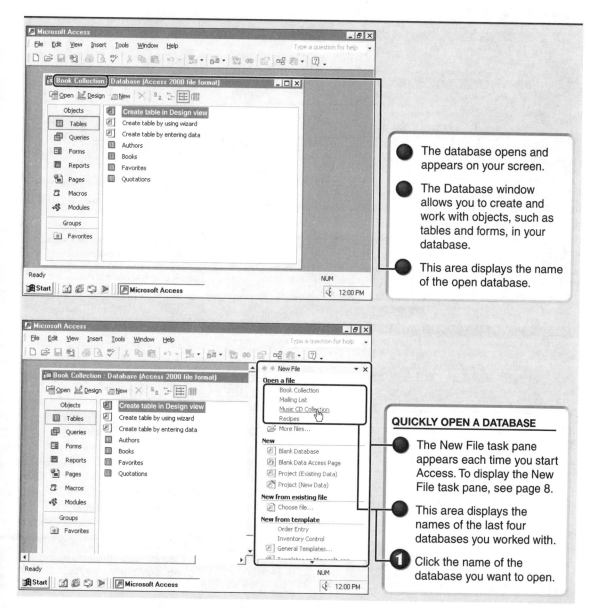

The database opens and appears on your screen.

The Database window allows you to create and work with objects, such as tables and forms, in your database.

This area displays the name of the open database.

QUICKLY OPEN A DATABASE

The New File task pane appears each time you start Access. To display the New File task pane, see page 8.

This area displays the names of the last four databases you worked with.

1 Click the name of the database you want to open.

CREATE A TABLE

A table stores a collection of information about a specific topic, such as a list of customer addresses. You can create a table to store new information in your database. When creating a table, you can specify the field names for the table. A field name identifies the information in a field.

CREATE A TABLE

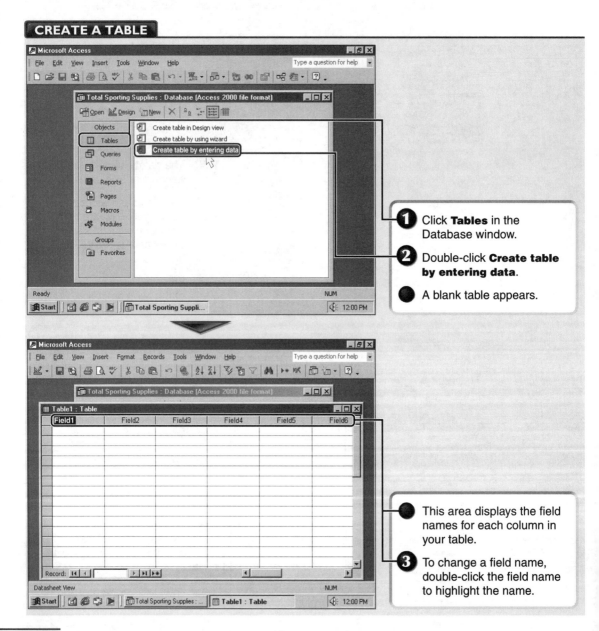

① Click **Tables** in the Database window.

② Double-click **Create table by entering data**.

● A blank table appears.

● This area displays the field names for each column in your table.

③ To change a field name, double-click the field name to highlight the name.

in an instant

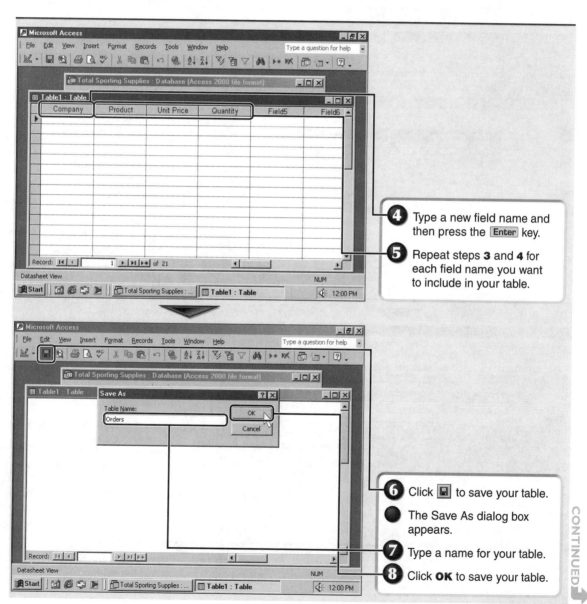

4 Type a new field name and then press the **Enter** key.

5 Repeat steps **3** and **4** for each field name you want to include in your table.

6 Click 🖫 to save your table.

● The Save As dialog box appears.

7 Type a name for your table.

8 Click **OK** to save your table.

CONTINUED

CREATE A TABLE

You can have Access create a primary key for your table. A primary key is one or more fields that uniquely identifies each record in a table, such as a field containing ID numbers. Each table in your database should have a primary key.

CREATE A TABLE (CONTINUED)

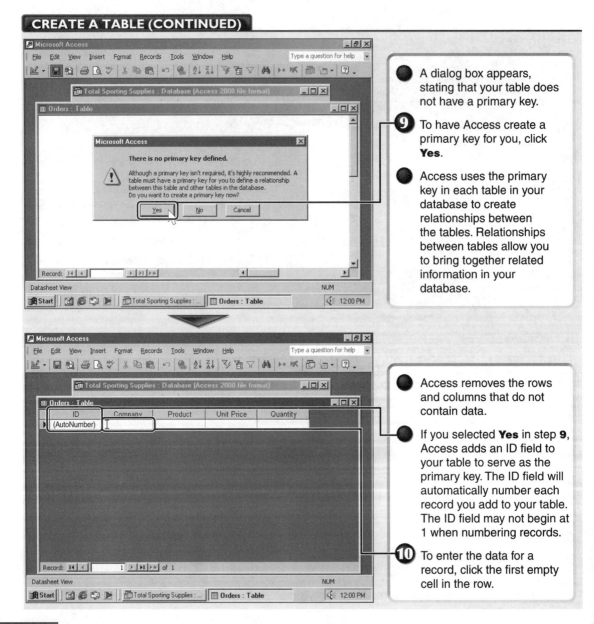

● A dialog box appears, stating that your table does not have a primary key.

9 To have Access create a primary key for you, click **Yes**.

● Access uses the primary key in each table in your database to create relationships between the tables. Relationships between tables allow you to bring together related information in your database.

● Access removes the rows and columns that do not contain data.

● If you selected **Yes** in step **9**, Access adds an ID field to your table to serve as the primary key. The ID field will automatically number each record you add to your table. The ID field may not begin at 1 when numbering records.

10 To enter the data for a record, click the first empty cell in the row.

in an *instant*

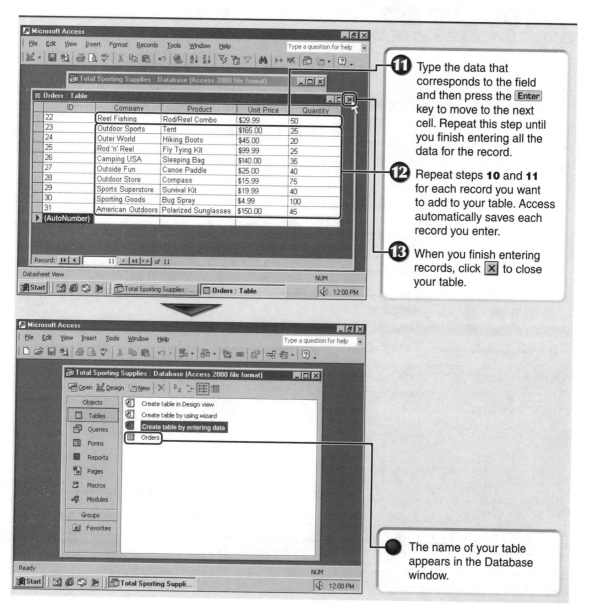

11 Type the data that corresponds to the field and then press the **Enter** key to move to the next cell. Repeat this step until you finish entering all the data for the record.

12 Repeat steps **10** and **11** for each record you want to add to your table. Access automatically saves each record you enter.

13 When you finish entering records, click ✕ to close your table.

● The name of your table appears in the Database window.

CHANGE COLUMN WIDTH

You can change the width of a column in your table. Increasing the width of a column lets you view data that is too long to display in the column. Reducing the width of a column allows you to display more fields on your screen at once.

CHANGE COLUMN WIDTH

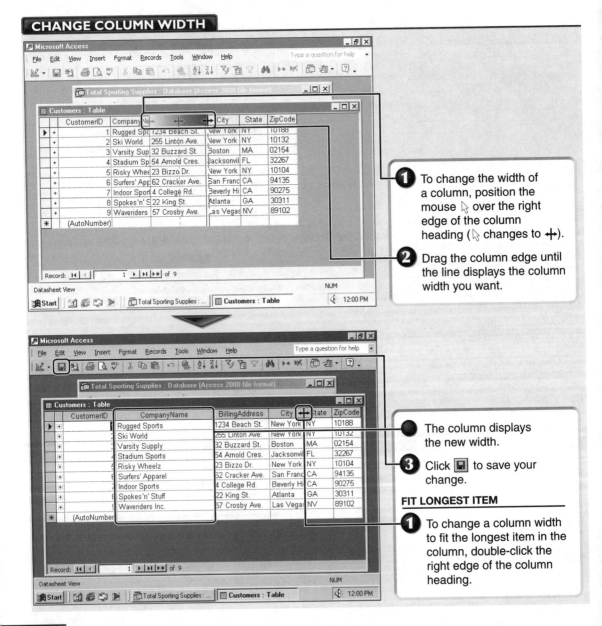

1 To change the width of a column, position the mouse ⍾ over the right edge of the column heading (⍾ changes to ✛).

2 Drag the column edge until the line displays the column width you want.

● The column displays the new width.

3 Click 🖫 to save your change.

FIT LONGEST ITEM

1 To change a column width to fit the longest item in the column, double-click the right edge of the column heading.

REARRANGE FIELDS

You can change the order of fields to better organize the
information in your table. After you change the order of
fields in your table, you must save the table to keep the
new arrangement of fields.

REARRANGE FIELDS

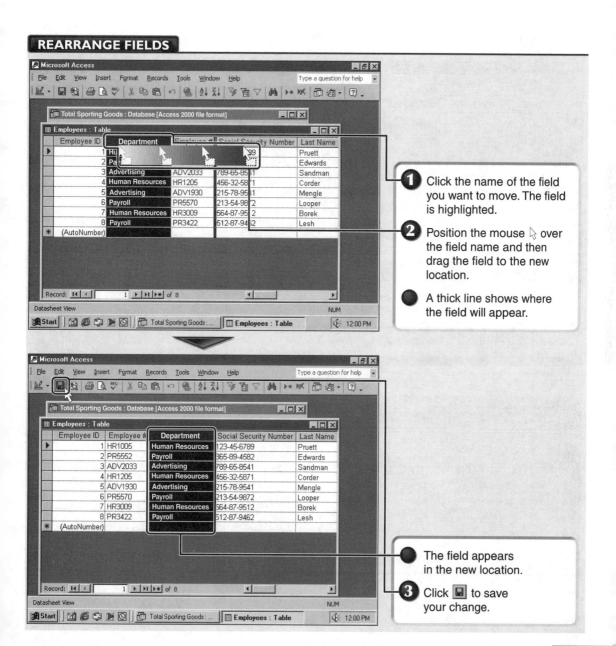

① Click the name of the field
you want to move. The field
is highlighted.

② Position the mouse ⌖ over
the field name and then
drag the field to the new
location.

● A thick line shows where
the field will appear.

● The field appears
in the new location.

③ Click 🖫 to save
your change.

ADD A FIELD

You can add a field to a table when you want to include an additional category of information. A field is a specific category of information in a table. For example, a field can contain the phone numbers of all your customers.

ADD A FIELD

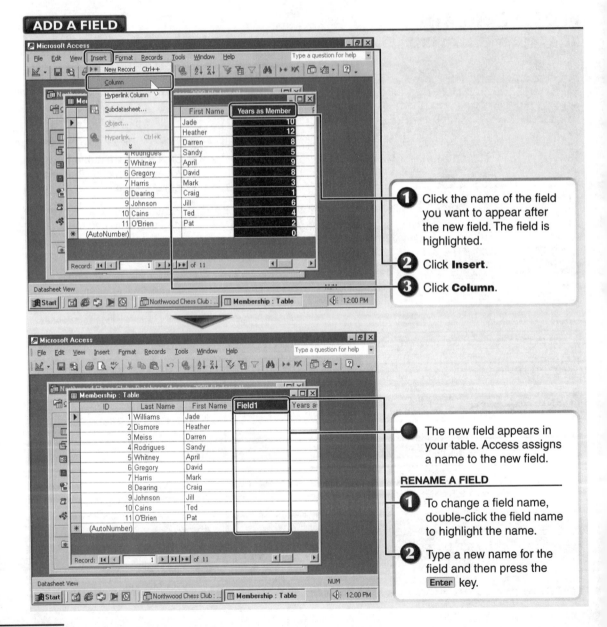

1 Click the name of the field you want to appear after the new field. The field is highlighted.

2 Click **Insert**.

3 Click **Column**.

■ The new field appears in your table. Access assigns a name to the new field.

RENAME A FIELD

1 To change a field name, double-click the field name to highlight the name.

2 Type a new name for the field and then press the Enter key.

If you no longer need a field, you can permanently delete the field from your table. Before you delete a field, make sure the field is not used in any other objects in your database, such as a query, form or report.

DELETE A FIELD

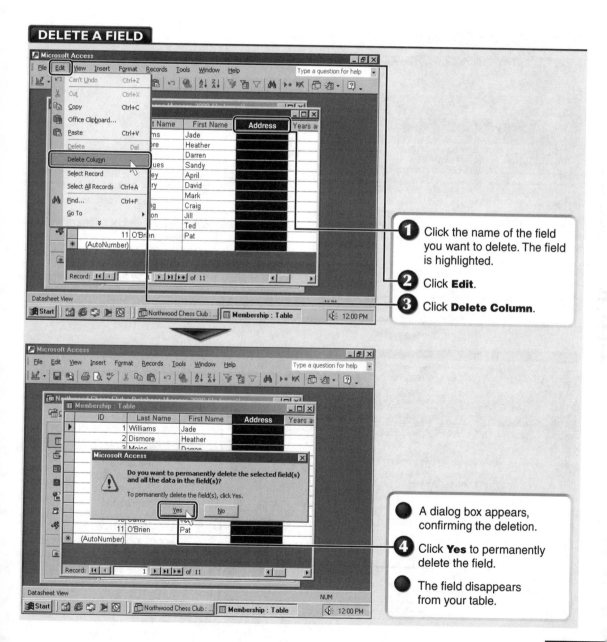

1 Click the name of the field you want to delete. The field is highlighted.

2 Click **Edit**.

3 Click **Delete Column**.

● A dialog box appears, confirming the deletion.

4 Click **Yes** to permanently delete the field.

● The field disappears from your table.

MOVE THROUGH DATA

You can move through the data in your table to review and edit information. If your table contains a lot of data, your computer screen may not be able to display all the data at once. You can scroll through fields and records to display data that does not appear on your screen.

MOVE THROUGH DATA

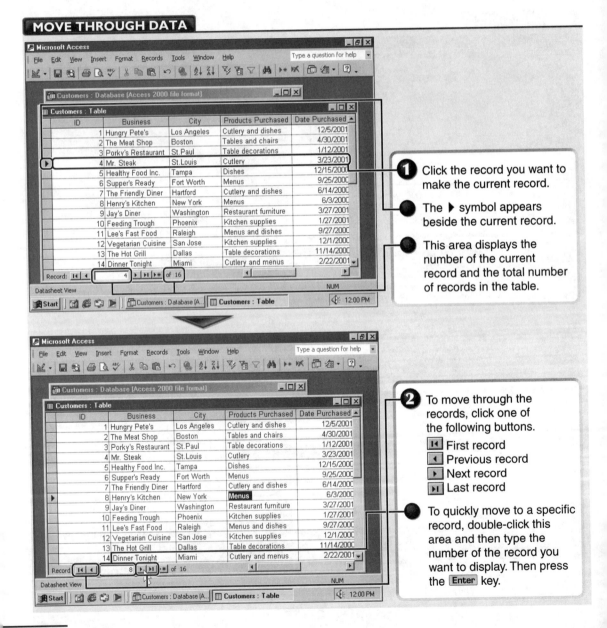

1 Click the record you want to make the current record.

The ▶ symbol appears beside the current record.

This area displays the number of the current record and the total number of records in the table.

2 To move through the records, click one of the following buttons.

⏮ First record
◀ Previous record
▶ Next record
⏭ Last record

To quickly move to a specific record, double-click this area and then type the number of the record you want to display. Then press the Enter key.

in an *Instant*

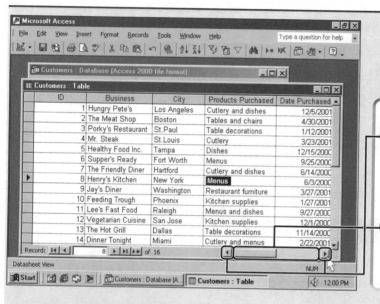

SCROLL THROUGH FIELDS

1 To scroll one field at a time, click ◄ or ►.

Note: You cannot scroll through fields if all the fields appear on your screen.

● To quickly scroll to any field, drag the scroll box along the scroll bar until the field you want to view appears.

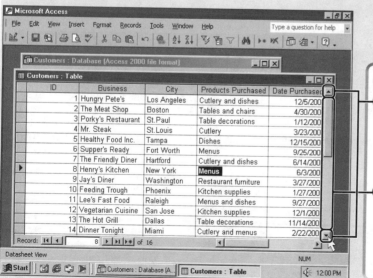

SCROLL THROUGH RECORDS

1 To scroll one record at a time, click ▲ or ▼.

Note: You cannot scroll through records if all the records appear on your screen.

● To quickly scroll to any record, drag the scroll box along the scroll bar until a yellow box displays the number of the record you want to view.

SELECT DATA

Before performing many tasks in a table, you must select the data you want to work with. Selected data appears highlighted on your screen. To deselect data in a table, click anywhere in the table.

SELECT DATA

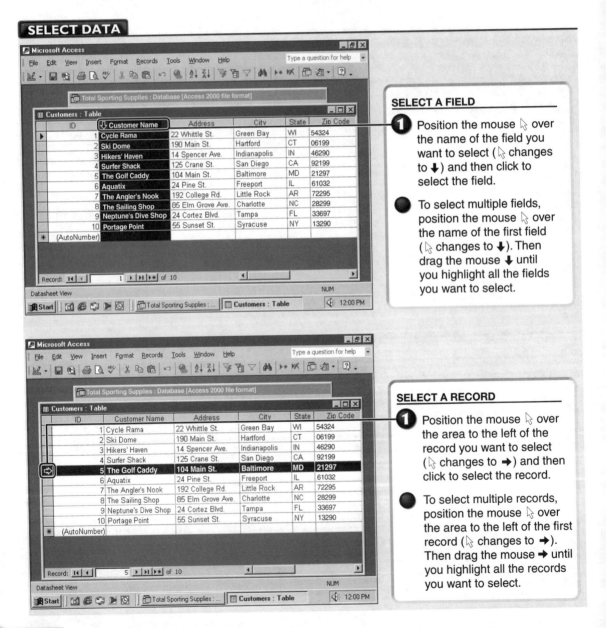

SELECT A FIELD

1 Position the mouse ⟋ over the name of the field you want to select (⟋ changes to ↓) and then click to select the field.

● To select multiple fields, position the mouse ⟋ over the name of the first field (⟋ changes to ↓). Then drag the mouse ↓ until you highlight all the fields you want to select.

SELECT A RECORD

1 Position the mouse ⟋ over the area to the left of the record you want to select (⟋ changes to →) and then click to select the record.

● To select multiple records, position the mouse ⟋ over the area to the left of the first record (⟋ changes to →). Then drag the mouse → until you highlight all the records you want to select.

in an *Instant*

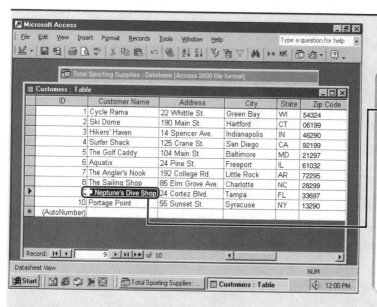

SELECT A CELL

1 Position the mouse I over the left edge of the cell you want to select (I changes to ⇦) and then click to select the cell.

● To select multiple cells, position the mouse I over the left edge of the first cell (I changes to ⇦). Then drag the mouse ⇦ until you highlight all the cells you want to select.

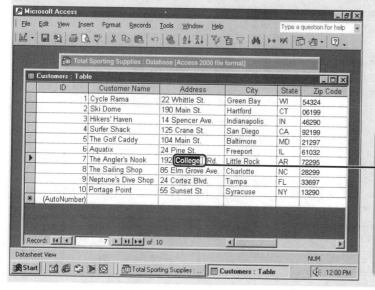

SELECT DATA IN A CELL

1 Position the mouse I over the left edge of the data and then drag the mouse I until you highlight all the data you want to select.

● To quickly select a word, double-click the word.

EDIT DATA

Access allows you to edit the data in a table to correct a mistake or update the data. You can add or remove characters in a cell. You call also replace all the data in a cell. Access automatically saves changes you make to data in a table.

EDIT DATA

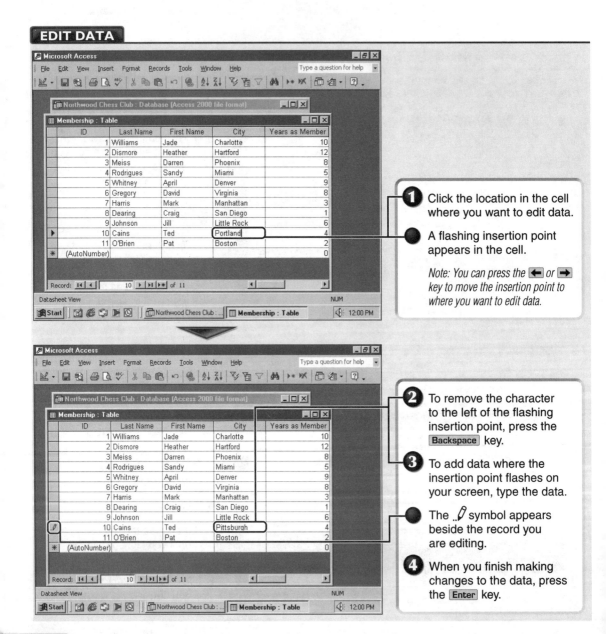

1 Click the location in the cell where you want to edit data.

■ A flashing insertion point appears in the cell.

Note: You can press the ◄ or ► key to move the insertion point to where you want to edit data.

2 To remove the character to the left of the flashing insertion point, press the Backspace key.

3 To add data where the insertion point flashes on your screen, type the data.

■ The ⌀ symbol appears beside the record you are editing.

4 When you finish making changes to the data, press the Enter key.

in an *Instant*

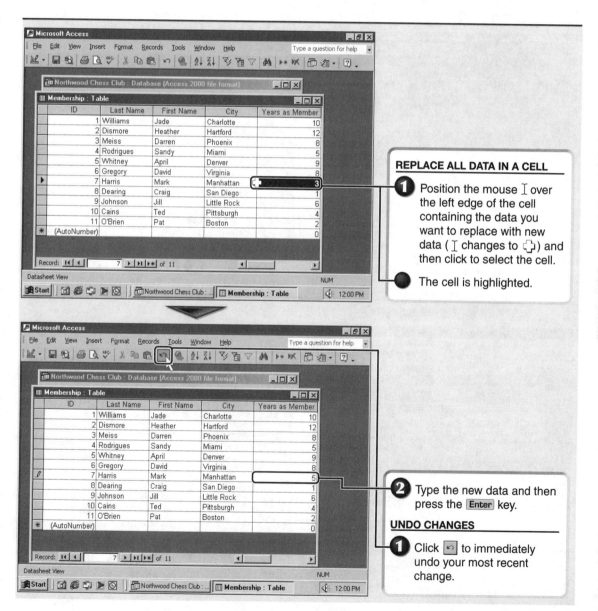

REPLACE ALL DATA IN A CELL

1 Position the mouse I over the left edge of the cell containing the data you want to replace with new data (I changes to ⇩) and then click to select the cell.

● The cell is highlighted.

2 Type the new data and then press the Enter key.

UNDO CHANGES

1 Click ↶ to immediately undo your most recent change.

ADD A RECORD

You can add a new record to insert additional information into your table. For example, you may want to add information about a new customer. You must add a new record to the end of your table. After adding a record, you can sort the records to change the order of the records. Access automatically saves each new record you add to your table.

ADD A RECORD

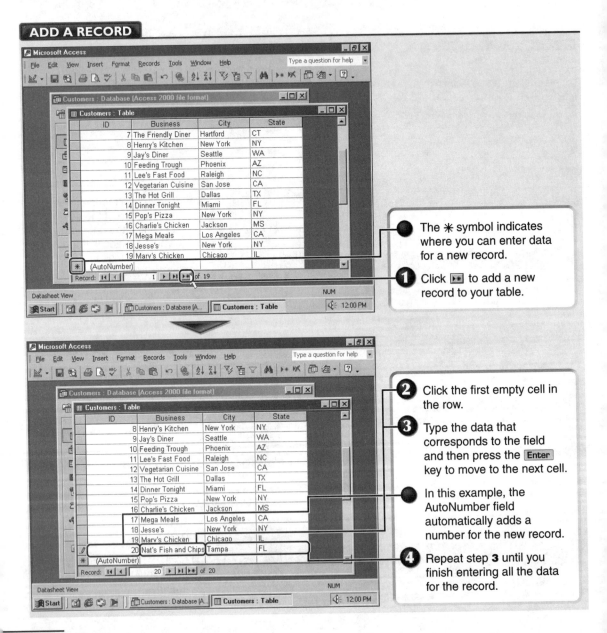

The ✳ symbol indicates where you can enter data for a new record.

❶ Click ▸✳ to add a new record to your table.

❷ Click the first empty cell in the row.

❸ Type the data that corresponds to the field and then press the `Enter` key to move to the next cell.

In this example, the AutoNumber field automatically adds a number for the new record.

❹ Repeat step **3** until you finish entering all the data for the record.

DELETE A RECORD

You can delete a record from a table to permanently remove information you no longer need. For example, you may want to remove information about a customer who no longer orders your products. Deleting records saves storage space on your computer and keeps your database from becoming cluttered with unnecessary information.

DELETE A RECORD

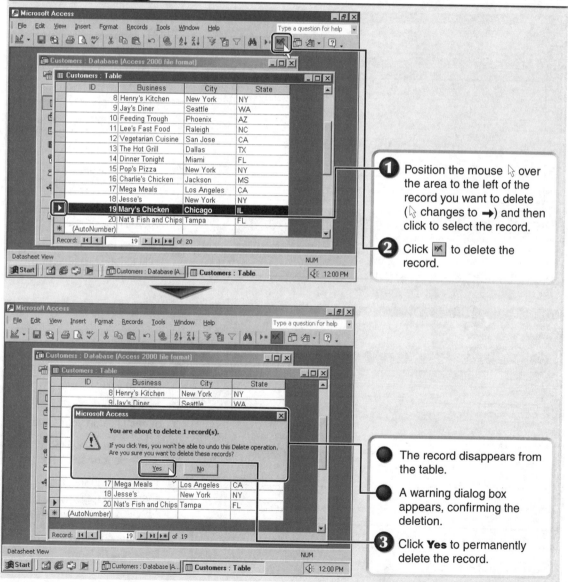

1 Position the mouse ⊷ over the area to the left of the record you want to delete (⊷ changes to ➡) and then click to select the record.

2 Click ✕ to delete the record.

■ The record disappears from the table.

■ A warning dialog box appears, confirming the deletion.

3 Click **Yes** to permanently delete the record.

CHANGE VIEW OF TABLE

Access allows you to quickly switch between the Datasheet and Design views of a table. The Datasheet view displays all the records in a table. You can enter, edit and review records in this view. The Design view displays the structure of a table. You can change the settings in this view to specify the kind of information you can enter into a table.

CHANGE VIEW OF TABLE

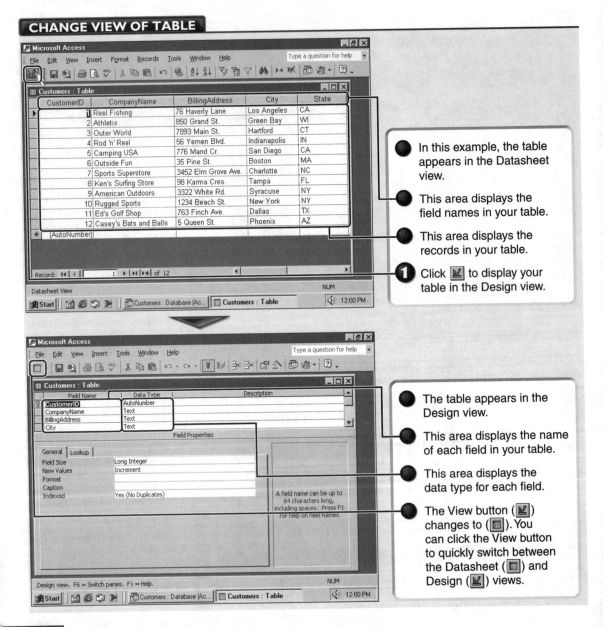

In this example, the table appears in the Datasheet view.

This area displays the field names in your table.

This area displays the records in your table.

1 Click 🖹 to display your table in the Design view.

The table appears in the Design view.

This area displays the name of each field in your table.

This area displays the data type for each field.

The View button (🖹) changes to (🔲). You can click the View button to quickly switch between the Datasheet (🔲) and Design (🖹) views.

SET THE PRIMARY KEY

A primary key is a field that uniquely identifies each record in a table. Each table in your database should have a primary key. Access uses the primary key in each table to create relationships between the tables. Relationships allow you to bring together related information in your database. You should not change the primary key in a table that has a relationship with another table.

SET THE PRIMARY KEY

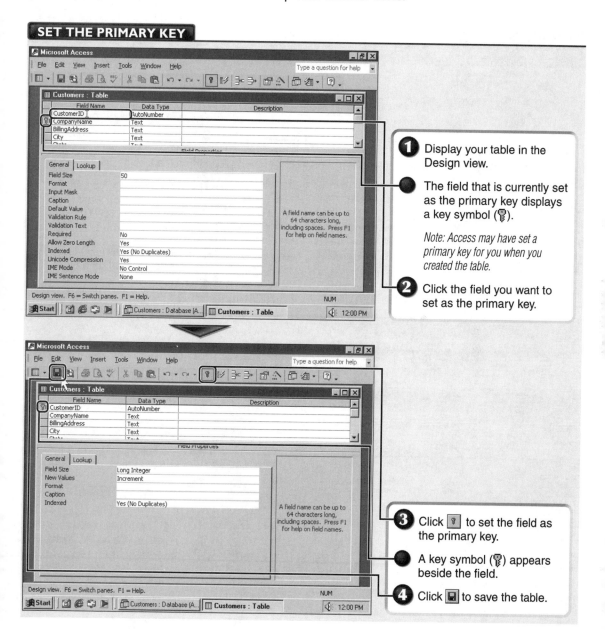

1 Display your table in the Design view.

The field that is currently set as the primary key displays a key symbol (🔑).

Note: Access may have set a primary key for you when you created the table.

2 Click the field you want to set as the primary key.

3 Click 🔑 to set the field as the primary key.

A key symbol (🔑) appears beside the field.

4 Click 🖫 to save the table.

CHANGE A FIELD'S DATA TYPE

You can change the type of data you can enter into a field.
Access will accept only entries that match the data type you
specify for a field. This helps prevent errors when entering
data. For example, you cannot enter text into a field with
the Number data type.

CHANGE A FIELD'S DATA TYPE

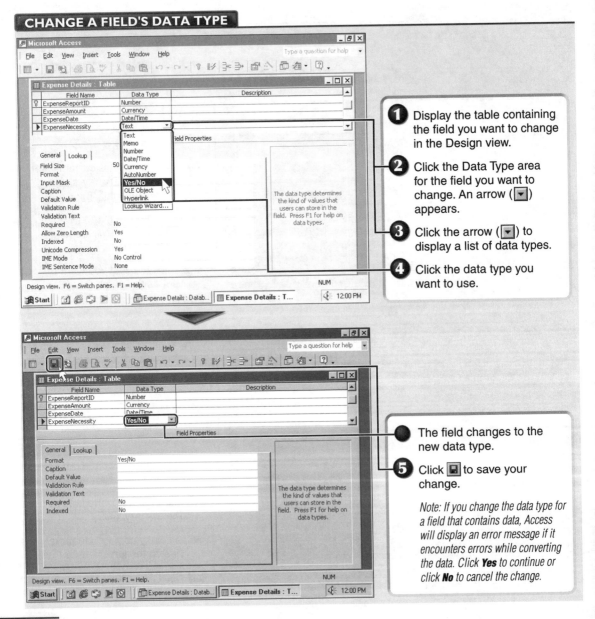

1 Display the table containing
the field you want to change
in the Design view.

2 Click the Data Type area
for the field you want to
change. An arrow (⏷)
appears.

3 Click the arrow (⏷) to
display a list of data types.

4 Click the data type you
want to use.

■ The field changes to the
new data type.

5 Click 🖫 to save your
change.

Note: If you change the data type for
a field that contains data, Access
will display an error message if it
encounters errors while converting
the data. Click **Yes** to continue or
click **No** to cancel the change.

in an instant

DATA TYPES

TEXT

Accepts entries up to 255 characters long that include any combination of text and numbers, such as an address. Make sure you use this data type for numbers you do not want to use in calculations, such as phone numbers or zip codes.

MEMO

Accepts entries up to 65,536 characters long that include any combination of text and numbers, such as notes, comments or lengthy descriptions.

NUMBER

Accepts numbers you can use in calculations.

DATE/TIME

Accepts only dates and times.

CURRENCY

Accepts only monetary values.

AUTONUMBER

Automatically numbers each record for you.

YES/NO

Accepts only one of two values—Yes/No, True/False or On/Off.

OLE OBJECT

Accepts OLE objects. An OLE object is an object created in another program, such as a document created in Word or a spreadsheet created in Excel. OLE objects can also include sounds and pictures.

HYPERLINK

Accepts hyperlinks you can select to jump to another document or a Web page.

CREATE RELATIONSHIPS BETWEEN TABLES

You can create relationships between tables. Relationships allow you to bring together related information in your database. Relationships between tables are essential for creating a form, query or report that uses information from more than one table in your database. If you used the Database Wizard to create your database, the wizard automatically created relationships between tables for you.

CREATE RELATIONSHIPS BETWEEN TABLES

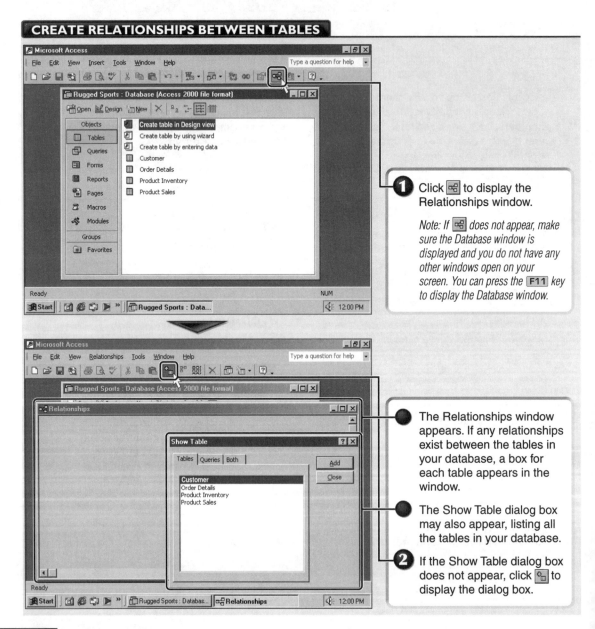

1 Click 🔲 to display the Relationships window.

Note: If 🔲 does not appear, make sure the Database window is displayed and you do not have any other windows open on your screen. You can press the F11 key to display the Database window.

● The Relationships window appears. If any relationships exist between the tables in your database, a box for each table appears in the window.

● The Show Table dialog box may also appear, listing all the tables in your database.

2 If the Show Table dialog box does not appear, click 🔲 to display the dialog box.

in an *instant*

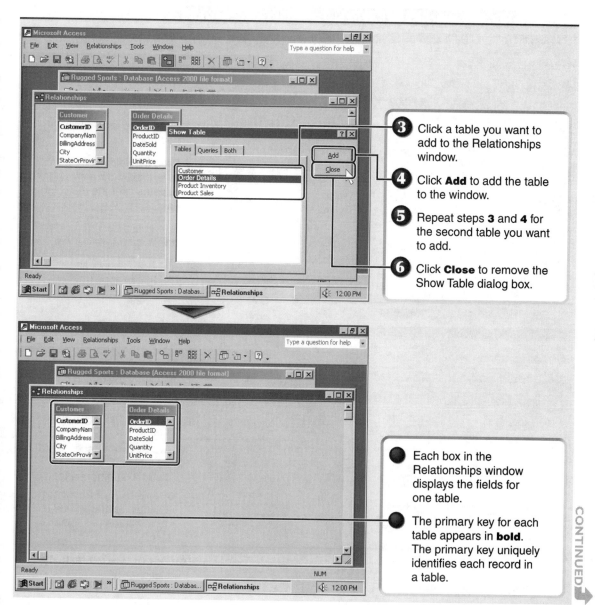

3 Click a table you want to add to the Relationships window.

4 Click **Add** to add the table to the window.

5 Repeat steps **3** and **4** for the second table you want to add.

6 Click **Close** to remove the Show Table dialog box.

● Each box in the Relationships window displays the fields for one table.

● The primary key for each table appears in **bold**. The primary key uniquely identifies each record in a table.

CONTINUED

You create a relationship between tables by identifying the matching fields in the tables. You will usually relate the primary key in one table to a matching field in the other table, creating a one-to-many relationship. In a one-to-many relationship, each record in a table relates to one or more records in another table. For example, each customer can have more than one order.

CREATE RELATIONSHIPS BETWEEN TABLES (CONTINUED)

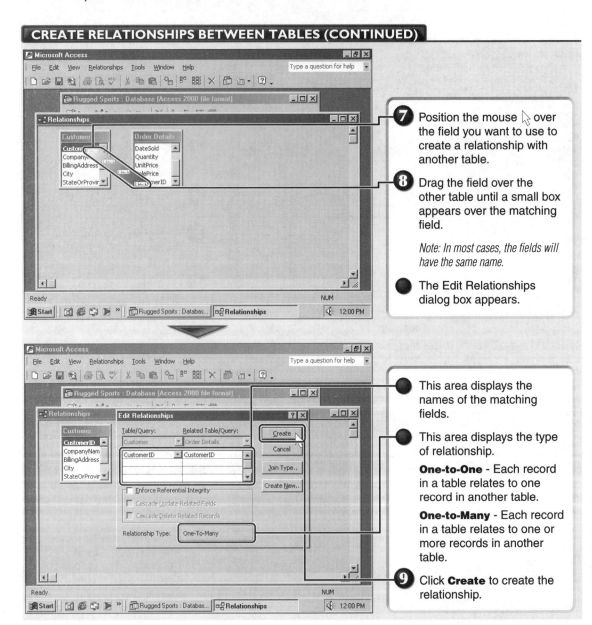

7 Position the mouse ↘ over the field you want to use to create a relationship with another table.

8 Drag the field over the other table until a small box appears over the matching field.

Note: In most cases, the fields will have the same name.

● The Edit Relationships dialog box appears.

● This area displays the names of the matching fields.

● This area displays the type of relationship.

One-to-One - Each record in a table relates to one record in another table.

One-to-Many - Each record in a table relates to one or more records in another table.

9 Click **Create** to create the relationship.

in an instant

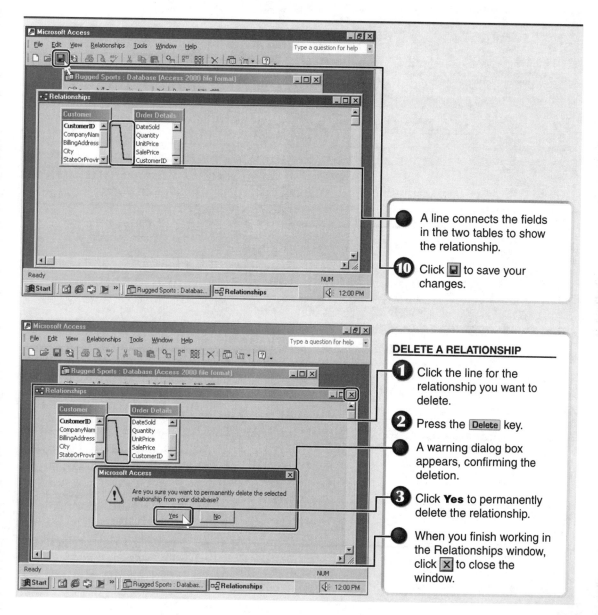

A line connects the fields in the two tables to show the relationship.

⑩ Click 🖫 to save your changes.

DELETE A RELATIONSHIP

① Click the line for the relationship you want to delete.

② Press the Delete key.

A warning dialog box appears, confirming the deletion.

③ Click **Yes** to permanently delete the relationship.

When you finish working in the Relationships window, click ☒ to close the window.

267

CREATE A FORM

You can use the Form Wizard to create a form that suits your needs. The wizard asks you a series of questions and then sets up a form based on your answers. A form presents data from a table in an attractive, easy-to-use format. You can use a form to view, change, add or delete data in a table.

CREATE A FORM

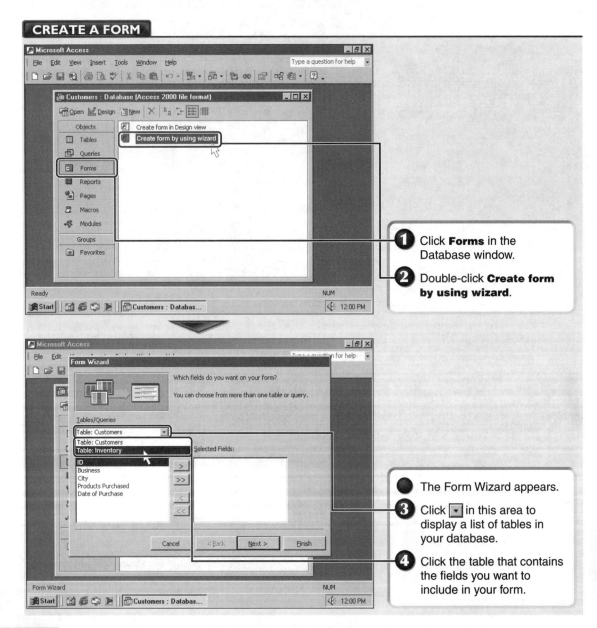

1 Click **Forms** in the Database window.

2 Double-click **Create form by using wizard**.

■ The Form Wizard appears.

3 Click ▾ in this area to display a list of tables in your database.

4 Click the table that contains the fields you want to include in your form.

in an *instant*

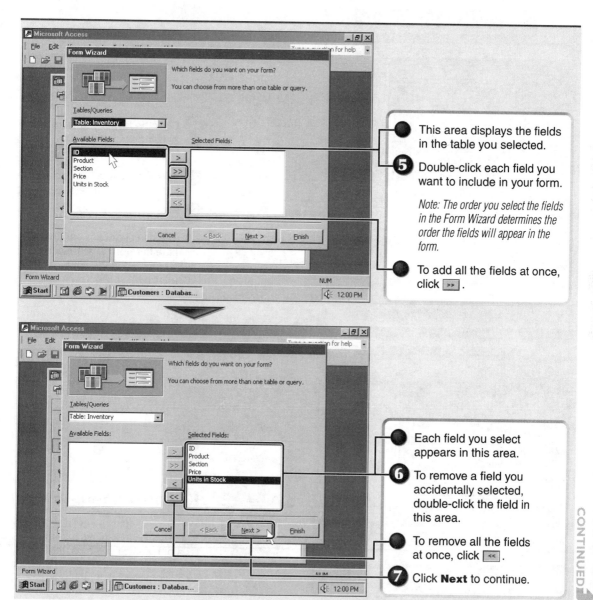

This area displays the fields in the table you selected.

5 Double-click each field you want to include in your form.

Note: The order you select the fields in the Form Wizard determines the order the fields will appear in the form.

To add all the fields at once, click ▸▸ .

Each field you select appears in this area.

6 To remove a field you accidentally selected, double-click the field in this area.

To remove all the fields at once, click ◂◂ .

7 Click **Next** to continue.

CONTINUED

269

CREATE A FORM

When creating a form, you can choose from several different layouts. The layout of a form determines the arrangement of information on the form. The Columnar and Justified layouts display one record at a time. The Tabular and Datasheet layouts display multiple records at a time.

CREATE A FORM (CONTINUED)

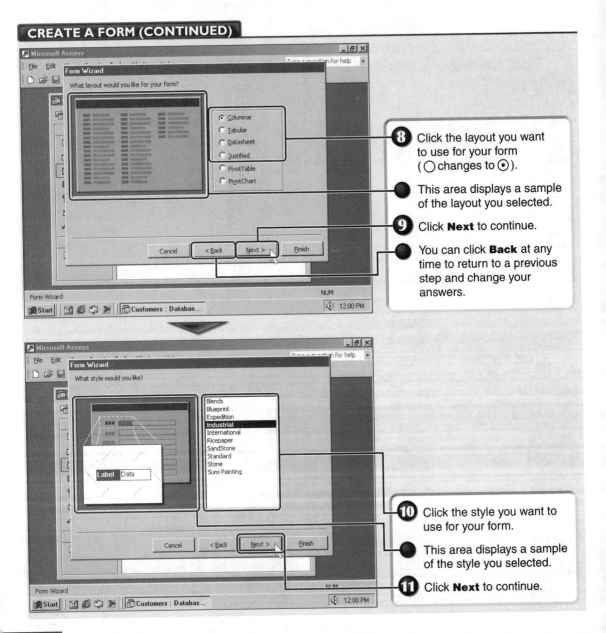

8 Click the layout you want to use for your form (○ changes to ⊙).

● This area displays a sample of the layout you selected.

9 Click **Next** to continue.

● You can click **Back** at any time to return to a previous step and change your answers.

10 Click the style you want to use for your form.

● This area displays a sample of the style you selected.

11 Click **Next** to continue.

in an *instant*

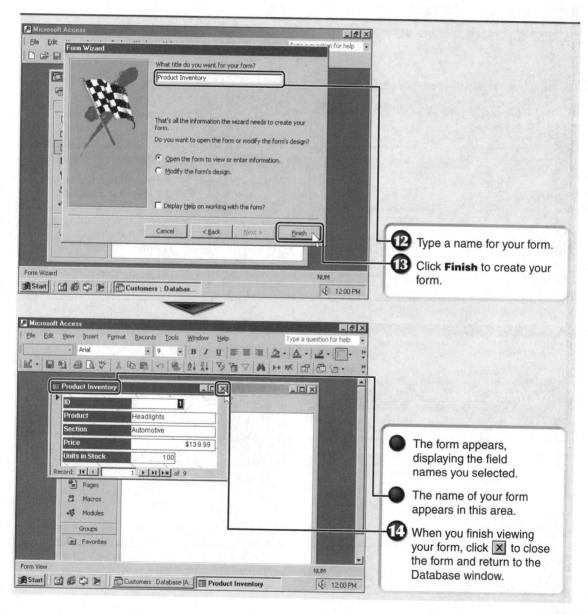

12 Type a name for your form.

13 Click **Finish** to create your form.

● The form appears, displaying the field names you selected.

● The name of your form appears in this area.

14 When you finish viewing your form, click ☒ to close the form and return to the Database window.

MOVE THROUGH RECORDS

Access allows you to move through the records displayed in a form to review or edit information. You can quickly move to the first, last, previous or next record. You can also move to a specific record displayed in a form.

MOVE THROUGH RECORDS

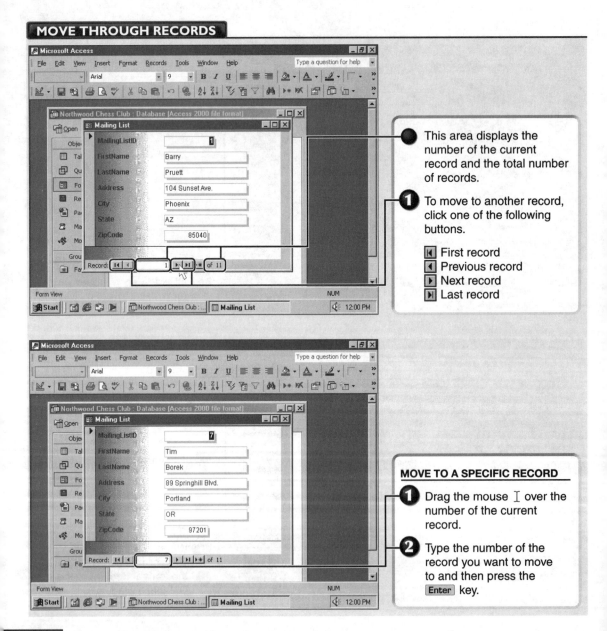

● This area displays the number of the current record and the total number of records.

1 To move to another record, click one of the following buttons.

- ⏮ First record
- ◀ Previous record
- ▶ Next record
- ⏭ Last record

MOVE TO A SPECIFIC RECORD

1 Drag the mouse I over the number of the current record.

2 Type the number of the record you want to move to and then press the [Enter] key.

You can edit data displayed in a form to correct a mistake
or update the data. When you change data in a form,
Access will also change the data in the table you used to
create the form. Access automatically saves changes you
make to data in a form.

EDIT DATA

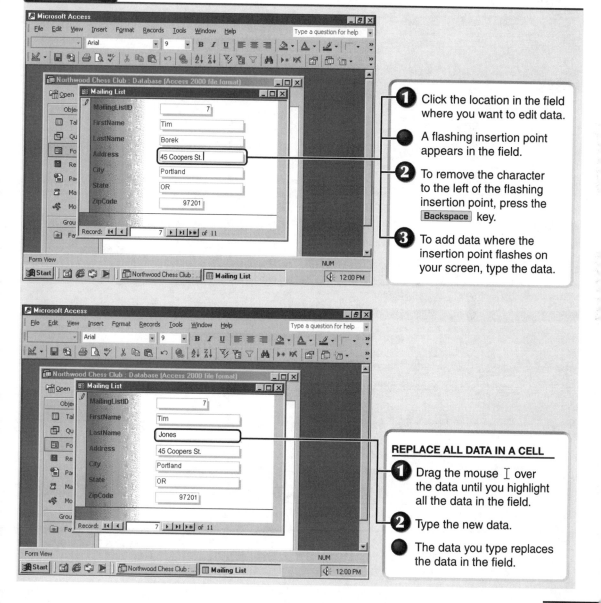

1 Click the location in the field where you want to edit data.

● A flashing insertion point appears in the field.

2 To remove the character to the left of the flashing insertion point, press the **Backspace** key.

3 To add data where the insertion point flashes on your screen, type the data.

REPLACE ALL DATA IN A CELL

1 Drag the mouse I over the data until you highlight all the data in the field.

2 Type the new data.

● The data you type replaces the data in the field.

ADD A RECORD

You can use a form to add a record to your database. For example, you may want to add a record to include information about a new client. When you use a form to add a record, Access adds the record to the table you used to create the form.

ADD A RECORD

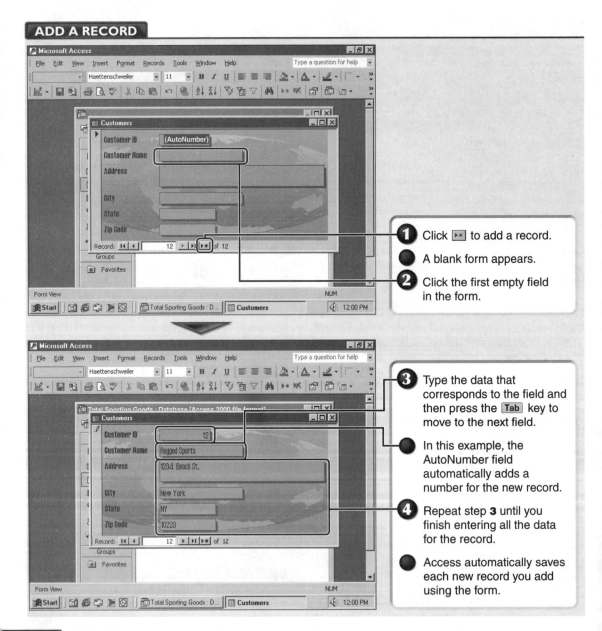

1 Click ►* to add a record.

● A blank form appears.

2 Click the first empty field in the form.

3 Type the data that corresponds to the field and then press the Tab key to move to the next field.

● In this example, the AutoNumber field automatically adds a number for the new record.

4 Repeat step 3 until you finish entering all the data for the record.

● Access automatically saves each new record you add using the form.

DELETE A RECORD

You can delete a record displayed in a form to permanently remove information you no longer need. Deleting records saves storage space on your computer and keeps your database from becoming cluttered with unnecessary information. When you delete a record displayed in a form, Access deletes the record from the table you used to create the form.

DELETE A RECORD

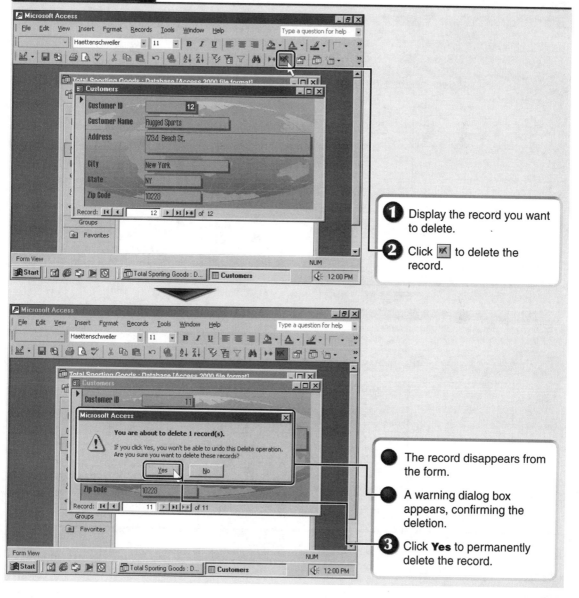

1 Display the record you want to delete.

2 Click 📉 to delete the record.

● The record disappears from the form.

● A warning dialog box appears, confirming the deletion.

3 Click **Yes** to permanently delete the record.

275

SORT RECORDS

You can change the order of records in a table, in a form or in the results of a query. This can help you find, organize and analyze data. You can use one or two fields to sort records.

SORT RECORDS

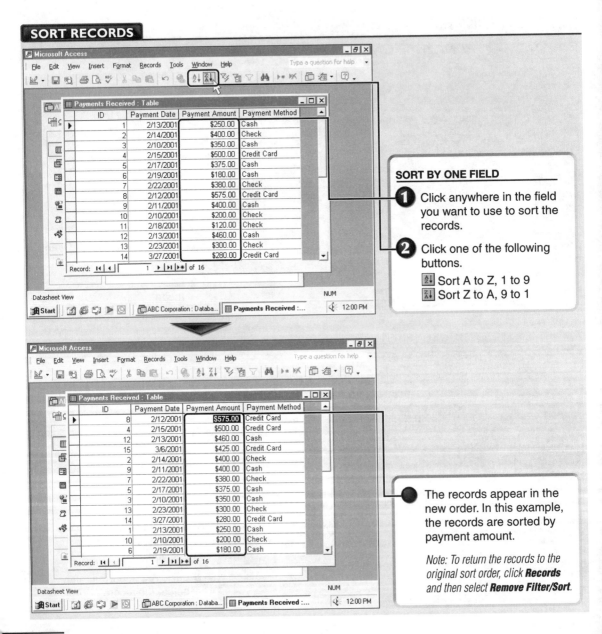

SORT BY ONE FIELD

1. Click anywhere in the field you want to use to sort the records.

2. Click one of the following buttons.

   Sort A to Z, 1 to 9
   Sort Z to A, 9 to 1

The records appear in the new order. In this example, the records are sorted by payment amount.

Note: To return the records to the original sort order, click **Records** and then select **Remove Filter/Sort**.

in an *instant*

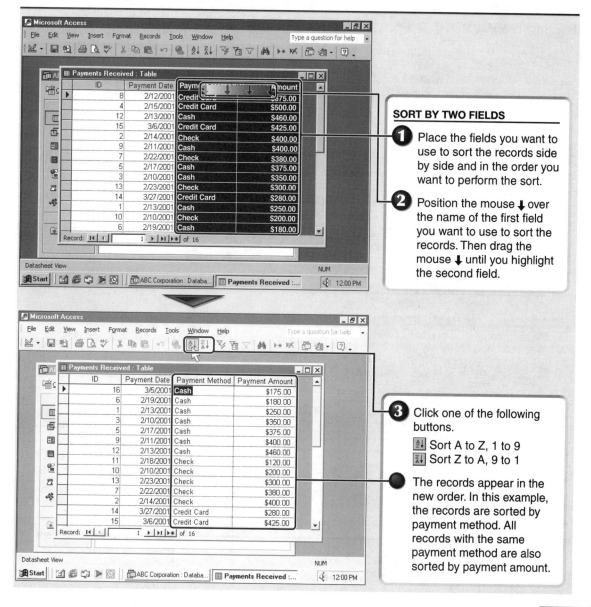

SORT BY TWO FIELDS

1 Place the fields you want to use to sort the records side by side and in the order you want to perform the sort.

2 Position the mouse ↓ over the name of the first field you want to use to sort the records. Then drag the mouse ↓ until you highlight the second field.

3 Click one of the following buttons.

▲↓ Sort A to Z, 1 to 9
▼↓ Sort Z to A, 9 to 1

● The records appear in the new order. In this example, the records are sorted by payment method. All records with the same payment method are also sorted by payment amount.

FIND DATA

You can search for data in a table, in a form or in the results of a query. After you start a search, Access finds and highlights the first instance of the data. You can continue the search to find the next instance of the data.

FIND DATA

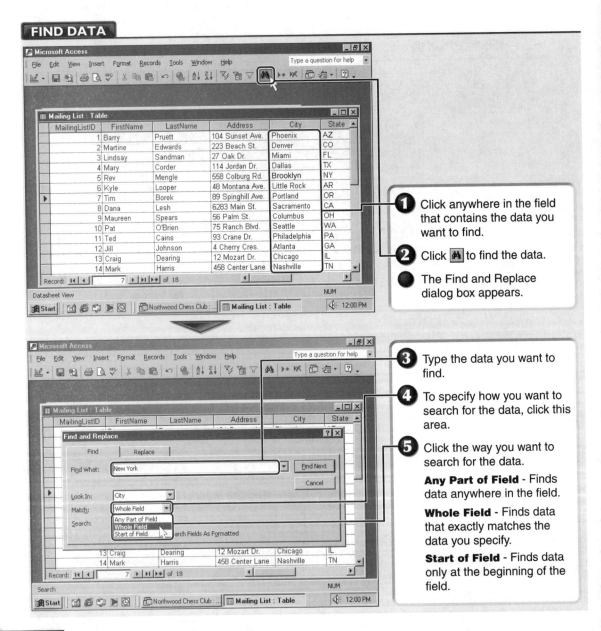

1 Click anywhere in the field that contains the data you want to find.

2 Click 🔍 to find the data.

● The Find and Replace dialog box appears.

3 Type the data you want to find.

4 To specify how you want to search for the data, click this area.

5 Click the way you want to search for the data.

Any Part of Field - Finds data anywhere in the field.

Whole Field - Finds data that exactly matches the data you specify.

Start of Field - Finds data only at the beginning of the field.

in an *Instant*

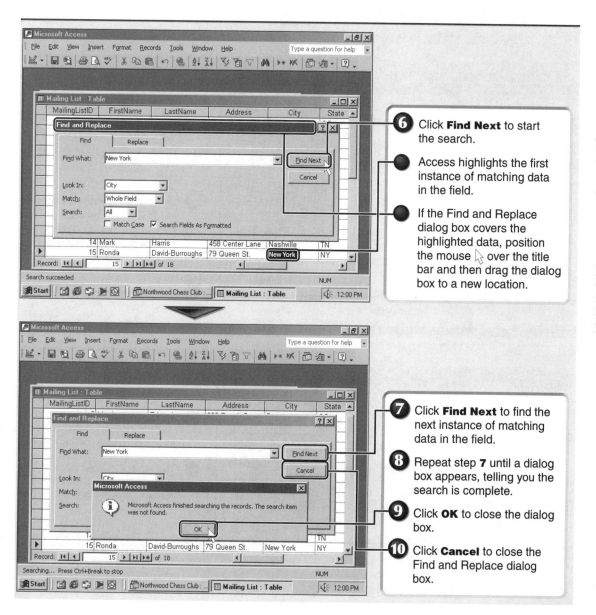

6 Click **Find Next** to start the search.

Access highlights the first instance of matching data in the field.

If the Find and Replace dialog box covers the highlighted data, position the mouse ⌖ over the title bar and then drag the dialog box to a new location.

7 Click **Find Next** to find the next instance of matching data in the field.

8 Repeat step **7** until a dialog box appears, telling you the search is complete.

9 Click **OK** to close the dialog box.

10 Click **Cancel** to close the Find and Replace dialog box.

FILTER DATA BY SELECTION

You can filter data in a table, in a form or in the results of a query to display only records containing data of interest. Filtering data can help you review and analyze information in your database. For example, you can display only the records for customers who live in California.

FILTER DATA BY SELECTION

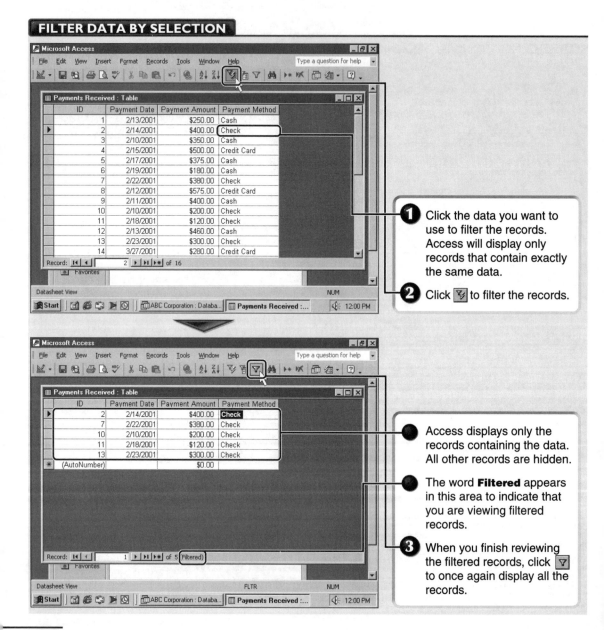

1 Click the data you want to use to filter the records. Access will display only records that contain exactly the same data.

2 Click [filter icon] to filter the records.

Access displays only the records containing the data. All other records are hidden.

The word **Filtered** appears in this area to indicate that you are viewing filtered records.

3 When you finish reviewing the filtered records, click [icon] to once again display all the records.

You can use criteria to filter data in a table, in a form or in the results of a query. Criteria are conditions that identify which records you want to display. For example, you can display only the records for customers who made purchases of more than $500.

FILTER DATA USING CRITERIA

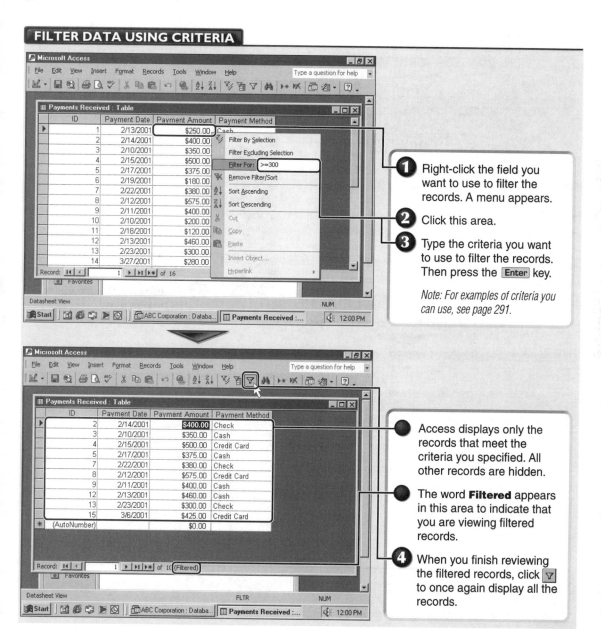

1 Right-click the field you want to use to filter the records. A menu appears.

2 Click this area.

3 Type the criteria you want to use to filter the records. Then press the Enter key.

Note: For examples of criteria you can use, see page 291.

Access displays only the records that meet the criteria you specified. All other records are hidden.

The word **Filtered** appears in this area to indicate that you are viewing filtered records.

4 When you finish reviewing the filtered records, click ▽ to once again display all the records.

CREATE A QUERY

You can create a query to find information of interest in your database. Creating a query allows you to ask Access to find information that meets certain criteria or conditions. When you create a query that uses information from more than one table in your database, the tables should be related.

CREATE A QUERY

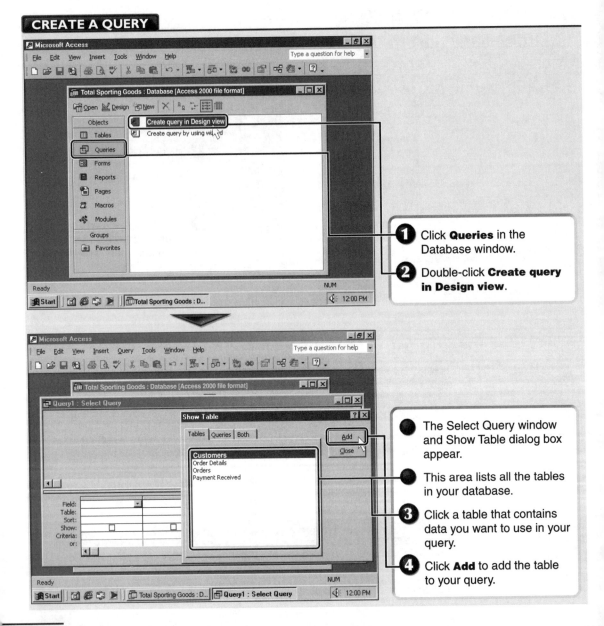

1 Click **Queries** in the Database window.

2 Double-click **Create query in Design view**.

■ The Select Query window and Show Table dialog box appear.

■ This area lists all the tables in your database.

3 Click a table that contains data you want to use in your query.

4 Click **Add** to add the table to your query.

in an instant

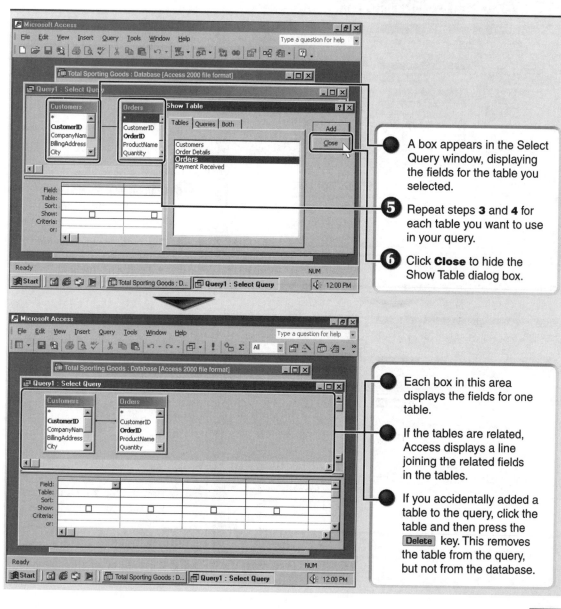

A box appears in the Select Query window, displaying the fields for the table you selected.

5 Repeat steps **3** and **4** for each table you want to use in your query.

6 Click **Close** to hide the Show Table dialog box.

Each box in this area displays the fields for one table.

If the tables are related, Access displays a line joining the related fields in the tables.

If you accidentally added a table to the query, click the table and then press the **Delete** key. This removes the table from the query, but not from the database.

CONTINUED

283

CREATE A QUERY

You can select the fields you want to include in your query. If you want to be able to run the query again at a later time, you can save the query. Each time you run a query, Access gathers the most current data from your database to determine the results of the query.

CREATE A QUERY (CONTINUED)

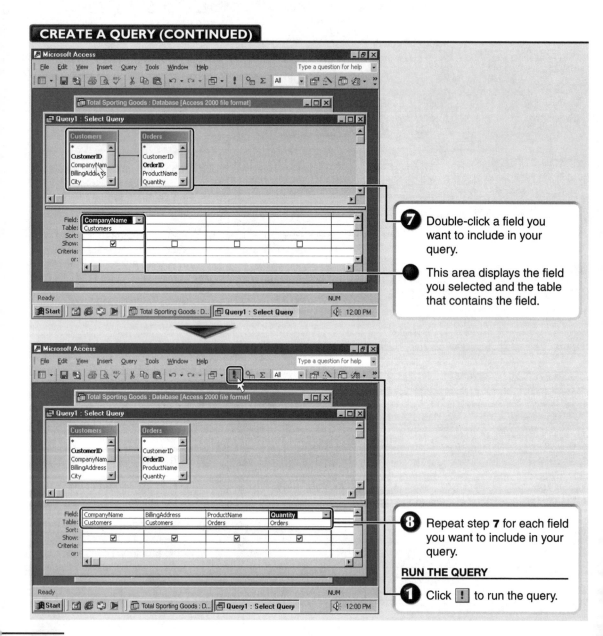

7 Double-click a field you want to include in your query.

● This area displays the field you selected and the table that contains the field.

8 Repeat step **7** for each field you want to include in your query.

RUN THE QUERY

1 Click ! to run the query.

in an *instant*

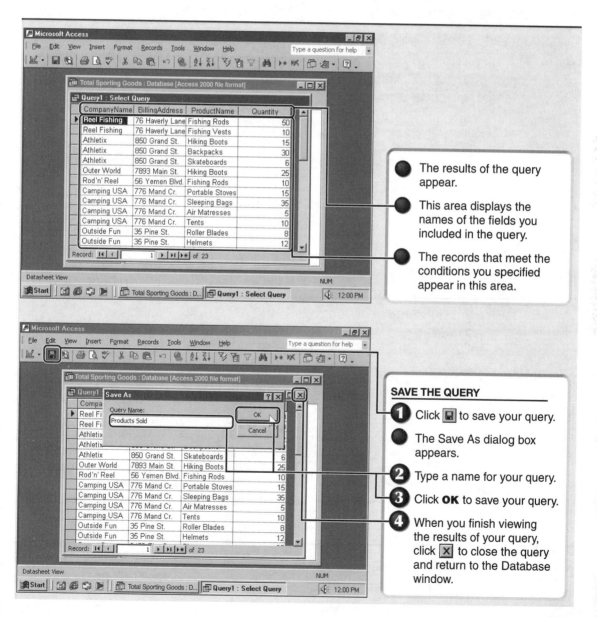

The results of the query appear.

This area displays the names of the fields you included in the query.

The records that meet the conditions you specified appear in this area.

SAVE THE QUERY

1 Click 🖫 to save your query.

The Save As dialog box appears.

2 Type a name for your query.

3 Click **OK** to save your query.

4 When you finish viewing the results of your query, click ✕ to close the query and return to the Database window.

CHANGE VIEW OF QUERY

Access allows you to quickly switch between the Datasheet and Design views of a query. The Datasheet view displays the results of your query. Each row shows the information for one record that meets the criteria or conditions you specified. The Design view allows you to plan your query. You can use this view to specify the data you want to find.

CHANGE VIEW OF QUERY

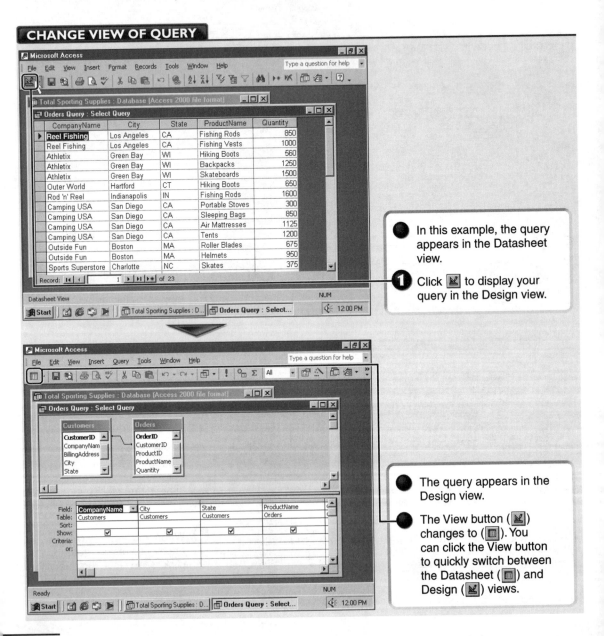

● In this example, the query appears in the Datasheet view.

1 Click 🖾 to display your query in the Design view.

● The query appears in the Design view.

● The View button (🖾) changes to (🔲). You can click the View button to quickly switch between the Datasheet (🔲) and Design (🖾) views.

SORT QUERY RESULTS

You can sort the results of a query to better organize the results. This can help you quickly find information of interest. You can sort the results of a query in ascending or descending order.

SORT QUERY RESULTS

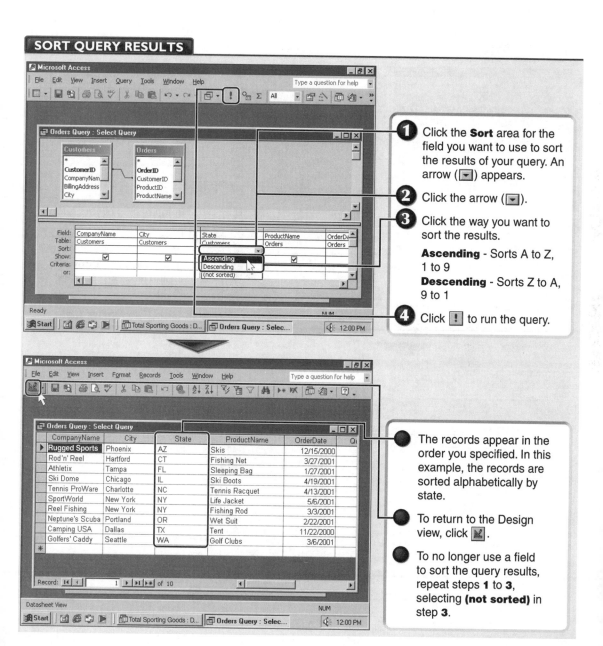

1 Click the **Sort** area for the field you want to use to sort the results of your query. An arrow (▼) appears.

2 Click the arrow (▼).

3 Click the way you want to sort the results.

Ascending - Sorts A to Z, 1 to 9

Descending - Sorts Z to A, 9 to 1

4 Click ❗ to run the query.

● The records appear in the order you specified. In this example, the records are sorted alphabetically by state.

● To return to the Design view, click 📐.

● To no longer use a field to sort the query results, repeat steps **1** to **3**, selecting **(not sorted)** in step **3**.

287

HIDE A FIELD

You can hide a field used in a query. Hiding a field is useful when you need a field to find information in your database, but do not want the field to appear in the results of your query. For example, you can hide the State field if you want to find clients in Florida, but do not want the State field to appear in the query results.

HIDE A FIELD

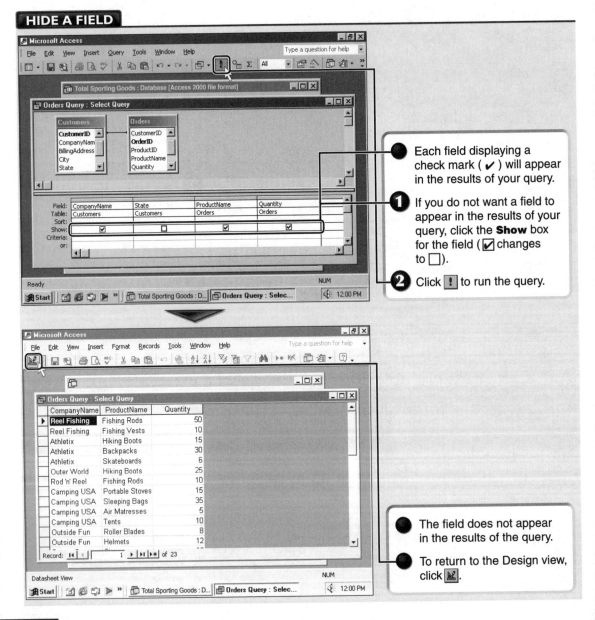

Each field displaying a check mark (✔) will appear in the results of your query.

1 If you do not want a field to appear in the results of your query, click the **Show** box for the field (☑ changes to ☐).

2 Click ! to run the query.

The field does not appear in the results of the query.

To return to the Design view, click .

You can delete a field you no longer need from your query. Deleting a field from a query does not delete the field from the table you used to create the query.

DELETE A FIELD

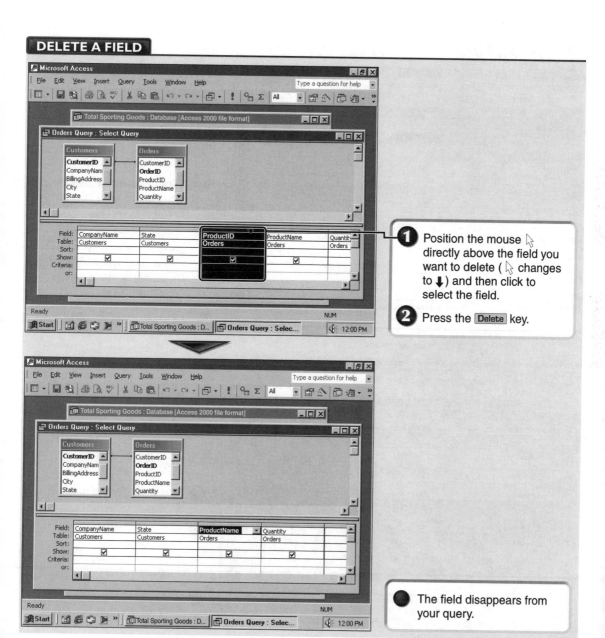

1 Position the mouse ⌖ directly above the field you want to delete (⌖ changes to ↓) and then click to select the field.

2 Press the Delete key.

● The field disappears from your query.

USING CRITERIA

You can use criteria to find specific records in your database. Criteria are conditions that identify which records you want to find. For example, you can use criteria to find customers who live in California.

USING CRITERIA

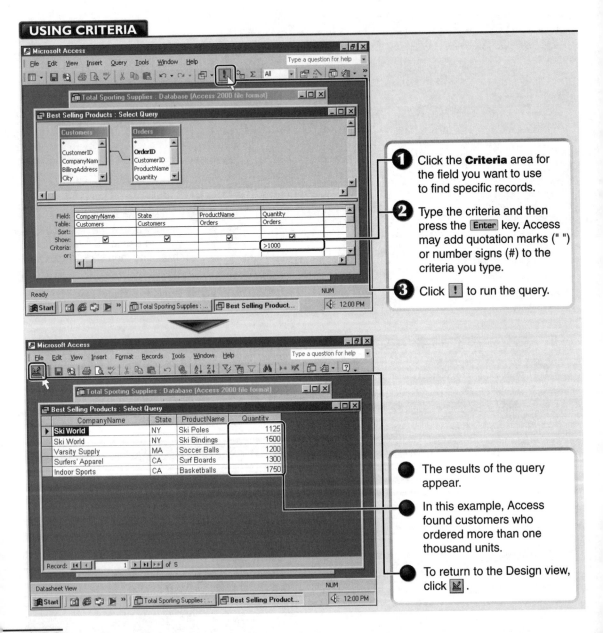

1. Click the **Criteria** area for the field you want to use to find specific records.

2. Type the criteria and then press the [Enter] key. Access may add quotation marks (" ") or number signs (#) to the criteria you type.

3. Click ! to run the query.

● The results of the query appear.

● In this example, Access found customers who ordered more than one thousand units.

● To return to the Design view, click ☒.

Here are examples of criteria that you can use to find records in your database.

EXAMPLES OF CRITERIA

EXACT MATCHES

=100	Finds the number 100.
=California	Finds California.
=5/9/2001	Finds the date 9-May-01.

LESS THAN

<100	Finds numbers less than 100.
<N	Finds text starting with the letters A to M.
<5/9/2001	Finds dates before 9-May-01.

LESS THAN OR EQUAL TO

<=100	Finds numbers less than or equal to 100.
<=N	Finds the letter N and text starting with the letters A to M.
<=5/9/2001	Finds dates on and before 9-May-01.

GREATER THAN

>100	Finds numbers greater than 100.
>N	Finds text starting with the letters N to Z.
>5/9/2001	Finds dates after 9-May-01.

GREATER THAN OR EQUAL TO

>=100	Finds numbers greater than or equal to 100.
>=N	Finds the letter N and text starting with the letters N to Z.
>=5/9/2001	Finds dates on and after 9-May-01.

NOT EQUAL TO

<>100	Finds numbers not equal to 100.
<>California	Finds text not equal to California.
<>5/9/2001	Finds dates not on 9-May-01.

EMPTY FIELDS

Is Null	Finds records that do not contain data in the field.
Is Not Null	Finds records that contain data in the field.

FIND LIST OF ITEMS

In (100,101)	Finds the numbers 100 and 101.
In (California,CA)	Finds California and CA.
In (#5/9/2001#, #5/10/2001#)	Finds the dates 9-May-01 and 10-May-01.

BETWEEN...AND...

Between 100 And 200	Finds numbers from 100 to 200.
Between A And D	Finds the letter D and text starting with the letters A to C.
Between 5/9/2001 And 5/15/2001	Finds dates on and between 9-May-01 and 15-May-01.

CREATE A REPORT

You can use the Report Wizard to create a professionally
designed report that summarizes data from your database. The
Report Wizard asks you a series of questions and then creates
a report based on your answers. You can use any table in your
database to create a report. When creating a report that uses
data from more than one table, the tables must be related.

CREATE A REPORT

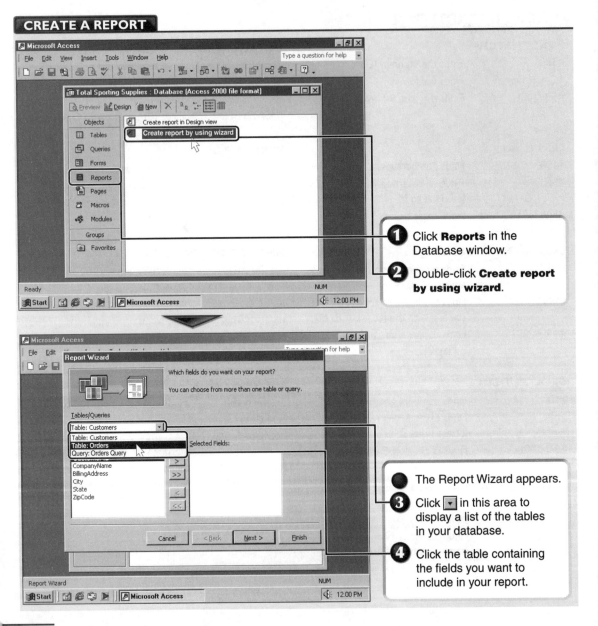

1 Click **Reports** in the
Database window.

2 Double-click **Create report
by using wizard**.

● The Report Wizard appears.

3 Click ▼ in this area to
display a list of the tables
in your database.

4 Click the table containing
the fields you want to
include in your report.

in an *instant*

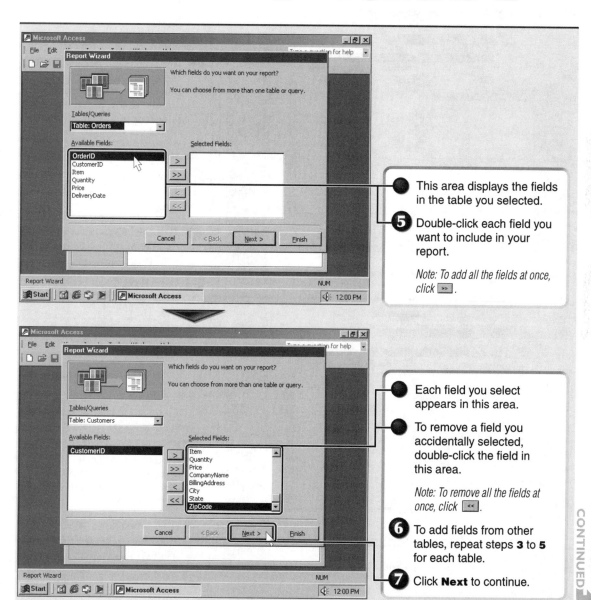

This area displays the fields in the table you selected.

5 Double-click each field you want to include in your report.

Note: To add all the fields at once, click ⧉.

Each field you select appears in this area.

To remove a field you accidentally selected, double-click the field in this area.

Note: To remove all the fields at once, click ⧉.

6 To add fields from other tables, repeat steps **3** to **5** for each table.

7 Click **Next** to continue.

CONTINUED

CREATE A REPORT

You can group data to better organize the data that will appear in your report. Grouping data allows you to place related data together in the report. For example, you can group data by the State field to place all the customers from the same state together.

CREATE A REPORT (CONTINUED)

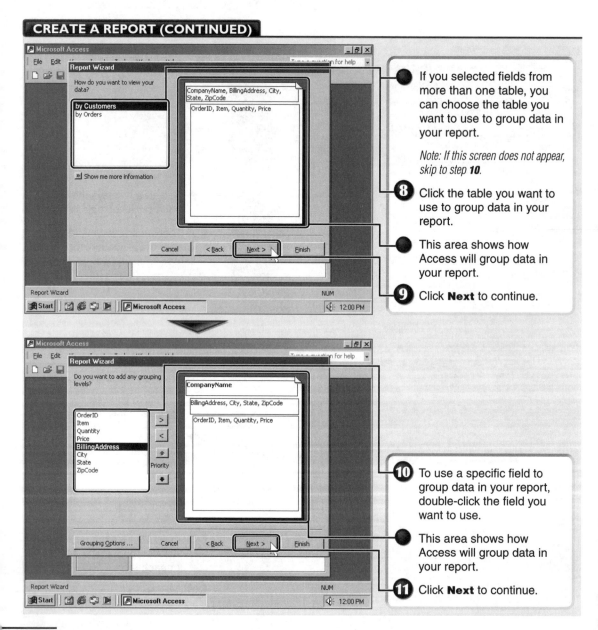

● If you selected fields from more than one table, you can choose the table you want to use to group data in your report.

Note: If this screen does not appear, skip to step 10.

8 Click the table you want to use to group data in your report.

● This area shows how Access will group data in your report.

9 Click **Next** to continue.

10 To use a specific field to group data in your report, double-click the field you want to use.

● This area shows how Access will group data in your report.

11 Click **Next** to continue.

in an instant

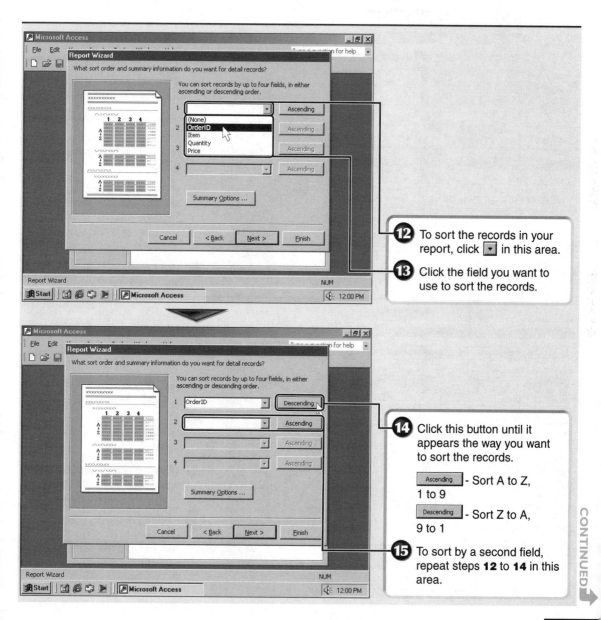

12 To sort the records in your report, click ▼ in this area.

13 Click the field you want to use to sort the records.

14 Click this button until it appears the way you want to sort the records.

Ascending - Sort A to Z, 1 to 9

Descending - Sort Z to A, 9 to 1

15 To sort by a second field, repeat steps **12** to **14** in this area.

CONTINUED ⯈

CREATE A REPORT

You can perform calculations to summarize the data in your report. When you perform calculations, you can have Access display all the records and the summary for each group of records or just the summary for each group in the report. You can also have Access display the percentage of the total that each group of records represents.

CREATE A REPORT (CONTINUED)

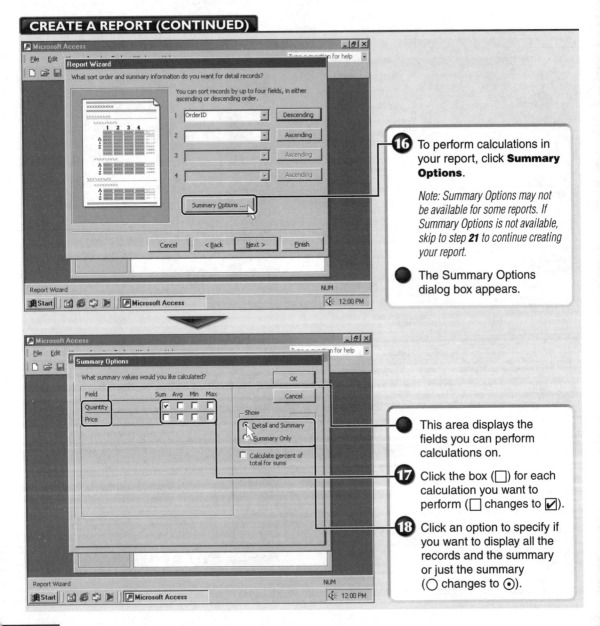

16 To perform calculations in your report, click **Summary Options**.

*Note: Summary Options may not be available for some reports. If Summary Options is not available, skip to step **21** to continue creating your report.*

● The Summary Options dialog box appears.

● This area displays the fields you can perform calculations on.

17 Click the box (☐) for each calculation you want to perform (☐ changes to ☑).

18 Click an option to specify if you want to display all the records and the summary or just the summary (○ changes to ⊙).

296

in an instant

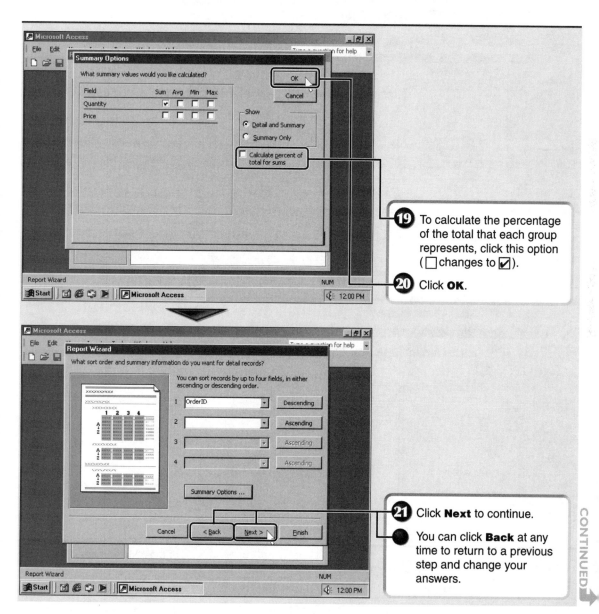

19 To calculate the percentage of the total that each group represents, click this option (☐ changes to ☑).

20 Click **OK**.

21 Click **Next** to continue.

● You can click **Back** at any time to return to a previous step and change your answers.

CREATE A REPORT

You can choose one of several different layouts for your report. The layout determines the arrangement of data in your report. After you finish creating your report, Access displays the report on your screen. Each time you open your report, Access will automatically gather the most current data from your database to create the report.

CREATE A REPORT (CONTINUED)

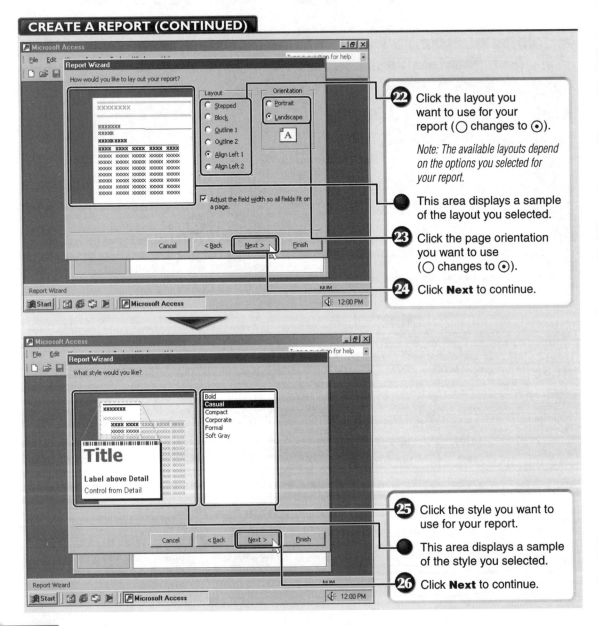

22 Click the layout you want to use for your report (○ changes to ⊙).

Note: The available layouts depend on the options you selected for your report.

● This area displays a sample of the layout you selected.

23 Click the page orientation you want to use (○ changes to ⊙).

24 Click **Next** to continue.

25 Click the style you want to use for your report.

● This area displays a sample of the style you selected.

26 Click **Next** to continue.

in an instant

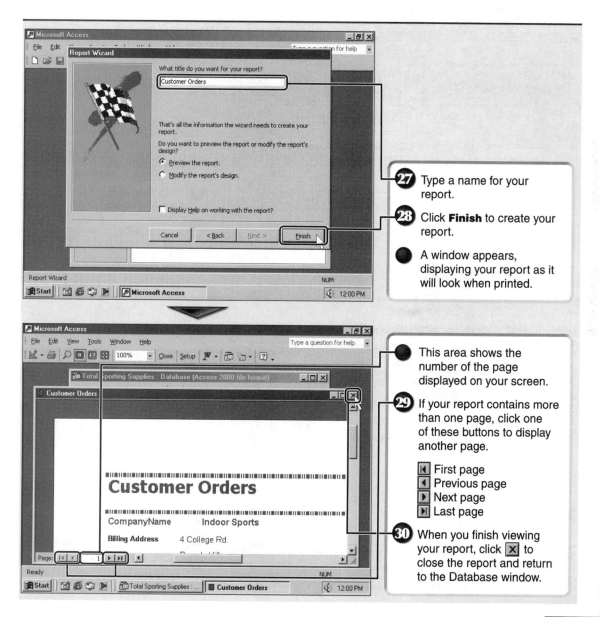

27 Type a name for your report.

28 Click **Finish** to create your report.

● A window appears, displaying your report as it will look when printed.

● This area shows the number of the page displayed on your screen.

29 If your report contains more than one page, click one of these buttons to display another page.

|◄| First page
|◄| Previous page
|►| Next page
|►| Last page

30 When you finish viewing your report, click |×| to close the report and return to the Database window.

299

PRINT A REPORT

You can produce a paper copy of the report displayed on your screen. You can also use the method described below to print a table, form or query in your database. Before printing, you should make sure your printer is turned on and contains paper.

PRINT A REPORT

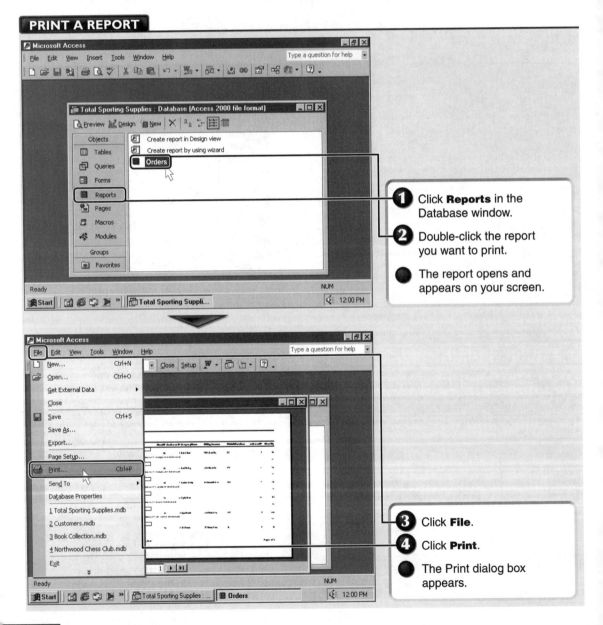

1 Click **Reports** in the Database window.

2 Double-click the report you want to print.

● The report opens and appears on your screen.

3 Click **File**.

4 Click **Print**.

● The Print dialog box appears.

300

in an *instant*

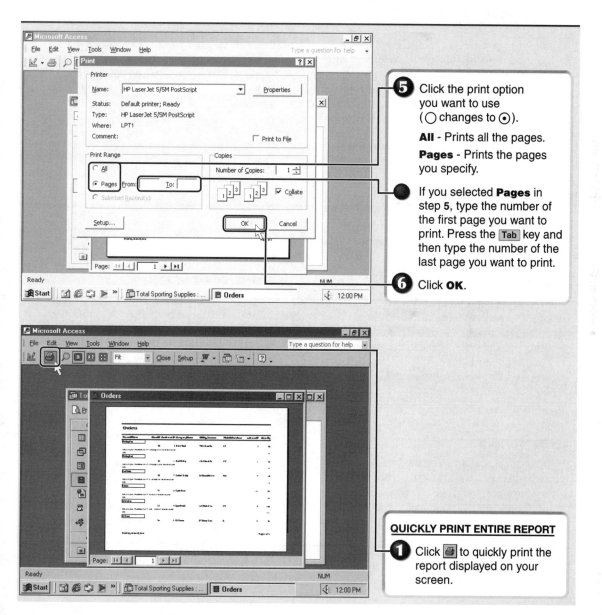

5 Click the print option you want to use (○ changes to ⊙).

All - Prints all the pages.

Pages - Prints the pages you specify.

If you selected **Pages** in step **5**, type the number of the first page you want to print. Press the Tab key and then type the number of the last page you want to print.

6 Click **OK**.

QUICKLY PRINT ENTIRE REPORT

1 Click 🖨 to quickly print the report displayed on your screen.

INTRODUCTION TO OUTLOOK

Outlook is an information management program that can help you keep track of your e-mail messages, appointments, contacts, tasks and notes.

EXCHANGE E-MAIL

You can use Outlook to exchange e-mail messages with friends, family members and colleagues. You can create a new message you want to send or reply to a message you have received. You can also forward a message you have received to another person who would be interested in the message.

You can attach a file, such as a document, picture or video, to a message you are sending. This is useful when you want to include additional information with a message.

MANAGE INFORMATION

Outlook's features allow you to manage several different types of information.

USING THE CALENDAR

You can use the Calendar to keep track of your appointments, such as business meetings, seminars and lunch dates. When using the Calendar, you can choose to view your appointments for the current day, the work week or the entire month.

USING CONTACTS

You can use Outlook's contact list to store information about your friends, colleagues and clients. When you add a contact to the list, you can include information such as the contact's full name, address, business phone number and e-mail address. After you add a contact to the list, you can update the information for the contact at any time.

USING TASKS

You can create an electronic to-do list of tasks that you want to keep track of until they are accomplished. Once you have accomplished a task, you can mark the task as complete. You can also delete a task you no longer want to accomplish.

USING NOTES

You can create electronic notes that are similar to paper sticky notes. Notes are ideal for storing reminders, questions or ideas. Outlook records the current date and time at the bottom of each note you create to help you keep track of your notes.

THE OUTLOOK WINDOW

The Outlook window displays several items
to help you perform tasks efficiently.

THE OUTLOOK WINDOW

Title Bar

Shows the name of the
Outlook feature you are
currently working with.

View Pane

Displays the Outlook
feature you are currently
working with.

Menu Bar

Provides access to
lists of commands
available in Outlook
and displays an area
where you can type
a question to get
help information.

Toolbar

Contains buttons
to help you select
common commands,
such as Print and
Delete.

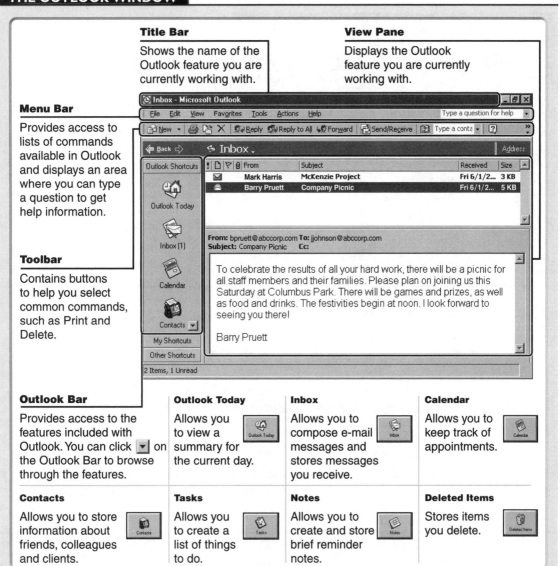

Outlook Bar

Provides access to the
features included with
Outlook. You can click ▼ on
the Outlook Bar to browse
through the features.

Outlook Today

Allows you
to view a
summary for
the current day.

Inbox

Allows you to
compose e-mail
messages and
stores messages
you receive.

Calendar

Allows you to
keep track of
appointments.

Contacts

Allows you to store
information about
friends, colleagues
and clients.

Tasks

Allows you
to create a
list of things
to do.

Notes

Allows you to
create and store
brief reminder
notes.

Deleted Items

Stores items
you delete.

303

READ MESSAGES

Outlook uses several folders to store your e-mail messages. The Inbox folder stores the messages you receive. The Drafts folder stores messages you have not yet completed. The Outbox folder temporarily stores messages that have not yet been sent and the Sent Items folder stores copies of messages that have been sent. You can open a message to read the contents of the message.

READ MESSAGES

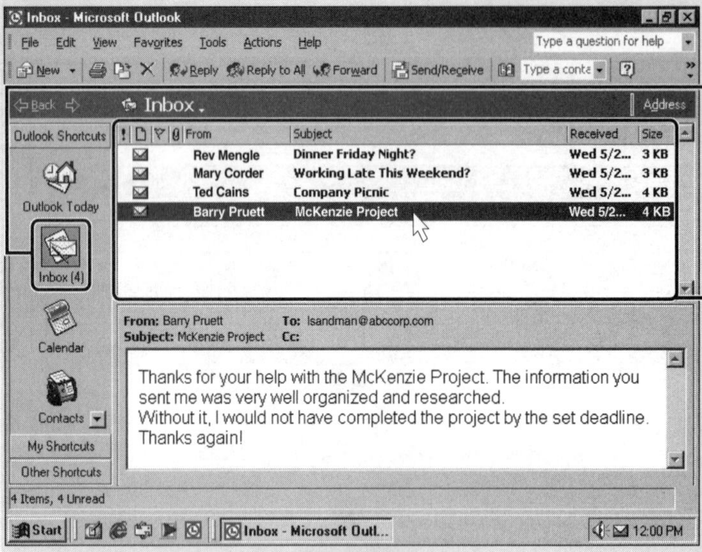

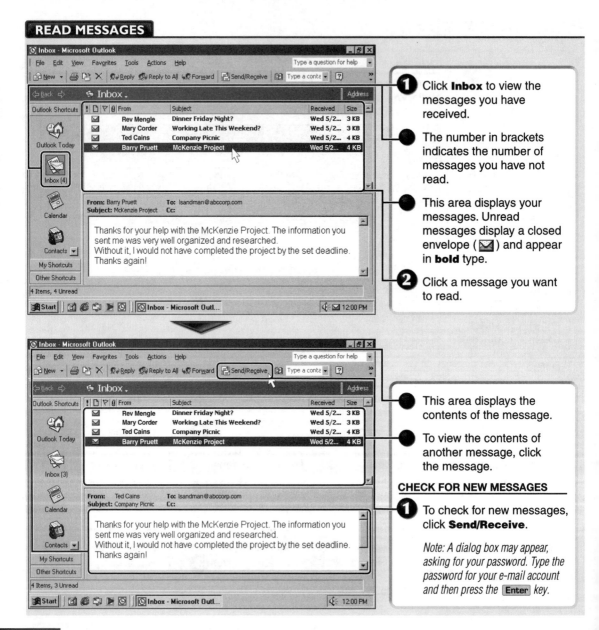

1. Click **Inbox** to view the messages you have received.

- The number in brackets indicates the number of messages you have not read.

- This area displays your messages. Unread messages display a closed envelope ( ) and appear in **bold** type.

2. Click a message you want to read.

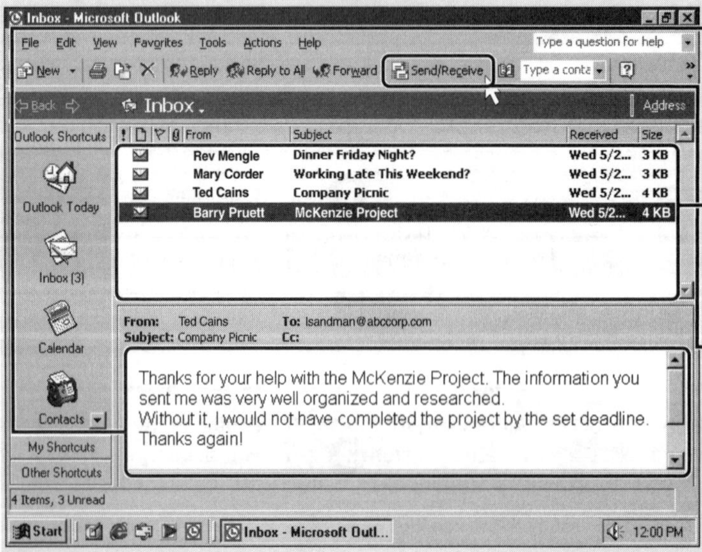

- This area displays the contents of the message.

- To view the contents of another message, click the message.

CHECK FOR NEW MESSAGES

1. To check for new messages, click **Send/Receive**.

Note: A dialog box may appear, asking for your password. Type the password for your e-mail account and then press the Enter *key.*

in an *Instant*

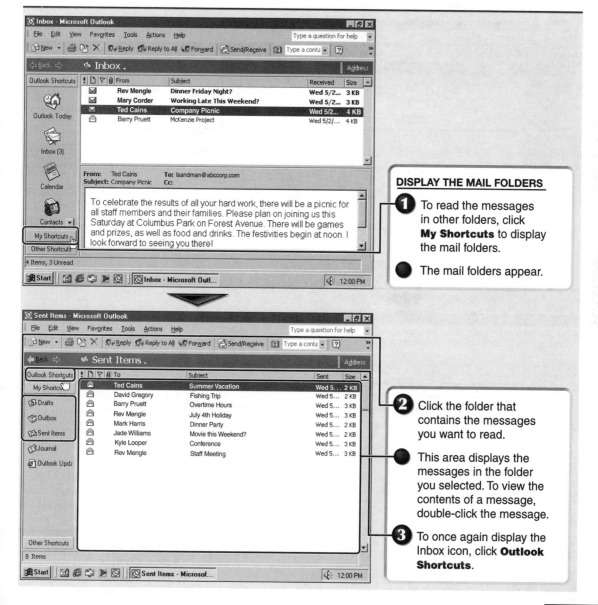

DISPLAY THE MAIL FOLDERS

1 To read the messages in other folders, click **My Shortcuts** to display the mail folders.

● The mail folders appear.

2 Click the folder that contains the messages you want to read.

● This area displays the messages in the folder you selected. To view the contents of a message, double-click the message.

3 To once again display the Inbox icon, click **Outlook Shortcuts**.

SEND A MESSAGE

You can send an e-mail message to express an idea or request information. When sending an e-mail message, you must specify the e-mail address of each person you want to receive the message. You can also send a copy of the message to people who are not directly involved but would be interested in the message.

SEND A MESSAGE

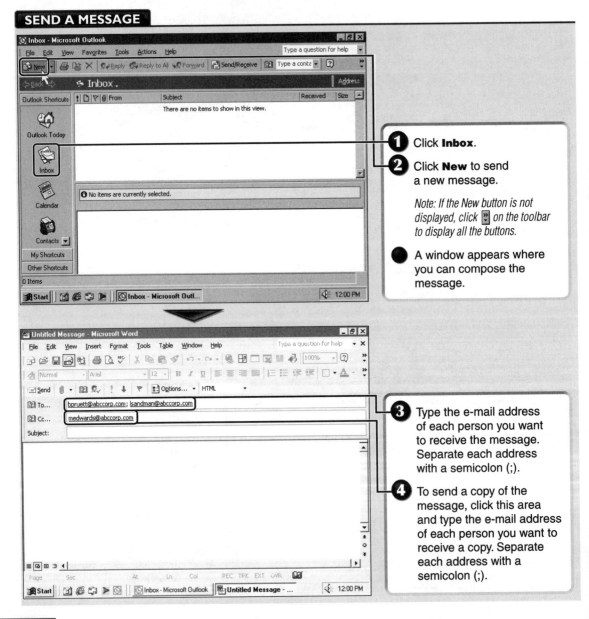

1 Click **Inbox**.

2 Click **New** to send a new message.

Note: If the New button is not displayed, click ☒ on the toolbar to display all the buttons.

● A window appears where you can compose the message.

3 Type the e-mail address of each person you want to receive the message. Separate each address with a semicolon (;).

4 To send a copy of the message, click this area and type the e-mail address of each person you want to receive a copy. Separate each address with a semicolon (;).

in an instant

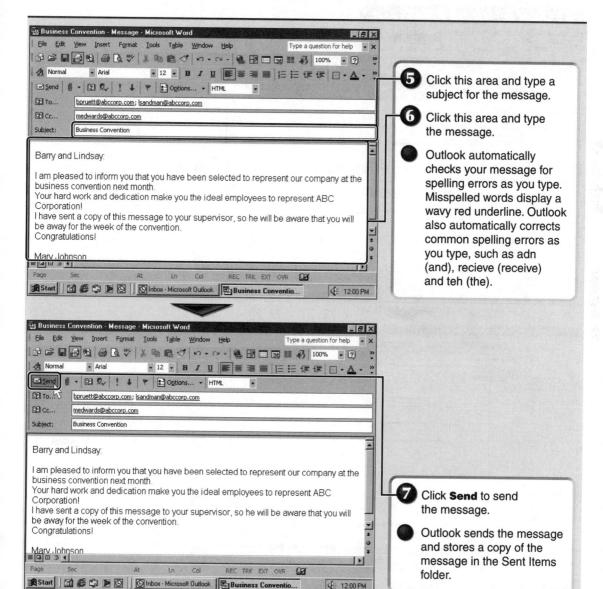

5 Click this area and type a subject for the message.

6 Click this area and type the message.

● Outlook automatically checks your message for spelling errors as you type. Misspelled words display a wavy red underline. Outlook also automatically corrects common spelling errors as you type, such as adn (and), recieve (receive) and teh (the).

7 Click **Send** to send the message.

● Outlook sends the message and stores a copy of the message in the Sent Items folder.

ATTACH A FILE TO A MESSAGE

You can attach a file to a message you are sending. Attaching a file is
useful when you want to include additional information with a message.
You can attach many types of files to a message, including documents,
pictures, videos and sounds. The computer receiving the message must
have the necessary hardware and software installed to display or play
the file you attached.

ATTACH A FILE TO A MESSAGE

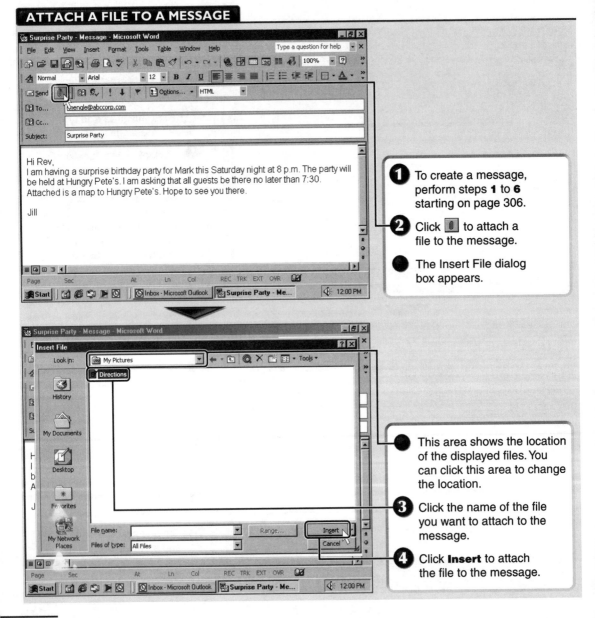

1 To create a message,
perform steps **1** to **6**
starting on page 306.

2 Click 📎 to attach a
file to the message.

■ The Insert File dialog
box appears.

■ This area shows the location
of the displayed files. You
can click this area to change
the location.

3 Click the name of the file
you want to attach to the
message.

4 Click **Insert** to attach
the file to the message.

in an *instant*

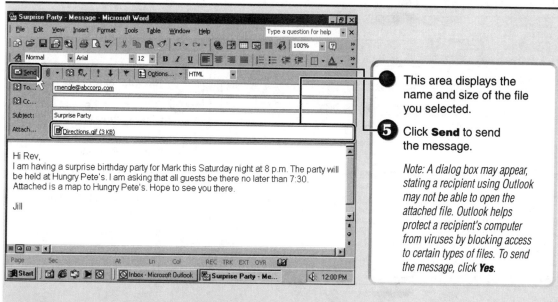

This area displays the name and size of the file you selected.

5 Click **Send** to send the message.

*Note: A dialog box may appear, stating a recipient using Outlook may not be able to open the attached file. Outlook helps protect a recipient's computer from viruses by blocking access to certain types of files. To send the message, click **Yes**.*

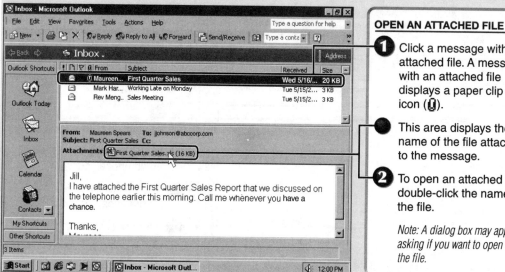

OPEN AN ATTACHED FILE

1 Click a message with an attached file. A message with an attached file displays a paper clip icon (📎).

This area displays the name of the file attached to the message.

2 To open an attached file, double-click the name of the file.

Note: A dialog box may appear, asking if you want to open or save the file.

REPLY TO A MESSAGE

You can reply to a message to answer a question, express an opinion or supply additional information. You can send a reply to just the person who sent the message or to the sender and everyone who received the original message.

REPLY TO A MESSAGE

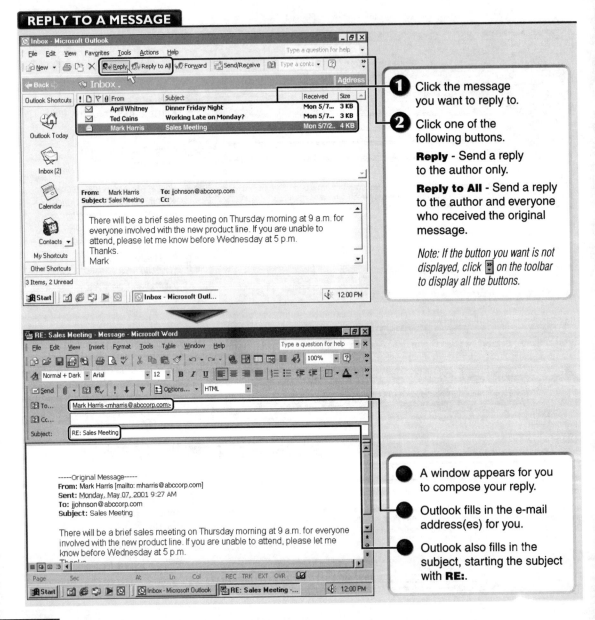

① Click the message you want to reply to.

② Click one of the following buttons.

Reply - Send a reply to the author only.

Reply to All - Send a reply to the author and everyone who received the original message.

Note: If the button you want is not displayed, click ☒ on the toolbar to display all the buttons.

● A window appears for you to compose your reply.

● Outlook fills in the e-mail address(es) for you.

● Outlook also fills in the subject, starting the subject with **RE:**.

in an instant

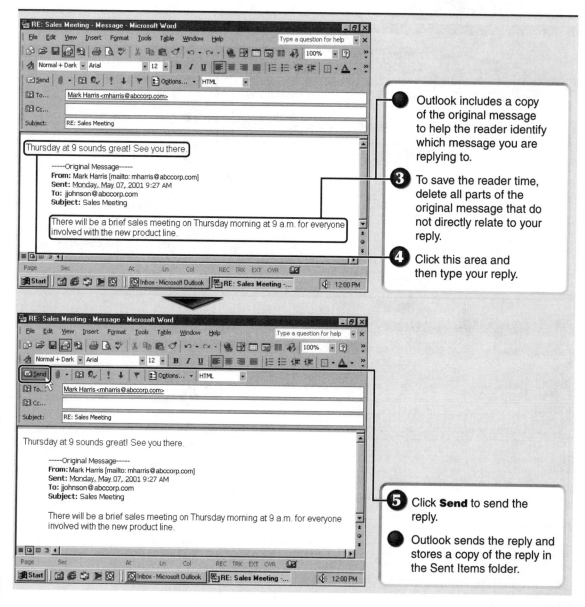

Outlook includes a copy of the original message to help the reader identify which message you are replying to.

3 To save the reader time, delete all parts of the original message that do not directly relate to your reply.

4 Click this area and then type your reply.

5 Click **Send** to send the reply.

Outlook sends the reply and stores a copy of the reply in the Sent Items folder.

FORWARD A MESSAGE

After reading a message, you can add comments and then
forward the message to a friend, family member or colleague.
Forwarding a message is useful when another person would
be interested in the contents of the message.

FORWARD A MESSAGE

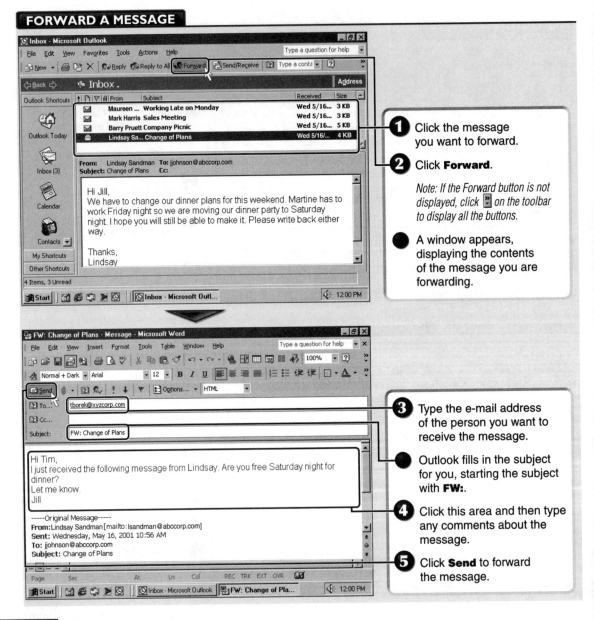

1 Click the message
you want to forward.

2 Click **Forward**.

Note: If the Forward button is not
displayed, click 🔽 on the toolbar
to display all the buttons.

● A window appears,
displaying the contents
of the message you are
forwarding.

3 Type the e-mail address
of the person you want to
receive the message.

● Outlook fills in the subject
for you, starting the subject
with **FW:**.

4 Click this area and then type
any comments about the
message.

5 Click **Send** to forward
the message.

You can delete messages you no longer need to prevent
your folders from becoming cluttered with messages.
Outlook places the messages you delete in the Deleted
Items folder. This folder stores all the items you delete
in Outlook.

DELETE A MESSAGE

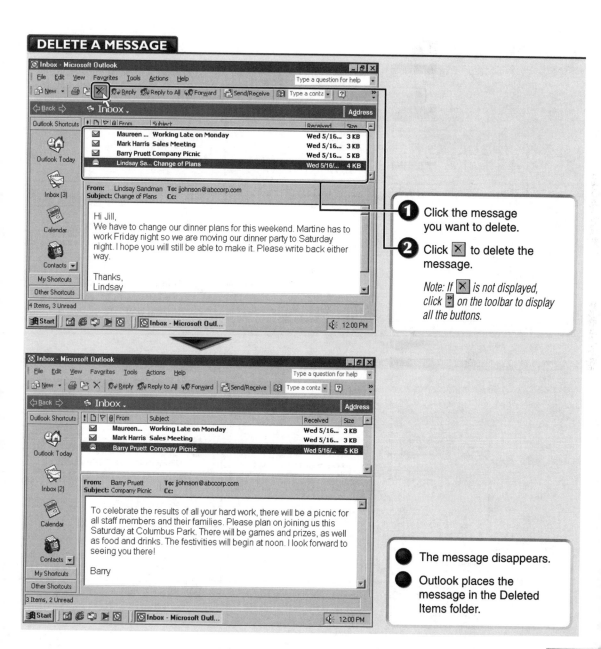

1 Click the message
you want to delete.

2 Click ☒ to delete the
message.

*Note: If ☒ is not displayed,
click ⁂ on the toolbar to display
all the buttons.*

● The message disappears.

● Outlook places the
message in the Deleted
Items folder.

USING THE CALENDAR

You can use the Calendar to keep track of your appointments, such as business meetings and lunch dates. Outlook uses the date and time set in your computer to determine today's date. To change the date and time set in your computer, refer to your Windows manual.

USING THE CALENDAR

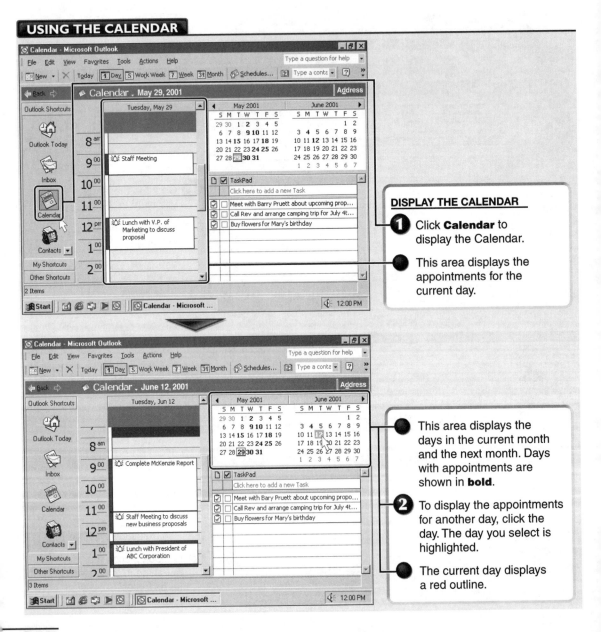

DISPLAY THE CALENDAR

1 Click **Calendar** to display the Calendar.

● This area displays the appointments for the current day.

● This area displays the days in the current month and the next month. Days with appointments are shown in **bold**.

2 To display the appointments for another day, click the day. The day you select is highlighted.

● The current day displays a red outline.

in an *instant*

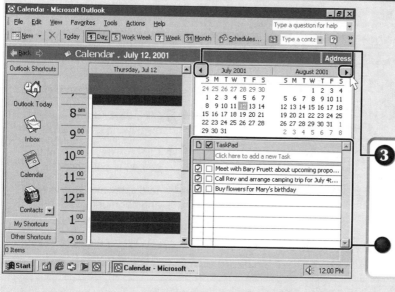

3 To display the days in another month, click one of the following options.

◀ Display previous month
▶ Display next month

● This area displays your tasks.

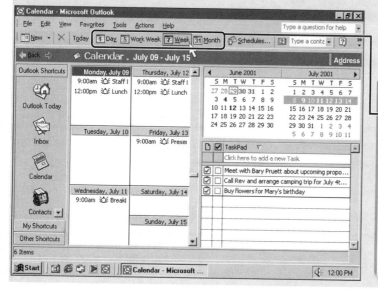

CHANGE VIEW OF CALENDAR

1 Click the button for the way you want to view the Calendar.

1 Day	Day
5 Work Week	Work Week
7 Week	Week
31 Month	Month

Note: If the button you want is not displayed, click ▸ on the toolbar to display all the buttons.

USING THE CALENDAR

You can add an appointment to the Calendar to have
Outlook remind you of an activity such as a seminar or
doctor appointment. You can also delete an appointment
that has been cancelled or that you no longer want to keep.

USING THE CALENDAR (CONTINUED)

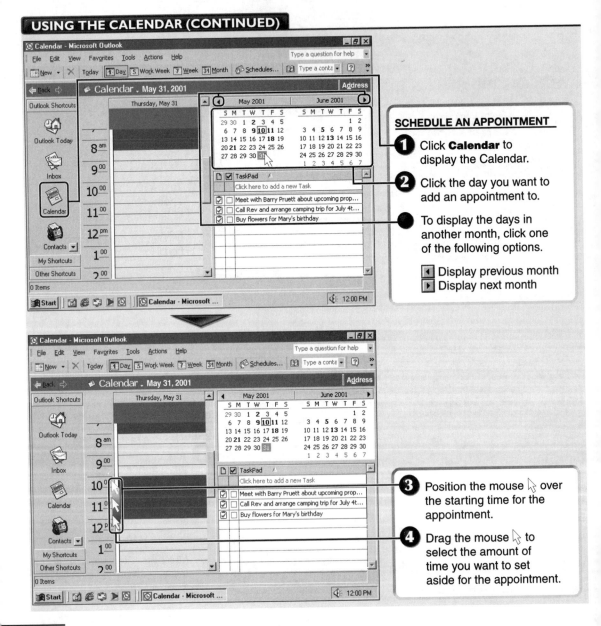

SCHEDULE AN APPOINTMENT

1 Click **Calendar** to
display the Calendar.

2 Click the day you want to
add an appointment to.

● To display the days in
another month, click one
of the following options.

◄ Display previous month
► Display next month

3 Position the mouse ⬚ over
the starting time for the
appointment.

4 Drag the mouse ⬚ to
select the amount of
time you want to set
aside for the appointment.

in an *instant*

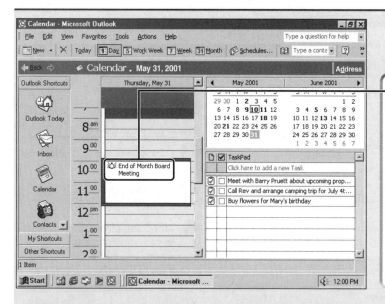

⑤ Type a subject for the appointment and then press the Enter key.

● To remind you of an appointment you have scheduled, Outlook will play a brief sound and display the Reminder dialog box 15 minutes before the scheduled appointment. To close the Reminder dialog box, click the **Dismiss** button.

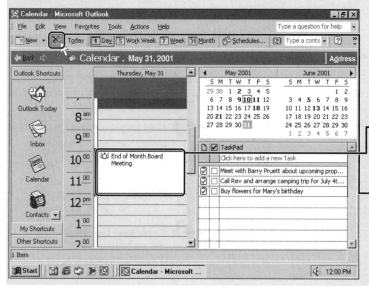

DELETE AN APPOINTMENT

① To select the appointment you want to delete, click the left edge of the appointment (↖ changes to ✥).

② Click ✕ to delete the appointment.

Note: If ✕ is not displayed, click ⁑ on the toolbar to display all the buttons.

USING CONTACTS

Outlook includes a contact list you can use to store information about your friends, family members, colleagues and clients. When you add a contact to the list, Outlook provides several areas where you can enter detailed information about the contact, such as the contact's full name, address, business phone number and e-mail address. You do not need to enter information in every area Outlook provides.

USING CONTACTS

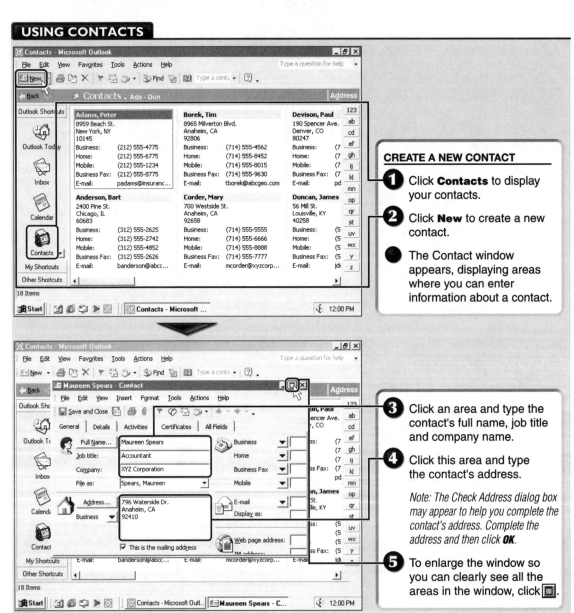

CREATE A NEW CONTACT

1 Click **Contacts** to display your contacts.

2 Click **New** to create a new contact.

● The Contact window appears, displaying areas where you can enter information about a contact.

3 Click an area and type the contact's full name, job title and company name.

4 Click this area and type the contact's address.

Note: The Check Address dialog box may appear to help you complete the contact's address. Complete the address and then click OK.

5 To enlarge the window so you can clearly see all the areas in the window, click ⬜.

in an instant

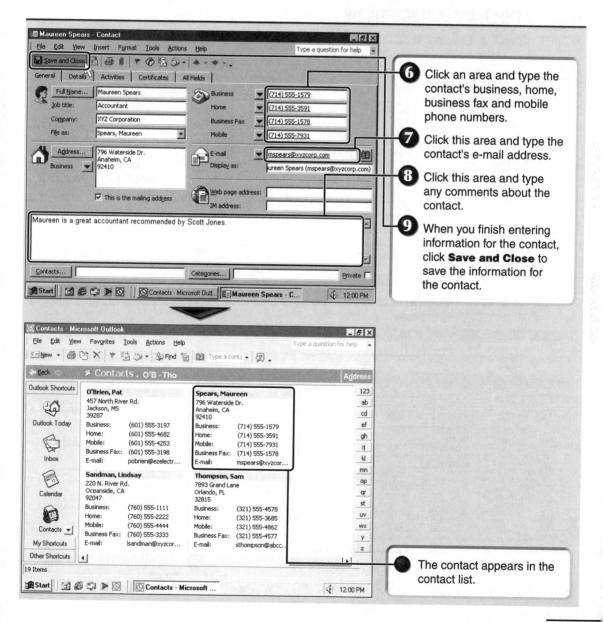

6 Click an area and type the contact's business, home, business fax and mobile phone numbers.

7 Click this area and type the contact's e-mail address.

8 Click this area and type any comments about the contact.

9 When you finish entering information for the contact, click **Save and Close** to save the information for the contact.

● The contact appears in the contact list.

USING CONTACTS

You can browse through your contacts to find the contact you want to work with. After you find the contact, you can remove the contact or update the information for the contact. Removing contacts you no longer need can help make the contact list smaller and easier to manage.

USING CONTACTS (CONTINUED)

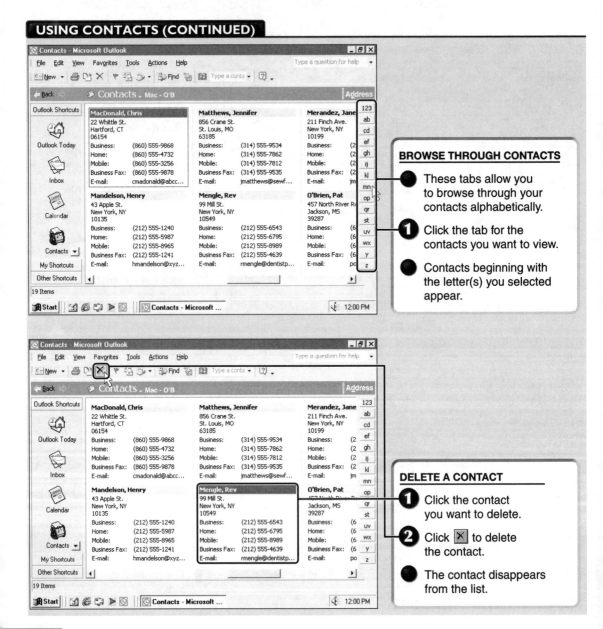

BROWSE THROUGH CONTACTS

● These tabs allow you to browse through your contacts alphabetically.

1 Click the tab for the contacts you want to view.

● Contacts beginning with the letter(s) you selected appear.

DELETE A CONTACT

1 Click the contact you want to delete.

2 Click ☒ to delete the contact.

● The contact disappears from the list.

in an instant

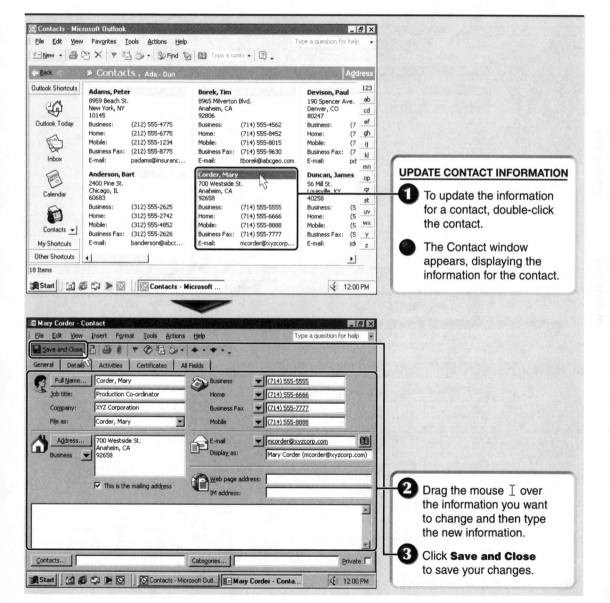

UPDATE CONTACT INFORMATION

1 To update the information for a contact, double-click the contact.

● The Contact window appears, displaying the information for the contact.

2 Drag the mouse I over the information you want to change and then type the new information.

3 Click **Save and Close** to save your changes.

USING TASKS

You can create an electronic to-do list of personal and work-related tasks that you want to accomplish. When adding a task to the list, you can specify a subject and due date for the task. Once you have accomplished a task, you can mark the task as complete.

USING TASKS

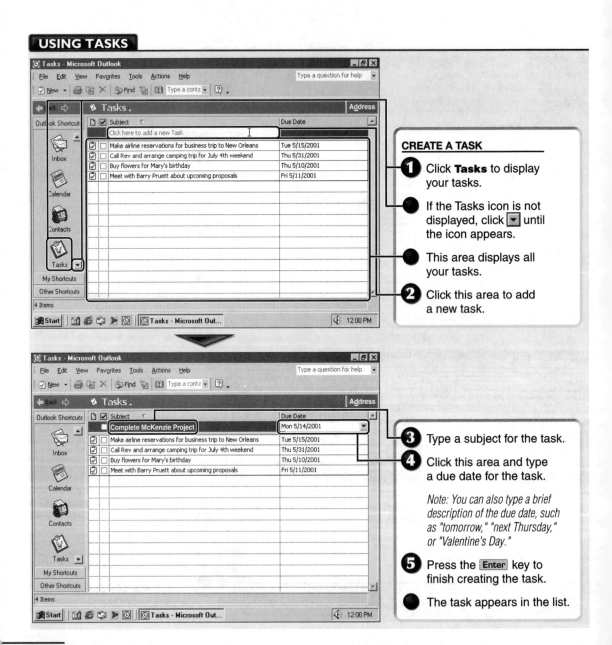

CREATE A TASK

1 Click **Tasks** to display your tasks.

● If the Tasks icon is not displayed, click ▼ until the icon appears.

● This area displays all your tasks.

2 Click this area to add a new task.

3 Type a subject for the task.

4 Click this area and type a due date for the task.

Note: You can also type a brief description of the due date, such as "tomorrow," "next Thursday," or "Valentine's Day."

5 Press the Enter key to finish creating the task.

● The task appears in the list.

in an instant

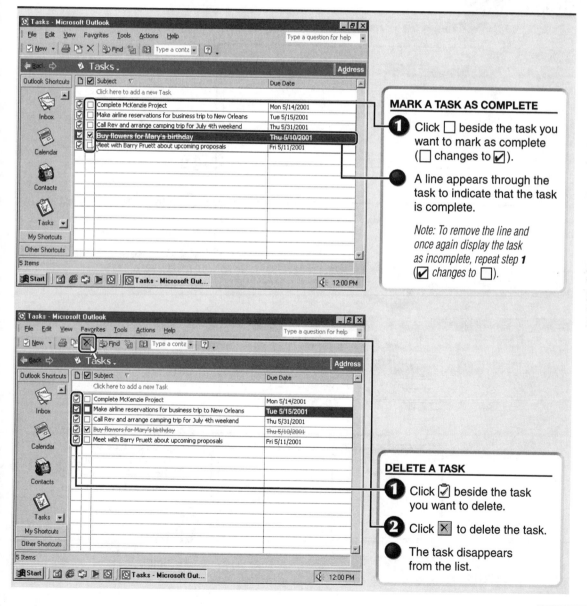

MARK A TASK AS COMPLETE

1 Click ☐ beside the task you want to mark as complete (☐ changes to ☑).

● A line appears through the task to indicate that the task is complete.

Note: To remove the line and once again display the task as incomplete, repeat step 1 (☑ changes to ☐).

DELETE A TASK

1 Click ☑ beside the task you want to delete.

2 Click ☒ to delete the task.

● The task disappears from the list.

323

USING NOTES

You can create electronic notes that are similar to paper sticky notes. Notes are useful for storing small pieces of information, such as reminders, questions, ideas or directions. When you create a note, Outlook records the current date and time at the bottom of the note. This information can help you identify notes that are no longer current.

USING NOTES

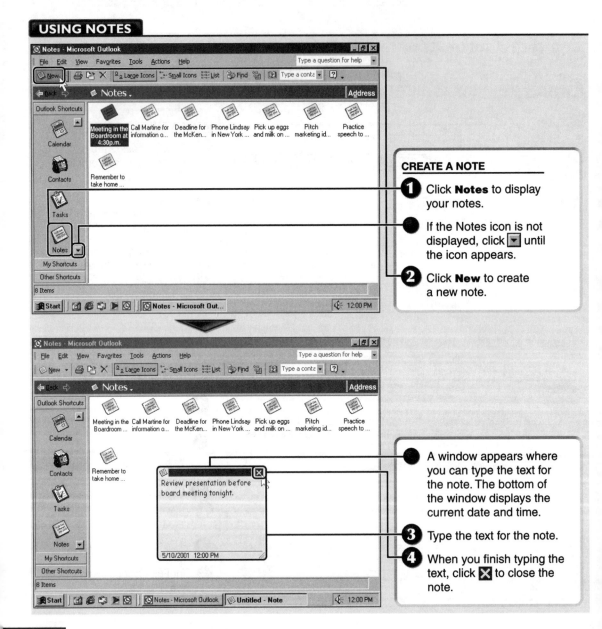

CREATE A NOTE

1 Click **Notes** to display your notes.

◆ If the Notes icon is not displayed, click ▼ until the icon appears.

2 Click **New** to create a new note.

◆ A window appears where you can type the text for the note. The bottom of the window displays the current date and time.

3 Type the text for the note.

4 When you finish typing the text, click ⊠ to close the note.

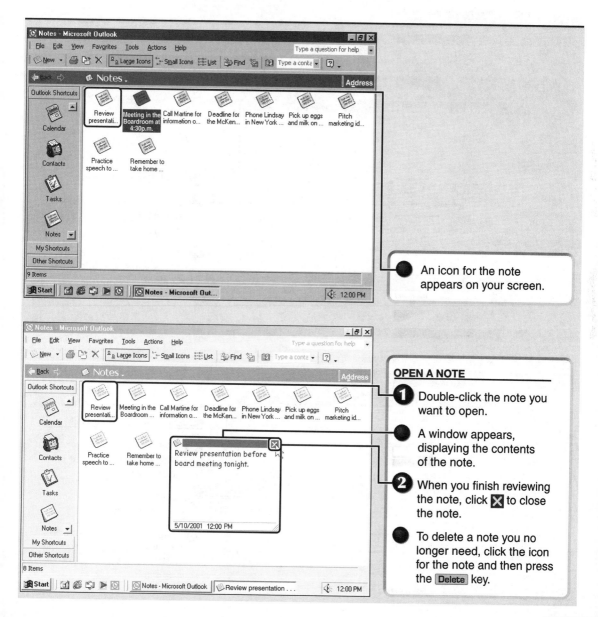

An icon for the note appears on your screen.

OPEN A NOTE

Double-click the note you want to open.

A window appears, displaying the contents of the note.

When you finish reviewing the note, click ⊠ to close the note.

To delete a note you no longer need, click the icon for the note and then press the Delete key.

USING DELETED ITEMS

The Deleted Items folder stores items you have deleted in Outlook. You can recover an item you accidentally deleted. You can also empty the Deleted Items folder to permanently remove all the items from the folder. You should regularly empty the folder to save space on your computer.

USING DELETED ITEMS

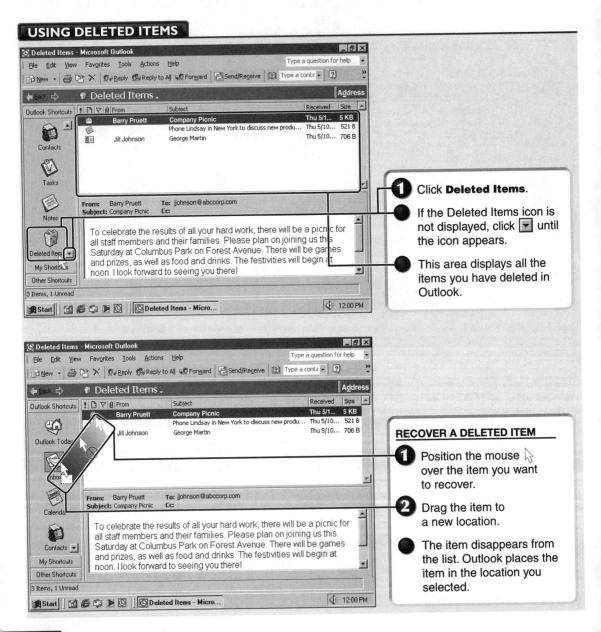

1 Click **Deleted Items**.

● If the Deleted Items icon is not displayed, click ▼ until the icon appears.

● This area displays all the items you have deleted in Outlook.

RECOVER A DELETED ITEM

1 Position the mouse ▷ over the item you want to recover.

2 Drag the item to a new location.

● The item disappears from the list. Outlook places the item in the location you selected.

in an *instant*

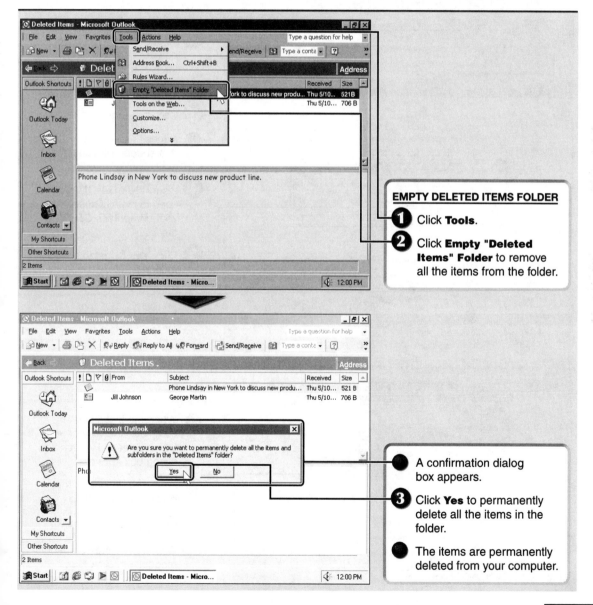

EMPTY DELETED ITEMS FOLDER

1 Click **Tools**.

2 Click **Empty "Deleted Items" Folder** to remove all the items from the folder.

● A confirmation dialog box appears.

3 Click **Yes** to permanently delete all the items in the folder.

● The items are permanently deleted from your computer.

SET UP SPEECH RECOGNITION

Speech recognition allows you to use your voice to enter text and select commands in Office programs. You should set up speech recognition in Word. Once speech recognition is set up, it will be available in all your Office programs. Before setting up speech recognition, make sure your microphone and speakers are connected to your computer. For best results, you should use a headset microphone.

SET UP SPEECH RECOGNITION

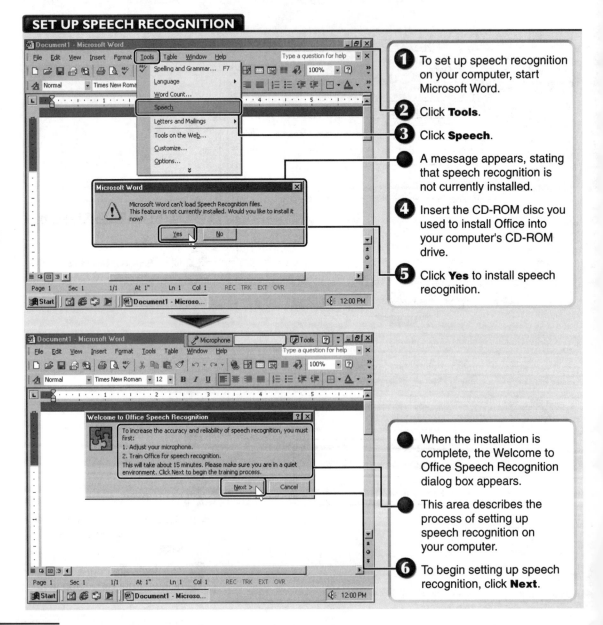

1 To set up speech recognition on your computer, start Microsoft Word.

2 Click **Tools**.

3 Click **Speech**.

● A message appears, stating that speech recognition is not currently installed.

4 Insert the CD-ROM disc you used to install Office into your computer's CD-ROM drive.

5 Click **Yes** to install speech recognition.

● When the installation is complete, the Welcome to Office Speech Recognition dialog box appears.

● This area describes the process of setting up speech recognition on your computer.

6 To begin setting up speech recognition, click **Next**.

in an *instant*

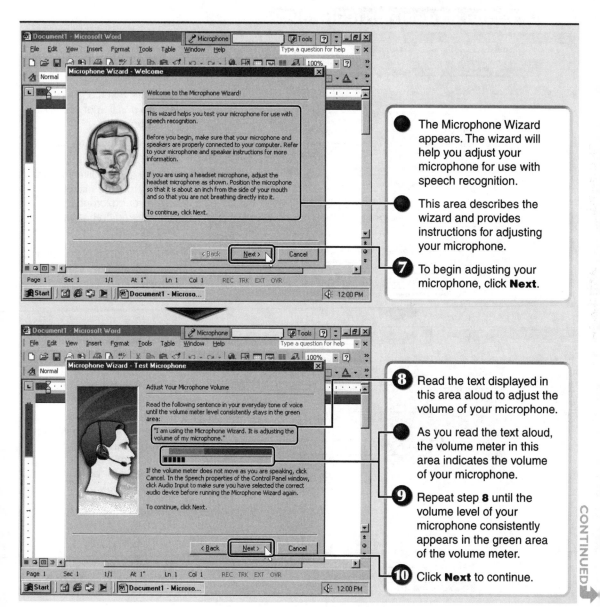

● The Microphone Wizard appears. The wizard will help you adjust your microphone for use with speech recognition.

● This area describes the wizard and provides instructions for adjusting your microphone.

7 To begin adjusting your microphone, click **Next**.

8 Read the text displayed in this area aloud to adjust the volume of your microphone.

● As you read the text aloud, the volume meter in this area indicates the volume of your microphone.

9 Repeat step **8** until the volume level of your microphone consistently appears in the green area of the volume meter.

10 Click **Next** to continue.

CONTINUED ▶

329

You can train speech recognition to recognize how you speak. The Microsoft Speech Recognition Training Wizard takes you step by step through the process of training speech recognition. During the training and when using speech recognition, you should speak in your everyday tone of voice, pronouncing words clearly and not pausing between words. You should also speak at a consistent speed.

SET UP SPEECH RECOGNITION (CONTINUED)

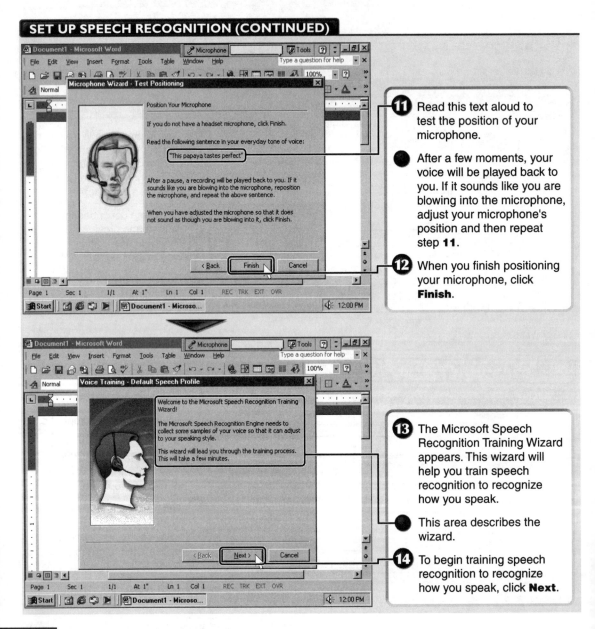

⓫ Read this text aloud to test the position of your microphone.

● After a few moments, your voice will be played back to you. If it sounds like you are blowing into the microphone, adjust your microphone's position and then repeat step **11**.

⓬ When you finish positioning your microphone, click **Finish**.

⓭ The Microsoft Speech Recognition Training Wizard appears. This wizard will help you train speech recognition to recognize how you speak.

● This area describes the wizard.

⓮ To begin training speech recognition to recognize how you speak, click **Next**.

in an *instant*

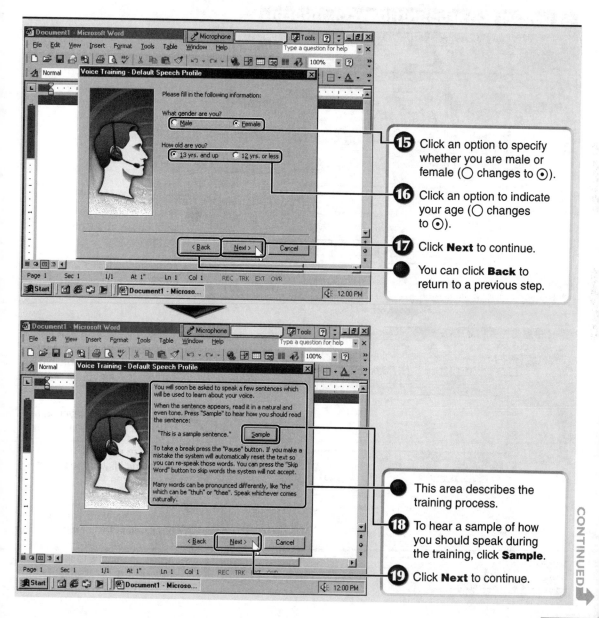

15 Click an option to specify whether you are male or female (○ changes to ⊙).

16 Click an option to indicate your age (○ changes to ⊙).

17 Click **Next** to continue.

● You can click **Back** to return to a previous step.

● This area describes the training process.

18 To hear a sample of how you should speak during the training, click **Sample**.

19 Click **Next** to continue.

CONTINUED

SET UP SPEECH RECOGNITION

The Microsoft Speech Recognition Training Wizard provides text you can read aloud to train speech recognition. You should train speech recognition in a quiet area so that background noise does not interfere with the sound of your voice. After you finish training speech recognition, a video introducing you to speech recognition will appear on your screen.

SET UP SPEECH RECOGNITION (CONTINUED)

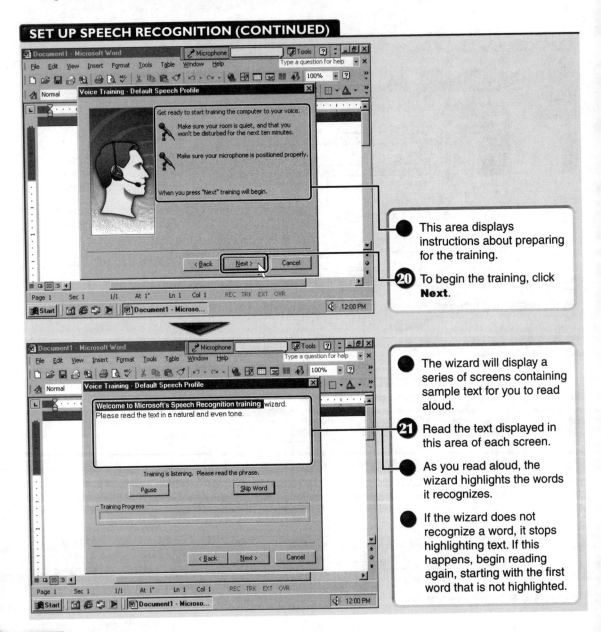

This area displays instructions about preparing for the training.

20 To begin the training, click **Next**.

The wizard will display a series of screens containing sample text for you to read aloud.

21 Read the text displayed in this area of each screen.

As you read aloud, the wizard highlights the words it recognizes.

If the wizard does not recognize a word, it stops highlighting text. If this happens, begin reading again, starting with the first word that is not highlighted.

in an instant

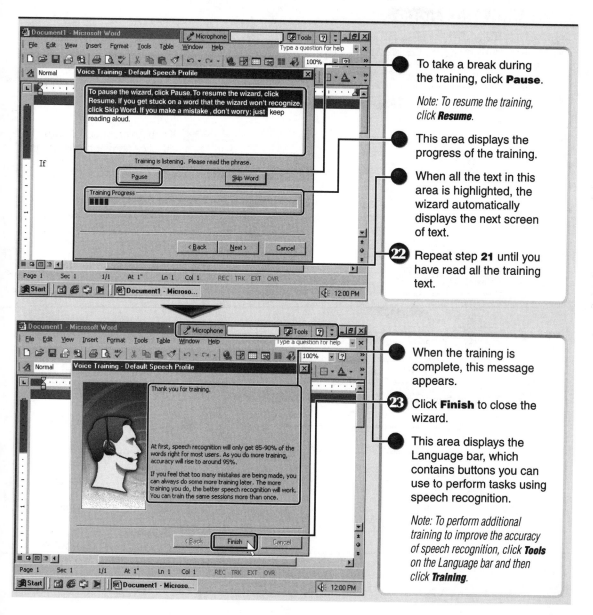

● To take a break during the training, click **Pause**.

*Note: To resume the training, click **Resume**.*

● This area displays the progress of the training.

● When all the text in this area is highlighted, the wizard automatically displays the next screen of text.

22 Repeat step **21** until you have read all the training text.

● When the training is complete, this message appears.

23 Click **Finish** to close the wizard.

● This area displays the Language bar, which contains buttons you can use to perform tasks using speech recognition.

*Note: To perform additional training to improve the accuracy of speech recognition, click **Tools** on the Language bar and then click **Training**.*

USING DICTATION MODE

Once you have set up speech recognition on your computer, you can use Dictation mode to enter text into an Office program using your voice. Speech recognition is designed to be used along with your mouse and keyboard. You can use your voice to enter text into an Office program and then use your mouse and keyboard to edit the text you entered.

USING DICTATION MODE

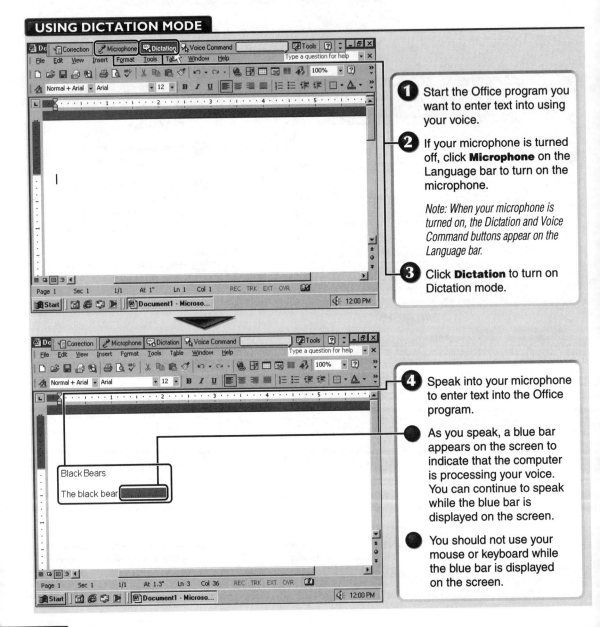

1 Start the Office program you want to enter text into using your voice.

2 If your microphone is turned off, click **Microphone** on the Language bar to turn on the microphone.

Note: When your microphone is turned on, the Dictation and Voice Command buttons appear on the Language bar.

3 Click **Dictation** to turn on Dictation mode.

4 Speak into your microphone to enter text into the Office program.

● As you speak, a blue bar appears on the screen to indicate that the computer is processing your voice. You can continue to speak while the blue bar is displayed on the screen.

● You should not use your mouse or keyboard while the blue bar is displayed on the screen.

in an instant

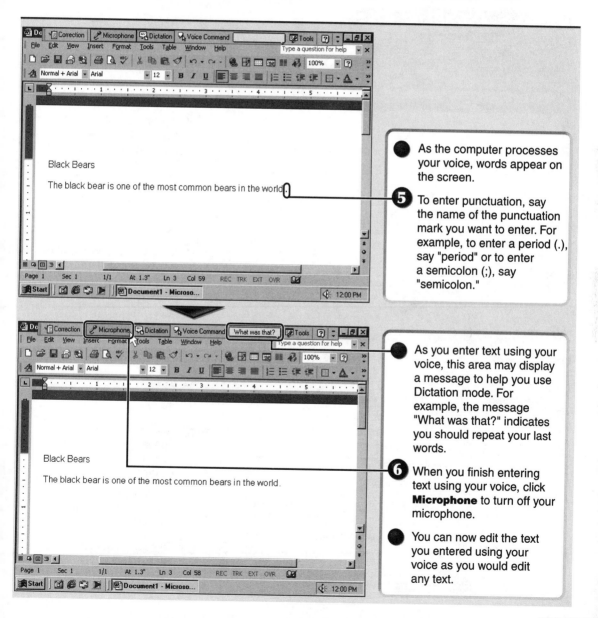

● As the computer processes your voice, words appear on the screen.

5 To enter punctuation, say the name of the punctuation mark you want to enter. For example, to enter a period (.), say "period" or to enter a semicolon (;), say "semicolon."

● As you enter text using your voice, this area may display a message to help you use Dictation mode. For example, the message "What was that?" indicates you should repeat your last words.

6 When you finish entering text using your voice, click **Microphone** to turn off your microphone.

● You can now edit the text you entered using your voice as you would edit any text.

USING VOICE COMMAND MODE

You can use Voice Command mode to select commands from menus and toolbars using your voice. You can also use Voice Command mode to select options in dialog boxes. For example, you can use Voice Command mode to select the Spelling and Grammar command from the Standard toolbar and then find and correct the spelling and grammar errors in your document.

USING VOICE COMMAND MODE

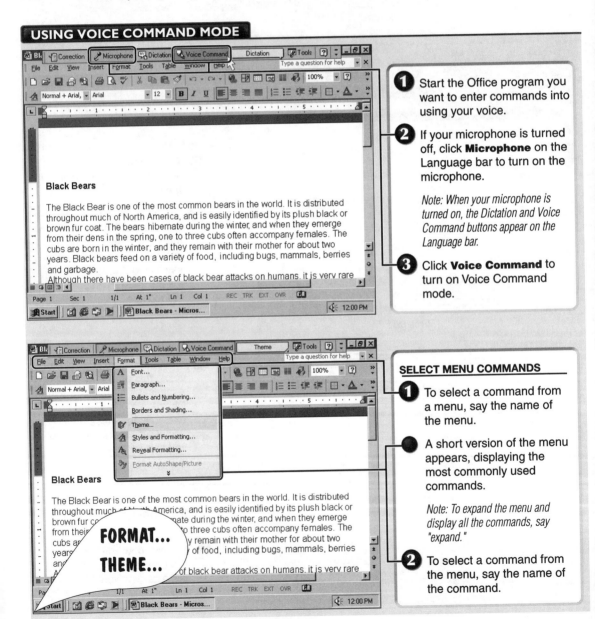

① Start the Office program you want to enter commands into using your voice.

② If your microphone is turned off, click **Microphone** on the Language bar to turn on the microphone.

Note: When your microphone is turned on, the Dictation and Voice Command buttons appear on the Language bar.

③ Click **Voice Command** to turn on Voice Command mode.

SELECT MENU COMMANDS

① To select a command from a menu, say the name of the menu.

● A short version of the menu appears, displaying the most commonly used commands.

Note: To expand the menu and display all the commands, say "expand."

② To select a command from the menu, say the name of the command.

in an instant

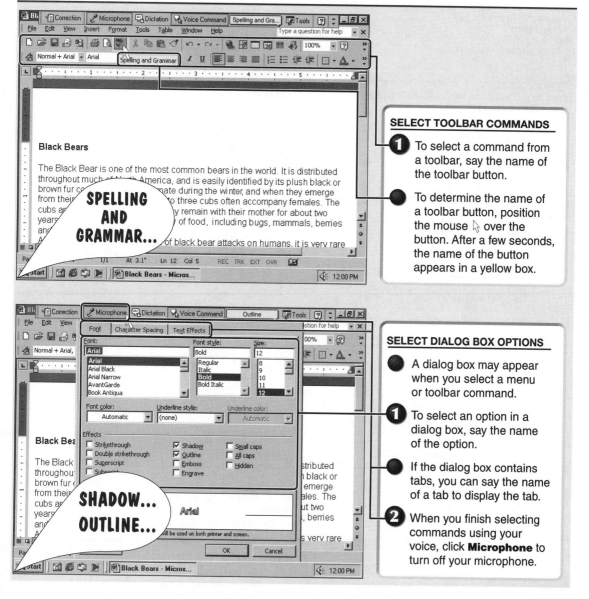

SELECT TOOLBAR COMMANDS

1 To select a command from a toolbar, say the name of the toolbar button.

● To determine the name of a toolbar button, position the mouse ⌖ over the button. After a few seconds, the name of the button appears in a yellow box.

SELECT DIALOG BOX OPTIONS

● A dialog box may appear when you select a menu or toolbar command.

1 To select an option in a dialog box, say the name of the option.

● If the dialog box contains tabs, you can say the name of a tab to display the tab.

2 When you finish selecting commands using your voice, click **Microphone** to turn off your microphone.

INDEX

INDEX

INDEX

Microphone Wizard, use to set up microphone, speech recognition, 328-330
Microsoft
    Access. *See* Access
    Excel. *See* Excel
    Office. *See* Office
    Outlook. *See* Outlook
    PowerPoint. *See* PowerPoint
    Word. *See* Word
misspelled words, correct, in PowerPoint, 186-187
move
    charts, in Excel, 156
    data, in Excel, 110-111
    insertion point, in Word, 20
    objects, in PowerPoint, 206
    text
        in PowerPoint, 184-185
        in Word, 38-39
    through. *See also* browse, through; scroll, through
        Calendar, in Outlook, 313-314
        data in tables, in Access, 252-253
        documents, in Word, 20-21
        records
            in forms, in Access, 272
            in reports, in Access, 299
            in tables, in Access, 252-253

N

Normal view
    in PowerPoint, 168
        create notes using, 224
    in Word, 22
not equal to (<>), criteria, in Access, 291
notes
    in Outlook
        create, 324-325
        deleted, recover, 326
        open, 325
        overview, 302, 303
    in PowerPoint
        browse through, 171
        create, 224-225
notes pages, in PowerPoint
    print, 228-229
    use, 224-225
Notes pane, in PowerPoint, 161
Number, data types, in Access, 263
numbers
    in Excel
        add, quickly, 127
        format, 134-135
    in Word
        add
            to lists, 58-59
            to pages, 74-75
        delete, from pages, 75

O

objects. *See also* specific object
    in Access
        databases
            open, 240-241
            rename, 241
        OLE, data types, 263

    in PowerPoint
        add to presentations, overview, 160
        color, change, 213
        move, 206
        size, 207
Office. *See also* specific subject or feature
    editions, 3
    overview, 2-3
    programs
        exit, 5
        getting help in, 12-13
        start, 4
    using speech recognition in, 328-337
        overview, 3
OLE Object, data types, in Access, 263
open
    in Access
        database objects, 240-241
        databases, 242-243
        forms, 240-241
        queries, 240-241
        reports, 240-241
        tables, 240-241
    in Excel, workbooks, 102-103
    in Outlook
        attached files, 309
        notes, 325
    in PowerPoint, presentations, 174-175
    in Word, documents, 26-27
operators, overview, 118
options
    dialog box, select, using speech recognition, 336-337
    print, change, in Excel, 150-151
orientation, of pages, in Excel, change, 148
Outbox folder, in Outlook, 304-305
Outline tab, in PowerPoint, 168
Outline view
    in PowerPoint, print, 228-229
    in Word, 23
Outlook. *See also* specific subject or feature
    overview, 3, 302
    window, parts of, 303
Outlook Bar, in Outlook, 303
Outlook Today, in Outlook, 303

P

page
    breaks, in Word
        delete, 69
        insert, 68-69
    numbers, in Word
        add, 74-75
        delete, 75
    orientation, in Excel, change, 148
pages. *See also* databases; presentations
    count, in Word, 41
    notes, use, in PowerPoint, 224-225
paragraphs, in Word
    count in documents, 41
    indent, 62-63
    select, 19
Percent, format, in Excel, 134-135
pictures. *See also* clip art; images
    add to slides, in PowerPoint, 196-197

343

INDEX

INDEX

toolbar
  buttons
    align text using, in Word, 60
    move or copy data using
      in Excel, 111
      in PowerPoint, 185
      in Word, 39
  commands, select, using speech recognition, 336-337
toolbars
  display or hide, 7
  in Excel, 87
  in Outlook, 303
  in PowerPoint, 161
  select commands using, 6
  in Word, 15
track changes, in Word, 48
training, for speech recognition, 330-333
transitions, add to slides, in PowerPoint, 220-221

U

underline
  data, in Excel, 140
  text
    in PowerPoint, 210
    in Word, 56
undo changes
  in Access, 257
  in Excel, 117
  in PowerPoint, 183
  in Word, 40
update, contacts, in Outlook, 321

V

view. *See also* **display**
  files attached to messages, in Outlook, 309
  slide shows, in PowerPoint, 222-223
view buttons, in PowerPoint, 161
View pane, in Outlook, 303
views, change
  for Calendar, in Outlook, 315
  for documents, in Word, 15, 22-23
  for presentations, in PowerPoint, 168-169
  for queries, in Access, 286
  for tables, in Access, 260
Voice Command mode, use with speech
  recognition, 336-337

W

watermarks, in Word, 76-77
Web Layout view, in Word, 22
width of columns, change
  in Excel, 130
  in Word, in tables, 80-81
window, parts of
  in Excel, 87
  in Outlook, 303
  in PowerPoint, 161
  in Word, 15

wizards
  AutoContent, in PowerPoint, 162-165
  Chart, in Excel, 152-154
  Database, in Access, 232-237
  Form, in Access, 268-271
  Microphone, in speech recognition, 328-333
  Microsoft Speech Recognition Training, in speech
    recognition, 330-333
  Reports, in Access, 292-299
Word. *See also specific subject or feature*
  overview, 2, 14
  window, parts of, 15
WordArt, add to slides, in PowerPoint, 194-195
words. *See also* **data; text**
  count, in documents, in Word, 41
  select
    in PowerPoint, 178
    in Word, 18-19
workbooks. *See also* **Excel; worksheets**
  close, 101
  create, 104
  e-mail, 106-107
  open, 102-103
  save, 100-101
  switch between, 105
worksheet tabs, browse through, 96
worksheets. *See also* **cells; columns; data; Excel; rows;**
  workbooks
  data, enter in, 90-91
  delete, 99
  edit, 108-109
  e-mail, 106-107
  format, overview, 86
  insert, 98
  margins, change, 149
  page orientation, change, 148
  preview, 144-145
  print, 146-147
  rename, 97
  scroll through, 89
  switch between, 96
  zoom in or out, 116

Y

Yes/No, data types, in Access, 263

Z

zoom, in or out, in Excel, 116

New from the Award-Winning Visual™ Series

in an instant

Fast

Focused

Visual

—and a great value!

- Zeroes in on the core tools and tasks of each application
- Features hundreds of large, super-crisp screenshots
- Straight-to-the-point explanations get you up and running—instantly

Titles In Series

Dreamweaver® 4 In an Instant
(0-7645-3628-1)
Flash™ 5 In an Instant
(0-7645-3624-9)
FrontPage® 2002 In an Instant
(0-7645-3626-5)
HTML In an Instant
(0-7645-3627-3)

Office XP In an Instant
(0-7645-3637-0)
Photoshop® 6 In an Instant
(0-7645-3629-X)
Windows® XP In an Instant
(0-7645-3625-7)

Other Visual Series That Help You Read Less - Learn More™

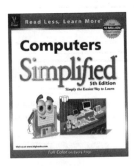

Simplified®

Teach Yourself VISUALLY™

Master VISUALLY™

Visual Blueprint

Available wherever books are sold

PC World—Winner of more editorial awards than any other PC publication!

Every issue is packed with the latest information to help you make the most of your PC—and it's yours risk-free!

Plus you will receive a FREE Hungry Minds/PC World CD wallet! It's perfect for transporting and protecting your favorite CDs.

Order Online Now!
www.pcworld.com/hungryminds

Hungry Minds and the Hungry Minds logo are trademarks or registered trademarks of Hungry Minds. All other trademarks are the property of their respective owners.

Send Today!

Here's how to order:

Cut and mail the coupon today to:
PC World, PO Box 37560, Boone, IA 50037-0560

- Call us at: (800) 825-7595

- Fax us at: (415) 882-0936

- Order online at: www.pcworld.com/hungryminds

PC WORLD

YOURS FREE!